Sports Hall of Fame
Grundy Center, Iowa
Established 2004

Profiles of

Athletes, Coaches, Administrators and Contributors

Inducted into the

Grundy Center Sports Hall of Fame

2004-2016

Compiled and written by David E. Pike

1

Sports Hall of Fame
Grundy Center, Iowa
Established 2004

Table of Contents

Dedication 5

Forward 6

Hall of Fame Class Lists by Year 9

The Charter Class of 2004 11

  Harold "Hal" Leffler 12

  Norman "Bud" Bergman 14

  Bill Smith 16

  Bob Stock 19

  Jim Basye 21

  Rick Kriz 24

  Greg Goodman 26

  Terry Crisman 28

  Dave Ehrig 30

  Kay Riek 32

  Jeff Dole 34

  Joel Crisman 36

  Kim Van Deest 38

Class of 2005 40

  Melvin "Fritz" Fritzel 41

  Arnold Reynolds 44

  Orville Allen 46

  Dennis Dirks 48

  Paul Eberline 50

  Tim Clark 52

  Dave Smoldt 54

  Tracey Voss 56

  Bobbi Sealman 58

Class of 2006 60

  Harold Engelkes 61

  Max Appel 64

  John Doak 67

  Dave Pike 70

  Lance Van Deest 73

Sports Hall of Fame
Grundy Center, Iowa
Established 2004

Mike Stumberg 76

Tim Baker 79

Scott Yoder 82

Class of 2007 85

Vernon Morrison 86

Leon Bockes 89

Glen Van Fossen 92

Al Harberts 95

Ivan Miller 97

Norm Riek 100

Class of 2008 103

Don Purvis 104

Wayne Wrage, Jr. 106

Kevin Ralston 108

Molly Thoren 110

Trina Dirks 112

Class of 2009 114

Dale Smith 115

Bob Smoldt 118

Harry Dole 121

Doug Stumberg 124

Andy Lebo 127

Todd Haupt 130

Class of 2010 132

Ed Palmer 133

Mark Eberline 136

Orrin Brown 139

Sarah Lynch 142

Brad Harms 145

Class of 2011 148

Melvin Heckt 149

Jack Basye 152

Tim Williamson 155

Carla Iverson 158

Class of 2012 161

Sports Hall of Fame
Grundy Center, Iowa
Established 2004

Forrest Meyers 162

J.A. Abels 164

Beth Stock 166

Lara Geer 169

Nicole VanderPol 171

Class of 2013 174

  Dick Lynch 175

  Charlie Peters 178

  Ron Coleman 181

  Matt Bockes 184

  Kylie Dirks 187

Class of 2014 190

  Roger Peters 191

  Randy Peters 194

  Clint Young 197

  Steve Bergman 200

  Dana Schmidt 203

Class of 2015 206

  Steve Ehlers 207

  Mike Draper 210

  Rick Ruebel 213

  Jordan Dirks 216

  Bobby Ayers 219

Class of 2016 222

  Dave Ralston 223

  Kurt Helmick 226

  Jeff Crisman 229

  Adrianne Alexia 232

  Phil Lebo 235

GC HOF Fun Facts as of 2016 238

Final Images 239

Sports Hall of Fame
Grundy Center, Iowa
Established 2004

Dedication

This book is dedicated to all the athletes, coaches, administrators and contributors who have given their time and talents to advance the athletic efforts of the Grundy Center Spartans as their teams and players strived to achieve success.

While this Grundy Center Sports Hall of Fame celebrates those who achieved a degree of greatness, we also salute and dedicate this book to all those who joined the Spartan teams, supported them, made the personal efforts to succeed, or assisted others in their quest for success for over 100 years. Go Spartans!

On a personal level, I dedicate this book to those who helped organize or participated with continuing this Hall of Fame. Rick Briggs has been the backbone of the Grundy Center Sports Hall of Fame. He and others like Dick Lynch, John Doak, Terry Haren, and Rollie Ackerman have kept the committee funded and running successfully.

John Doak was also my high school wrestling coach and he and his wife, Mary, have been generous supporters of Spartan athletics over the decades. They also donated the Spartan helmet sculpture that stands outside the high school gym as shown in the photo below.

This book is also dedicated to my father, Bud Pike, who supported me all though my sports career and beyond. He was a loyal fan of Spartans' sports for decades.

Many thanks to Brian Thies (my fraternity pledge dad from college and retired journalism teacher) and Mary Doak for editing this book before it was published.

David Pike with Rick Briggs (left) John Doak (center) and his dad, Bud Pike (right).

-David Pike

Sports Hall of Fame
Grundy Center, Iowa
Established 2004

Forward

Sports have long played an important role in the community of Grundy Center, Iowa. A great deal of civic pride has been derived directly from the efforts and the successes of the athletes, coaches, and teams that have entertained the city's residents over the decades.

The Grundy Center Sports Hall of Fame was founded to remember the accomplishments and contributions of those who have been involved in or supported the athletic programs in the City of Grundy Center and, particularly, Grundy Center Community High School.

This book is a written record of those athletes, coaches, administrators, and contributors who have been elected to the Grundy Center Sports Hall of Fame. Nominations for election to the Hall of Fame are made by the public, often from relatives, friends, or coaches of the nominees. Anyone can nominate any qualifying candidate who has either graduated from Grundy Center High School or has been a coach, administrator or contributor to the school's athletic programs

Upon election, each Hall of Fame inductee has a 5" x 7" brushed steel plaque created with a career summary and a photo which is added to the Hall of Fame wall located at Grundy Center High School. This further commemorates their accomplishments and helps add to the legacy of Spartan athletics.

Since its founding in 2004, the Hall of Fame has inducted new members at a public ceremony during the annual Felix Grundy Festival held in July. Each inductee had a sports biography created in an oral style and delivered at the ceremony. The biographies in this book are adaptions from those presentations.

The Grundy Center Sports Hall of Fame is operated by a committee of mostly local volunteers and former athletes. This group solicits nominations, elects the inductees, conducts fund raising activities, plans and executes the induction ceremony, and creates the plaques for the Hall of Fame wall at the high school.

Disclaimer: The Hall of Fame Committee has made a conscious effort to be reasonably sure the information and statistics provided in the nominations and the resulting biographies are accurate. A good faith effort is made to corroborate the information with the nominees and with school records that exist. While the information contained in these biographies is believed to be accurate, we cannot be absolutely certain in every instance. Where possible, we have consulted with news sources, school sources, nominators, teammates, and the inductees. If errors are brought to our attention, they will be corrected in the future editions.

Sports Hall of Fame
Grundy Center, Iowa
Established 2004

Induction Cermonies

Crowds gather annually for the Hall of Fame induction ceremonies at the Court House.

Newly elected members awaited their turn to be inducted in 2015.

Jason Eslinger, a frequent Emcee for the induction programs, read the sports biography of Beth Stock, who was presented with her HOF plaque by Terry Haren in 2012.

Sports Hall of Fame
Grundy Center, Iowa
Established 2004

A Gathering of Grundy Greats in 2006

Some existing Hall of Famers joined the third class of new inductees at the 2006 ceremony. Pictured here in the front row: Lillian Appel (representing her husband Max Appel) and Carol and Maxine Engelkes (representing their father Harold Engelkes). Second row: Scott Yoder, John Doak, Lance Van Deest, Tim Baker, and Mike Stumberg. Third row: Dorothy Reynolds (representing her husband Arnie Reynolds), Terry Crisman, Paul Eberline, and Dave Pike. Back row: Bud Bergman, Tim Clark, Rick Kriz, Jeff Dole and Dennis Dirks.

Sports Hall of Fame
Grundy Center, Iowa
Established 2004

Hall of Fame Class Lists by Year

Below is a listing of the classes as they were elected to the Grundy Center Sports Hall of Fame and the year they graduated from Grundy Center High School or years of service for administrators, contributors and Spartan coaches. Only athletes were eligible for the first two years. Coaches, administrators, and contributors were eligible beginning in 2006.

Charter Class of 2004: Harold Leffler* 1937; Bud Bergman 1954; Bill Smith 1959; Bob Stock 1962; Jim Basye* 1963; Rick Kriz 1965; Greg Goodman 1973; Terry Crisman 1977; Dave Ehrig 1978; Kay Riek 1980; Jeff Dole 1985; Joel Crisman 1989; Kim VanDeest 1989.

Class of 2005: Melvin Fritzel* 1926; Arnold Reynolds* 1939; Orville Allen* 1952; Dennis Dirks 1971; Paul Eberline 1972; Tim Clark 1977; Dave Smoldt 1980; Tracey Voss 1992; Bobbi Sealman 1992.

Class of 2006: Harold Engelkes* 1943-1978; Max Appel* 1943; John Doak 1961-1974; Dave Pike 1969; Lance Van Deest 1982; Mike Stumberg 1985; Tim Baker 1986; Scott Yoder 1993.

Class of 2007: Vernon Morrison* 1921; Leon Bockes* 1945; Glen Van Fossen 1954; Al Harberts 1957; Ivan Miller 1966; Norm Riek 1972;

Class of 2008: Don Purvis* 1935; Wayne Wrage, Jr. 1966; Kevin Ralston 1975; Molly Thoren 1989; Trina Dirks 1998.

Class of 2009: Dale Smith* 1929; Bob Smoldt 1963; Harry Dole 1967-1995; Doug Stumberg 1983; Andy Lebo 1995; Todd Haupt 2003.

Class of 2010: Ed Palmer 1969; Mark Eberline 1972; Orrin Brown 1975; Sarah Lynch 1990; Brad Harms 1996.

Class of 2011: Melvin Heckt 1942; Jack Basye 1960; Tim Williamson 1971; Carla Iverson 1998.

Class of 2012: Forrest Meyers* 1916; J.A. Abels 1962; Beth Stock 1970; Lara Geer 2001; Nicole VanderPol 2005.

Class of 2013: Dick Lynch 1963; Charlie Peters 1965; Ron Coleman 1977; Matt Bockes 1999; Kylie Dirks 2000.

Class of 2014: Roger Peters* 1937; Randy Peters, 1964; Clint Young 1971-1980; Steve Bergman 1976; Dana Schmidt 2007.

Class of 2015: Steve Ehlers 1966; Mike Draper 1975; Rick Ruebel 1980; Jordan Dirks 1995; Bobby Ayers 2005.

Class of 2016: Dave Ralston 1974; Kurt Helmick 1977; Jeff Crisman 1978; Adrianne Alexia 2010; Phil Lebo, 1980-2006.

*Deceased

Sports Hall of Fame
Grundy Center, Iowa
Established 2004

Sports Biographies
of the
Athletes, Coaches,
Administrators & Contributors
inducted into the
Grundy Center Sports Hall of Fame

The wall plaques for members of the Hall of Fame are located at Grundy Center High School just outside the principal's office and organized by decades of graduation.

Sports Hall of Fame
Grundy Center, Iowa
Established 2004

The Charter Class of 2004

Harold Leffler* 1937

Bud Bergman 1954

Bill Smith 1959

Bob Stock 1962

Jim Basye* 1963

Rick Kriz 1965

Greg Goodman 1973

Terry Crisman 1977

Dave Ehrig 1978

Kay Riek 1980

Jeff Dole 1985

Joel Crisman 1989

Kim Van Deest 1989

The Charter Class of the Grundy Center Sports Hall of Fame was elected in the spring of 2004 and inducted during Felix Grundy Festival activities that July. This photo of the original inductees includes L-R front row: Greg Goodman, Sue Basye (representing her husband, Jim Basye), Rick Kriz, and Bud Bergman. Second row: Kay Riek, Terry Crisman and Bob Stock. Back row: Dave Ehrig, Kim Van Deest, Joel Crisman and Jeff Dole. Not pictured: Hal Leffler and Bill Smith.

Harold "Hal" Leffler

Hal Leffler is shown left in his high school graduation photo in 1937 and at right in his adult years. Hal was elected for gymnastics at the University of Iowa (shown above in 1941 and 1942) and as a contributor to racquetball which he promoted for decades in Europe.

Harold "Hal" Leffler is a great example of what the Grundy Center Sports Hall of Fame is all about. Few remember his exploits as a Grundy athlete because he didn't earn his Hall of Fame credentials for what he did as a Spartan.

Hal graduated from high school in 1937. His athletic accomplishments in high school were modest. He was a forward on the Spartan basketball team that won the County and Sectional basketball crowns, but there is no evidence he was a star on that team.

He was runner-up in the Conference singles tennis tournament when tennis was more like a "club" sport in the mid-1930s. To look at Hal's high school sports achievements in football, basketball, and tennis, he participated, but certainly didn't appear to establish "Hall of Fame" credentials.

It wasn't until college that Hal found his sport. Enrolling at the University of Iowa as a Physical Education major, Hal went out for gymnastics. By the time he graduated from Iowa in 1941, he earned three letters in the sport, earned Big Ten all-conference honors, and was named Hawkeye team captain his senior season.

Leffler, elected in the Charter Class in 2004, is the only gymnastics athlete in the Grundy Center Sports Hall of Fame as of 2016. But he is also recognized as a Hall of Fame "Contributor" for another sport uniquely represented among the membership of this group.

After graduation, Hal accepted the patriotic call for World War II. He enlisted in the Army Air Corps and became a B-29 pilot completing 35 combat missions in the

Pacific theater. One of the B-29s he commanded was named the "City of Grundy Center." In 1961, after a successful insurance career, Hal moved to Germany to work with Military Personnel. Because of his strong interest in sports, he started volunteering to help with sports activities on various U.S. Military bases.

Racquetball was all but unknown in Europe. A player and promoter of racquetball, Hal persuaded the U.S. Military to build portable racquetball courts in America and ship them to military bases in Europe. Not only was he working with the U.S. Military in Germany, he contacted the French Ministry of Sports and also Belgium's Military Headquarters.

Hal Leffler and a few fellow enthusiasts founded the European Racquetball Association in 1975. Hal was chosen as its first Administrator. During his tenure, Hal expanded the sport of racquetball to southern Europe, France, Germany, the Mediterranean, Italy, northern Europe, Belgium and Holland. He has been called the "Father of European Racquetball".

Hal coached, arranged, promoted, and ran racquetball tournaments. He has also put on workshops and clinics in most of those European countries and was technical consultant for the 1989 World Games in Karlsruhe, West Germany.

Hal spent the rest of his life in retirement in Germany and passed away there on July 4, 2010. He was cremated and his ashes scattered in Germany and Grundy Center.

Leffler was the most senior member of the Charter Class of the Grundy Center Sports Hall of Fame in 2004 as both an athlete and contributor making him one of the most unique members of this body.

The 1942 Iowa gymnastics team is shown above with Hal Leffler (circled) as Captain.

Norman "Bud" Bergman

Bud Bergman was an all-around athlete in high school and a basketball player at Iowa State University. He was elected to this Hall of Fame as an "Athlete", but is also a Hall of Fame basketball coach with 519 wins in his coaching career.

Who would have thought a Grundy Center basketball player would play a key role in beating the #1 college team in the nation led by one of the greatest NBA basketball players of all time?

It happened to Norman "Bud" Bergman, a 1954 graduate while he was playing basketball for Iowa State where he was a three-year letterman. That NBA Hall of Famer was Wilt Chamberlin.

Wilt Chamberlin, a 7'2" center, played one season of college basketball for Kansas in 1956 before turning pro. He led the Jayhawks, ranked #1 most of the season, to the finals of the NCAA tournament where they lost for only the second time all year. The other loss was to Iowa State in the regular season.

Grundy Center's Bud Bergman scored 14 points in that game and afterwards the Kansas coach specifically attributed the loss of the game to the key baskets Bud made in the upset.

Bud Bergman was one of those athletes from the Spartans' past who could do it all. He played football and baseball in addition to basketball while in high school playing on some very successful teams.

The Spartans' 1953 football team in Bud's senior year went undefeated and was ranked 31st in the state by the Des Moines Register prep poll back when there were no classes of schools. Bud was first team all-conference and named third team all-state playing in the backfield along with fellow Hall of Famer Glen Van Fossen.

Grundy also had a strong baseball team in 1954 going 10-1 and winning the NICL Conference Championship where Bud pitched and played shortstop. The Spartans also won a Sectional Championship.

Basketball was Bud's forte and he was one of the Spartans' all-time greats. As a sophomore during the 1951-52 season, Bergman teamed with and learned from senior leader and Hall of Famer Orville Allen. The team went undefeated in the regular season and finished 24-1 with their only loss at the State tournament where there were still no classes separating small schools from large schools.

The Spartans put up another impressive record in Bud's junior season at 20-3. They won the conference title and Sectionals before losing in the District finals.

Bergman set a school scoring record his senior season of 1953-54 for most points scored in a game with 41. The Spartans tied for the conference championship and won another Sectional title before losing at Districts and finishing with a 19-2 record. So for Bud's three years as a varsity basketball player, the Spartans were 63-6!

Following graduation from high school, Bud went on to Iowa State where he played both baseball and basketball. He lettered one year in baseball before an injury to his throwing arm forced him to drop the sport. He continued playing basketball lettering three years and led the Cyclones to the huge upset over Wilt Chamberlain's Kansas Jayhawks.

Bergman went on to a highly successful coaching career and put up hall of fame numbers there as well. He is best known as the coach of Waverly-Shell Rock where he posted the vast majority of his 519 career basketball victories and had a 73% winning percentage. He was inducted into the Hall of Fame with the Charter Class of 2004.

Interestingly, Bud's nephew and Grundy Center graduate Steve Bergman, also won over 500 career basketball victories in his coaching career and surpassed his Uncle Bud. That's more than 1000 wins for the coaching Bergmans. Steve joined Bud in the Grundy Center Sports Hall of Fame 2014.

Bill Smith

Bill Smith, left in 1958, averaged 12 yards per carry that fall on the undefeated Spartan football team. Center is a 1957 track photo from Smith's sophomore year. Right, he's shown as a senior basketball player. Bill once broke a glass backboard in pre-game basketball warm-ups trying to dunk the ball.

When local sports enthusiasts talk about the greatest athletes to ever compete for Grundy Center, veteran Spartan fans invariably put forward Bill Smith, a 1959 graduate, who left an indelible mark on the football and track teams of the late 1950s. Smith was not only big and powerful at 6' 2" and over 200 pounds, he also had speed which translated into records in track and field.

Bill lettered all four years in track setting the school's shot put record as a sophomore in 1957 at 51' 10-1/2". Then using his speed in the 180 yard low hurdles, he set another school record with a time of 22.2 seconds. As a team, the Spartans finished fourth in the State track meet that spring. During his junior year of 1958, Smith was part of a school record-setting Medley Relay team as the Spartans finished eighth at the State meet.

As a senior in 1959, Bill continued to dominate in track with four more school records. He knocked a full second off his own 180 yard hurdles mark, he added a few inches to his shot put record exceeding 52', and he set a record for the football throw. The fourth record was with the Mile Relay team. It was a great way to end his high school athletic career.

While basketball wasn't his best sport, Bill's strength showed up during warm-ups for a home game in 1959 when he tried to dunk the ball. Whether he successfully

completed the dunk or not was lost in the chaos of hitting the rim with such force that it totally shattered the glass backboard into a million pieces that scattered all over the gym floor! The game was delayed nearly an hour while a substitute metal backboard was installed. With Smith's size, speed and strength, Spartan wrestling fans can only wonder what Bill could have done on the wrestling mat if Grundy Center had that sport in the late 1950s.

It was the gridiron where Bill Smith made his reputation by terrorizing conference opponents at running back and linebacker. Bill lettered all four years and was a starter at least three of them. The Spartans were an undefeated 8-0 in 1956 and a respectable 6-2 in 1957.

Statistics from his early career are very sketchy, but as a senior on the Spartans' undefeated 1958 squad, Smith gained 1,326 in 106 carries over eight games with an astonishing average of 12.5 yards per carry and an average of over 165 yards per game! Bill scored 19 touchdowns, 16 point-after attempts, and totaled 130 points himself. Smith also led the team in tackles with 111 coming up from his linebacker position, an average of over 14 tackles per game.

Bill Smith (#35) is shown left in 1958 lining up in the backfield where he struck fear in opposing defenses averaging over 12 yards per carry using both speed and power.

Smith took the field with some outstanding teammates like Jack Stumberg, Daryl Connell, Darrell Diehl, Jim Lynch, Bob Grimmius, Jack Basye, and Jim Terrell under Coach Bub Bitcon. The fall of 1958 saw the Spartans score 312 points for an average of 39 points per game. Defensively, they only gave-up 73 points, an

average of less than 10 points a game. The Spartans' three-year record with Bill Smith in the starting line-up was an impressive 22-2.

The last game of their senior season, the Spartans were playing arch rival Reinbeck. Grundy Center came into the game undefeated and playing for the conference championship against a tough Reinbeck team. The Rams' star player took the opening kick-off and started up the sideline when Smith leveled him at full speed knocking the player out of the game. It was downhill from there for Reinbeck as the Spartans shut-down the Rams offense and battered their defense in a lopsided shut-out of their rivals by a score of 51-0.

Bill Smith was considered the premier running back in the area and was a unanimous first team all-conference selection. He was then named first-team all-state in an era when there was only one class for football.

After graduation, Bill went on to Iowa State University and played football for Coach Clay Stapleton as a running back and linebacker. He graduated with a degree in Education. Bill Smith remains a Spartan football legend.

This 1958 Spartan football team went undefeated, averaged 39 points a game. They were led by senior running back Bill Smith (circled) and coached by the late Lawrence "Bub" Bitcon. There are two Hall of Famers in this photo and the fathers of two others.

Sports Hall of Fame
Grundy Center, Iowa
Established 2004

Bob Stock

The legacy of Grundy Center tennis all started with Bob Stock. He was Grundy Center's first State tennis champion and went on to play in college and professionally. He is shown center playing at Wimbledon in 1972 and right in 1999

The legacy of Grundy Center boys tennis started in the late 1950s and early 1960s with Bob Stock. He blazed the trail for the Spartan tennis stars under Coach John Doak that lasted through the 1960s with Steve Ehlers and Ed Palmer and on into the early 1970s with Norm Riek and Dave Ralston. From this tennis influence of Bob Stock, all the aforementioned tennis players are also in this Hall of Fame, including Coach Doak and Bob's sister, Beth Stock.

Bob Stock remembered growing up in Grundy Center and playing basketball at Preach Basye's house next to the Methodist Church. There was always a pick-up game going on and the skills and competition honed in Basye's driveway made a positive contribution to not only the future success that Bob had, but for many of the Grundy athletes of that era. It was common to see Jack and Jim Basye hosting the likes of Bob Smoldt, Dick Lynch, Daryl Connell, and Ken Dirks among others playing a hard pick-up game of hoops. Not surprisingly, Bob turned out to be a pretty good guard on the basketball team lettering two years.

But it was tennis where Bob had a Hall of Fame career and started the Spartans tennis legacy. Steve Ehlers attributes his interest in tennis to Bob. Living across the street from the swimming pool park where there were two concrete tennis courts, a ten year old Steve would often wake up to the rhythmic *"thwack, thwack, thwack"* of Bob practicing by himself against the wooden backboards.

And the practice paid off. Bob won the State singles title in 1962 when there was only one class size for the entire State. He went on to win the Missouri Valley Singles championship that year, an area that covered five states.

Bob initially chose to follow Horace Greeley's famous advice, "Go west, young man." He went all the way to UCLA where he lettered for the Bruins. However, he later transferred to the University of Tennessee where he lettered and earned Honorable Mention All-American for the Volunteers.

After college, Bob made a career out of tennis beginning as a teaching pro, but also playing professionally on the European tour for 18 months. His proudest accomplishment was qualifying for and playing in the main draw at Wimbledon in 1972 along with playing twice in the U.S. Open tournament during the years he was ranked in the World singles standings.

In view of all these great individual tennis accomplishments, one of Bob's favorite memories brought him back to Grundy Center and his high school days. He fondly remembered bringing his little sister, Beth, over to the courts at the old swimming pool park when she was only 6-7 years old and teaching her how to play tennis. Bob was a great teacher as Beth went on to her own Hall of Fame tennis career in high school, college, and beyond in adult and seniors' level competition.

The tennis legacy of Grundy Center from the late 1950s into the mid-1970s under Coach John Doak all started with Bob Stock. His name is legendary and the memories strong of the young man who started it all in Spartan sports lore. While others had success in high school, college, and as adults, Bob Stock did it first. And he may have been the best. At a minimum, he set the bar very high.

Following Bob's State title, Grundy Center boys' tennis qualified at least one person for the State tournament for the next 12 consecutive years. Competing in one class against the largest schools in the state, Bob paved the way for 17 qualifiers, most of whom took summer recreational tennis lessons from him as they grew-up. Those legacy players of Ehlers, Palmer, Riek, Ralston, as well as his sister Beth, all looked-up to the one who started that tremendous tennis tradition, the legendary Bob Stock.

After retiring to Alabama, Stock built his own clay court on his property. Bob continued to play competitive senior tennis into his 70s claiming he still had the "*fire in the belly.*"

Jim Basye

Jim Basye is shown left #32 as a freshman in 1959 with older brother Jack, center #45 as a senior football player in 1962. An all-around athlete, Jim was elected to the Hall of Fame for football and track and earned 15 letters for the Spartans. He also played football for the University of Northern Iowa as a kicker and defensive lineman and was a Captain on the Panthers' squad.

Jim Basye was a big guy and a big eater growing up in Grundy Center in the 1950s and early 1960s. With his older brother, Jack, Jim often played sports with the older kids who dubbed him "Chow". But those pick-up games of football and basketball helped set the stage for future athletic success for the Spartans and beyond.

Jim Basye, son of the local Methodist minister, was a hometown hero at football, basketball, track and baseball. He could do it all and do it well. Jim earned 15 letters for the Spartans. In basketball, he lettered all four years and was all-conference as a junior and senior. With his size and bulk, he was hard to move out from under the basket.

Over his high school basketball career, the Spartans were 67-17 with more than half of those losses just from his freshman season. Their three year record was 49-9 and during Jim's junior and senior seasons, they posted 39 wins against just 4 losses.

Under Coach Marv Ott, the Spartans hoopsters won the North Iowa Cedar League Conference during Basye's sophomore, junior and senior campaigns. It took big city teams, primarily Marshalltown, to keep the Spartans out of the State tournament series in the days before there were class sizes. Success in all these team sports wasn't just because of Jim Basye. He had a cast of quality athletes around him

including fellow Hall of Famers Bob Smoldt, Bob Stock, and Dick Lynch along with Arlen Kruger and Chris DenOuden. And it didn't matter whether it was basketball, football, or baseball.

Grundy Center also had some strong football teams under the late Coach Greg Bice. Dick Lynch was in the same backfield with Basye, playing halfback to Jim's fullback. An outstanding and powerful running back, opponents would key on Basye being the big, bruising runner he was. So when the much smaller, but faster Lynch would get the ball, he benefitted from the defenses keying on Basye. Lynch felt as a quick, smaller back, he was hard for defenses to pick-out when Jim was running a fake or leading the blocking. They were a dynamic backfield rushing duo.

But even when defenses were keying on Jim Basye, he was hard to stop. While not a speedster, he had a powerful lower body, great hands as a receiver, and he was a smart, versatile player. In one game, Jim not only ran for a touchdown, he caught a touchdown pass and threw for another one! He was also the Spartans' middle linebacker to boot. And when it came to "booting", Jim had quite a leg for that often sending his kick-offs into the end zone.

The 1962 Spartan football team under head coach, Greg Bice, went undefeated with its only blemish being a tie with LaPorte City. They finished the season 7-0-1 and Jim Basye along with Dick Lynch and center Gary Appel earned first team all-conference honors. Only two teams scored more than one touchdown against the tough Spartan defense with stalwarts like tackle Noel Rewerts, end Gerry Long, and guard Glen Popes, all second team all-conference selections.

FIRST ROW: Manager Mitchell, Coach Bice, R. Kruse, S. Ford, Popes, Myers, Wical, Long, Tack, Jim Basye, Lynch, Rewerts, Shaw, Coach Ott, Manager Miller. SECOND ROW: Hulne, Odenthal, Sheller, McMartin, Saddoris, Heltibridle, Smith, John Basye, R. Peters, C. Kruse, Augustine, Behrens, Mast, Fisher, C. Peters, Dudden, Bertram. THIRD ROW: Vogt, Lage, Reedholm, Meents, Stover, K. Ford, Wrage.

The 1962 Spartans are shown above and finished their season undefeated at 7-0-1. This team features six future Hall of Famers. Jim Basye is circled.

Track was another avenue for Jim's talents. He broke Hall of Famer Bill Smith's shot put record with a 53' 8" toss as a senior in 1963 that still stands as of 2016. He also won the State Indoor shot put title as a junior in 1962. Basye set the discus record as a junior beating Roger Hook's record from 1957 by 2 ½ feet. The following season in 1963, Jim then beat his own record by six feet. That record stood until it was beaten in 1968 by Jim Clark. Additionally, Jim was also a four year letterman in baseball.

Basye finished his formal sports career at the University of Northern Iowa. He played defensive tackle and also handled the kicking chores for Coach Stan Sheriff. Despite playing through some back injuries, Jim was elected a team captain for the Panthers and completed an outstanding career.

After graduation, Jim had a long career teaching and coaching, primarily in Hampton, Iowa. He died of cancer in November 2003 and was the inspiration for starting the Grundy Center Hall of Fame. He was elected to the Charter Class of 2004 for football and track. He will long be remembered for his many contributions and accomplishments as a Grundy Center Spartan as well as a great teammate and friend.

Coach Greg Bice (center) is celebrating a hard-fought win over Jesup in 1962 with his players. Clockwise from lower-left are Jim Basye, Gerry Long, Gary Appel, Dick Lynch and Denny Wical. Jim Basye's Prep All-American plaque is shown above recognizing him as one of the outstanding football players in the country in the fall of 1962.

Sports Hall of Fame
Grundy Center, Iowa
Established 2004

Rick Kriz

Rick Kriz is shown in a 1965 team basketball photo (left), in the minor leagues (center), and in 2013 with classmate, football teammate, and fellow Hall of Fame member Charlie Peters (right). Rick was elected to the Hall of Fame as a baseball and softball player. He is also a member of the Iowa Fast Pitch Softball Hall of Fame.

Rick Kriz made his Hall of Fame credentials on the baseball diamond. A great left-handed batter who hit for both batting average and power for the Spartans, he took his skills to college and the professional ranks before turning his talents to fast pitch softball.

Rick was a good all-around athlete. He was a two-year starting guard on the basketball team and earned first team all-conference honors his senior season of 1964-65. Coach Marv Ott made Rick a team captain.

The gridiron was also a place where Rick excelled. He was first team in 1964 while playing receiver and defensive back for Coach Ott. The Spartans posted a strong 6-2 record and boasted two Hall of Fame linemen/linebackers in classmate Charlie Peters and Wayne Wrage, Jr. The Spartans also featured Jim Hulne, Don Mackey, Ron Shoup, and the late Don Dudden, all of whom shared the baseball diamond with Rick.

Again, playing for Coach Marv Ott, Rick showcased his talents as a four year letter winner. He pitched two no-hitters for the Spartans, including a perfect seven inning game as a sophomore. When he wasn't on the mound, he batted nearly .400 dispelling the adage that "pitchers can't hit."

Back in the 1960s, the Spartans played at the old Tom Patten baseball field down by the bus barns of the day. They played without fences in the outfield and it wasn't

uncommon to see opponents chase long-balls hit by Rick and his teammates into yards of houses across the street.

FIRST ROW: Haren, Peters, Schroder, Halstead, Mr. Ott, Kriz, Hulne. SECOND ROW: Kell, Dietch, Clark, Dudden, Waldo, Mackey, Brower. THIRD ROW: Slinker, Rewerts, Wrage, Meents, Henze.

Rick played for Marv Ott the 1965 Spartan baseball team and later at Northern Iowa.

Following graduation, Rick started in centerfield for two years at Ellsworth Junior College in Iowa Falls. Rick and his Ellsworth teammates finished third in the 1966 National Junior College World Series. The following year at Ellsworth, Rick was named to the All-Star team for the North Central District of Junior College baseball and was also Ellsworth's Most Valuable Player.

Rick's next stop was the University of Northern Iowa where he continued to play centerfield for the Panthers and put up some impressive statistics. He was all-conference in both 1968 and 1969. He led the Panthers in at-bats, hits, RBIs, doubles, triples, and home runs. His two year batting average at UNI was an impressive .404! Rick capped his college career by being named to the Topps College Division All-Star team for UNI's district in 1969.

After graduation, Rick was drafted by the New York Yankees and he spent two years in their minor league organization.

While finishing his formal baseball career, Rick also started playing fast pitch softball, something he continued for many years. He played for perennial State champions Butt'r Top. The legendary Butt'r Top team named Rick to their "All Decade 1970s" team and he was later inducted into the Iowa Fast Pitch Hall of Fame.

Rick will be remembered in the history of Spartan baseball and softball players as one of Grundy Center's greatest of all-time.

Sports Hall of Fame
Grundy Center, Iowa
Established 2004

Greg Goodman

Greg Goodman was an outstanding basketball player in high school who became an accomplished triathlon athlete as an adult. He competed in five "Iron Man" triathlons. He's shown left-to-right in basketball, cross country, in his Hall of Fame plaque portrait, and as an adult biking.

Hall of Fame Coach Harry Dole's first basketball team in Grundy Center was the 1967-68 season and they posted a winning record while learning a new system. His 1968-69 team, led by Alvin Everts and Ed Palmer, won the conference and just missed making it to State with a 19-2 record.

The 1970-71 Spartan team took it to all the way to State with Hall of Famer Dennis Dirks, Jerry Appel, Rod Ragsdale, Darrel Dirks, and a sophomore guard named Greg Goodman. With the level of talent on that 1970-71 Spartan team, it was clear that any underclassman who got playing time was pretty good. And Greg proved he was, not only in basketball, but other sports as well.

Greg Goodman played baseball and ran track and cross country. Then as a senior, he went out for football for the first time. That was a gutsy thing to do as the Spartans only had two other seniors on the team. Greg played running back on the team that soon after developed into an area powerhouse.

However, in the fall of 1972, they weren't quite there yet. Greg likes to say they were 4-4 that season, before going on to explain he meant four losses at home and four losses on the road!

After a tough season on the gridiron, Goodman was happy to get back to basketball. Greg was first team all-conference as a junior and senior and earned all-state honors as a senior. He was both the playmaker and the "go-to guy" to put points on the

board. The pressure for that role was increased during Greg's senior season when star center Orrin Brown broke his arm.

Greg gives high praise to Hall of Fame Coach Harry Dole who always had his teams well-prepared and well-conditioned. Greg vividly remembers one of his first varsity practices under Coach Dole. They just finished a workout where they were playing very well, running the offense, diving for loose balls, and making free throws. Then Harry pulled the team together and told them how well they practiced and that they were going "run a little bit."

After about 45 minutes of rims, defensive slides, and sprints, Greg looked up at senior Jerry Appel who said, "Just think what would happen if we had a BAD practice!" That moment taught Greg that there is no substitute for work and it's the price you pay for success.

After graduating from high school in 1974, Greg initially went to the University of Northern Iowa to play basketball before transferring and finishing his college career at Central Missouri State. He redshirted one year and played one more where he averaged 16 points per game and earned all-conference honors.

Greg graduated from Central Missouri State and stayed on to earn a Master's Degree in Exercise Science and Sports. This led to his lifelong commitment to fitness that dominated his adult life.

He developed a new interest and started competing in triathlons and then "Iron Man" triathlons. That's where competitors swim 2.4 miles, ride a bike for 112 miles, then run a full 26 mile marathon. Goodman completed five "Iron Man" competitions and finished as high as 38th overall and third in his age division.

Besides his triathlon competitions, Greg was a teacher and a coach for over 25 years showing the same dedication he had for fitness to youth sports programs. Among his fond coaching memories is his tenure as the Springboard Diving coach for Blue Springs, Missouri. He coached two State Champions and numerous all-state divers. That's particularly impressive since Grundy Center didn't have any swimming or diving in high school.

.

Sports Hall of Fame
Grundy Center, Iowa
Established 2004

Terry Crisman

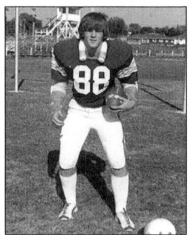  

Terry Crisman is the oldest of three brothers in the Hall of Fame. He earned 12 letters in high school football, basketball, baseball, track and tennis. He went on to play football at Drake University as a defensive tackle earning four more letters.

Terry "Red" Crisman is the oldest of a family of great athletes, including sister Nadine, Hall of Fame brother Jeff, and fellow Hall of Famer, little brother, Joel!
And like his siblings, Terry was talented in several sports in the mid-1970s. He lettered three years each in baseball, basketball, and football as well as picking up two letters in track and a letter in tennis. After high school, he picked up another four football letters at Drake University.

Terry was a tight end for Rod Nelson's teams from 1974-77. As a 215 pound junior, he caught 21 passes for 287 yards and four touchdowns. Red was also a crunching blocker and Coach Nelson ran most of his plays over Terry's side of the line where he played next to fellow Hall of Fame tackle, Dave Ehrig. No opponents liked lining up against those guys! But of course, Kurt Helmick, another Hall of Fame member, loved it as he racked up the Spartan record for rushing yardage running behind Crisman and Ehrig!

Terry's junior year in the fall of 1975, the Spartans finished 8-1 and Terry was named all-area first team at tight end, first team all-conference and honorable mention. The class of 1977 was very strong and Terry gives credit to a talented supporting cast of athletes like Tim Clark, Ron Coleman, Kent Hitchings, Bill Itzen, Don Appel, Dave Voss and Steve Hamm. With talent like that, it's no wonder Grundy Center won so often in so many sports!

As a senior, Terry weighed in at 230 pounds and threw his weight around the gridiron once again. In the wake of another successful season where the Spartans went 7-2, Terry was again first-team all-conference and named to the team. He was second team all-state on defense for Class 2A. And behind all that beef, Kurt Helmick was named conference back of the year.

"Big Red" also had a successful basketball career playing for Jim Brousard. In fact, one of Terry's best memories of his Grundy Center days was the success his class, the Class of 1977, had on the basketball court. During his four years, they never lost a conference game! They were undefeated as a freshman squad in 1974 and as a junior varsity team in 1975.

Terry was a letter winner on the 1975 State runner-up team as a sophomore. He took on a starting role his junior year as the team rolled-up a 20-3 record, winning the North Iowa Cedar League Conference, Sectionals, and Districts. For his efforts, Terry was named first team all-conference.

The 1976-77 basketball season was almost an instant replay of his junior year as Jim Brousard's team went 21-2, winning the conference, sectionals and districts. Once again as a senior, Terry was first team all-conference.

As a bittersweet footnote, the most crushing defeat Terry remembered in his high school career was a sub-State basketball loss to Waverly-Shell Rock, coached by none other than Spartan Hall of Famer, Bud Bergman.

Terry is very proud of the fact that he was a Spartan during an era when football went from last in the conference to conference champs, where basketball won three conference titles and finished runner-up at State, and the baseball team made two State appearances and also finished second in the State. That's quite a legacy Terry and his teammates contributed to Spartan sports history.

With football being his best sport, Terry went to Drake University in Des Moines where he chalked up four more letters in the trenches as a defensive tackle. He contributed to Drake's most successful season ever in 1981 when they tied for the Missouri Valley championship with a 10-1 record. Terry was also honored as a team captain for Coach Chuck Sheldon.

Sports Hall of Fame
Grundy Center, Iowa
Established 2004

Dave Ehrig

Dave Ehrig was Grundy Center's only two-time State wrestling champion. He also starred as a lineman in football and was a starting offensive tackle for the University of Northern Iowa. He was elected to the Hall of Fame for football, wrestling, and track.

Dave Ehrig was another great Spartan athlete who excelled in numerous sports. In nominating Dave for the Hall of Fame, his Hall of Fame high school wrestling coach, Clint Young, noted Dave was one of the most gifted athletes he ever coached. Young further noted that Dave could use his power and quickness not only in wrestling, but also in football and track.

Dave was a four-year letterman on the Spartan track team. He showed his power by finishing fourth in the State shot. As a senior in 1977, Dave showed his speed and quickness as part of the 4x200 meter relay team that finished sixth in the State track meet. Ehrig was also proud he could run competitively in the 220 yard dash and the 440 while weighing over 220 pounds.

A three year letterman on the Spartans' football team, Dave excelled on the gridiron playing in the offensive line and knocking open holes for runners like Hall of Famer Kurt Helmick and Vince Klosterboer. As a defensive tackle, he was often able to fight off double and triple team blocking to secure tackles on opponent's running backs. One year, LaPorte City not only triple teamed him at times, the Eldora Tigers literally ran every play to the opposite side of where Dave lined up!

Dave earned first team all-conference honors and was chosen to play in the high school Shrine All-Star game after graduating. He received football scholarship offers from the University of Iowa, Illinois State and the University of Northern Iowa, and chose UNI where Dave became an offensive lineman for the Panthers.

During his college career, Dave was part of an offensive line that helped UNI's star running back, Kelly Ellis, set a single game Division 1-AA rushing record in 1979. As a sophomore, Dave was named 2nd team all-conference.

Ehrig also excelled on the wrestling mat mostly at heavyweight for Coach Clint Young. Dave fondly remembered first learning about wrestling in Doug Van Gelder's kids wrestling program held on Saturday mornings. And that start, plus Coach Young's tutelage, developed Dave into a three-time State place winner and two-time State champion. Dave remains as of 2016 the only Spartan wrestler to win two State championships.

Dave Ehrig was a four year wrestling letterman from 1974-1978 when Coach Young produced a number of powerhouse teams. During Dave's tenure, the Spartans notched a dual meet record of 35-5! This was highlighted by the team's 1976 second place finish at the State tournament. If Iowa had started their State dual meet tournament during this era, the Spartans might have seen even more team trophies with formidable wrestlers like Ehrig, Todd Stumberg, Todd Geer, Todd Onnen, Mike Krull, and fellow Hall of Famers Mike Draper, Kevin Ralston, Kurt Helmick and Rick Ruebel.

As a freshman in 1975, Dave learned a good lesson on the mat. He was wrestling at 167 pounds and pinned the eventual 1975 State champion at the Spartan Invitational Tournament. Dave was so happy that he hugged the guy he pinned! Well, not surprisingly, that angered his opponent and Dave learned that you share your joy with teammates and not the vanquished. So as a senior when he came from behind and pinned his opponent to win his second State championship, he just shook hands and saved the hugs for his coaches.

This four picture sequence shows Dave Ehrig taking down his opponent and pinning him in the State finals his senior season of 1978 for his second State heavyweight championship.

Dave's individual accomplishments were significant and he held many team records when he graduated and still owned a few as of this printing. He graduated with two State championships and went undefeated his senior year at 31-0. Ehrig held records for most career wins, pins in a season, career pins, most points in a season, and points in a career. He has the distinction of being the only wrestler elected in the Hall of Fame's Charter Class of 2004.

Sports Hall of Fame
Grundy Center, Iowa
Established 2004

Kay Riek

Kay Riek (left in 1980) had an outstanding high school sports career before concentrating on basketball at Drake (center), where she started for Coach Carol Baumgarten. She went on to her own coaching career at both the college and high school levels (right).

Kay Riek has the distinction, along with Kim Van Deest, of being the first women elected to the Grundy Center Sports Hall of Fame. With Kay coming from a family of brothers and sports enthusiasts, it's not surprising she turned out to be such a great athlete herself and garnered so many honors as a basketball player and coach. Her brothers likely take credit for that!

Kay was royalty in Grundy Center wherever she held court and it didn't matter if it was the basketball court, the tennis court, or even the volleyball court! She held your interest with outstanding performances in all three.

Volleyball didn't start in Grundy Center until Kay's junior year. By the time she was a senior in 1980, she was already first team all-conference and honorable mention all-state as the Spartan ladies finished second in the conference with an 18-8 record.

Of course, it's hard to be a Riek and not play tennis! Kay shined in tennis, too. A four year letter winner, she made three appearances at State and placed twice, including a third place finish in 1977.
.

But it was the other court, the basketball court, where Kay Riek truly excelled. She won three letters for Coach Dan Malloy. As a sophomore, the 1978 team finished a respectable 14-9 as Kay was named first team all-conference and honorable mention all-state.

Her junior year in 1979, the team improved to 21-5 and tied for the conference championship. They won both Sectionals and Districts before finishing runner-up in the Regional. Kay was again named first team all-conference as well as first team all-state!

Capping off her Spartan career in 1980, Kay led the team to a 20-3 record nearly duplicating the previous year as conference co-champions, Sectional and District winners, and once again, regional runner-up. And again, Kay earned first team all-conference and first team all-state honors to end her remarkable high school athletic career.

But Kay wasn't done competing. Drake coach Carol Baumgarten recruited Kay for the Lady Bulldogs and she headed for Des Moines. During her career, Drake made it to the Final 8 in the NCAA Tournament in 1982 and Kay also earned an Academic All American honor for her accomplishments in sports and the classroom. And just for fun, Kay played tennis at Drake and lettered all four years! She even won the conference championship for #4 singles as a senior.

In addition to her outstanding basketball career, Kay followed the Riek family tennis tradition and was an accomplished player both in high school and at Drake University.

Upon graduating from Drake, Kay did graduate work at Nichols State in Louisiana and served two years as a graduate assistant for women's basketball. She then moved to Indiana State University where she spent three years as an assistant before taking over the head coaching duties for another six years.

Kay returned to Iowa and took a teaching and coaching position at Iowa City West High School where she found a fellow Grundy graduate from her era in Hall of Famer Steve Bergman, coaching the boys basketball team. It is indeed a small world.

Kay was elected to the Hall of Fame for basketball, tennis and volleyball.

Sports Hall of Fame
Grundy Center, Iowa
Established 2004

Jeff Dole

 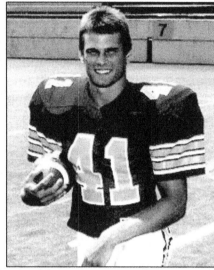 

Jeff Dole was one of the greatest athletes to wear a Spartan uniform. He earned 16 letters in four sports before going on to a great college football career at Iowa State where he earned honorable mention All-American for the Cyclones.

When the locals talk about the greatest all-around athletes to ever come out of Grundy Center, they have to include Jeff Dole. In Jeff's high school career, he earned an astonishing 16 letters! That was four letters each in football, basketball, track and baseball. But he wasn't just good enough to letter, Jeff earned all-conference honors three times in each sport.

Jeff's parents, Hall of Fame coach and administrator Harry Dole and wife Jean, moved to Grundy Center in 1967. Harry was the high school math teacher and coached basketball and baseball. By choosing to spend the rest of his career in Grundy Center, the Spartans won the sports lottery with Jeff! And the success Grundy Center athletics had during the time Jeff competed in high school rivals the best years Grundy Center had since the golden years of the 1950s.

In track, Jeff qualified for the State meet all four years and culminated his track career as a senior when he finished second in the long jump and second in the 400 meter hurdles at the State track meet.

In baseball, Jeff played shortstop, left field, and occasionally pitched for Coach Don Kramer. Besides being named all-conference three times, Jeff was all-state honorable mention in baseball and was chosen the Spartans' Most Valuable Player as a senior.

In basketball, Jeff was again a three-time all-conference player and he was part of the State runner-up team his senior year of 1985.

But Jeff Dole's best sport was football playing for Coach Don Knock. He led the Spartans to the Class 2A semi-finals as a junior and to Grundy's first state football championship in the fall of 1984 as a senior. That year, Dole set the season rushing record with 1711 yards in 12 games, an average of 142 yards per game. Jeff was the conference Most Valuable Player for three straight years and his senior year was named first team all-state in two separate polls.

Football isn't a sport you do by yourself and Jeff credited his teammates in the trenches of the offensive line who made it possible to accomplish what he did. Those Spartan linemen included Hall of Famer Mike Stumberg, Mark Fogt, David Hook, Kevin Venenga, Paul Samo, Lee Walters and Chris Stanley.

After graduation, Jeff followed his dad's footsteps and went on to Iowa State as a freshman walk-on. After only one season, Jeff earned a full scholarship for the Cyclones. He not only lettered all four years as a defensive back and punt returner, but he noted one of his proudest accomplishments was playing in all 45 games while he was on the team! That was a great testimony, not only to his talent, but to his durability.

Jeff continued to shine for the Cyclones his last two seasons. He led the team in tackles both years and was a team captain as a senior in 1988. That year, he set the team record for tackles by a defensive back and was third on the Iowa State list for career punt returns. He was named All-Big Eight second team on defense and an honorable mention All-American. Jeff wrapped up his college career by playing in the Blue-Grey game as a starting defensive back.

Not quite ready to give up football, Jeff had free-agent NFL tryouts with the New York Jets and Minnesota Vikings and then played two years of Arena football.

Jeff Dole will long be remembered as one of the greatest athletes in Grundy Center sports history and was elected to the Hall Fame for football and track.

Sports Hall of Fame
Grundy Center, Iowa
Established 2004

Joel Crisman

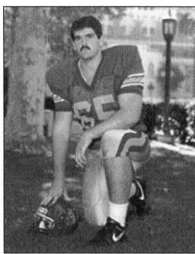

Joel Crisman is shown left in high school, center in a press photo from the University of Southern California during college, and right in 2016. He was elected to the Hall of Fame as a football player and is the youngest of three Crisman brothers inducted.

Grundy Center sports have a long history of families that have made names for Spartan teams over the years. Bergman, Basye, Eberline, Riek, Stumberg and Dirks are among those that come to mind along with the Crisman brothers.

Older brothers Terry and Jeff are members of the Grundy Center Sports Hall and so is little brother, Joel, though it's been a long time since anyone considered him "little".

Many long-time local Spartan sports fans considered the 1950s sports teams a "golden era". The 1980s deserve the same consideration, especially in football.

Grundy Center football was already established as a powerhouse team in the mid-1980s led by Hall of Famer Jeff Dole. The team finished runner-up in 1983 and won it all in 1984. But it got even better when Joel Crisman took the field for the Spartans.

Joel lettered three years in football playing primarily defensive tackle. During that time, the Spartans went 30-3 and won back-to-back State championships. On the defensive side of the ball, Joel was a major impact player. As a junior, he made 113 tackles, seven sacks, two fumble recoveries and even managed an interception.

In the fall of 1988 his senior season, Joel punished opponent's backfields with 154 tackles, 13 sacks, and two more fumble recoveries. As an offensive tackle, he also did some effective blocking for Spartan running backs.

As a high school player, Joel was such a dominating lineman that Grundy coaches could line him up defensively whichever side of the line of scrimmage they wanted and knew Joel could handle it. This allowed the Spartans to stack the other side of the line and shore up any weakness they had.

Joel was not only selected first team all-conference and Most Valuable Lineman his junior and senior seasons, he was named first team all-state both years as a tackle. The acclaim came from outside of Iowa, too. The USA Today named Joel an All-USA Honorable Mention tackle in 1987 as a junior and he made Super Prep Magazine's second team All-Midwest in 1988 as a senior. He was also invited to play in the 1989 Shriner's game.

Crisman was a sought-after college recruit. While Horace Greeley is famous for saying "*Go west, young man, go west*", when the University of Southern California coach John Robinson said it to Joel, his answer was, "*California here I come!*"

Joel lettered three years for the Trojans and earned All-PAC 10 honors before heading to a professional career in the NFL.

As of this printing, Joel Crisman has the distinction of not only being the first Grundy Center athlete to play in the NFL, but the only one. Joel played as an offensive center, mostly for the Tampa Bay Buccaneers under coaches Sam Wyche and Tony Dungee. Jeff's football career literally spanned the country from Iowa to California to Florida.

In the laurels of Spartan linemen including Charlie Peters, Wayne Wrage, Dave Ehrig, Jim Basye, and brothers Terry and Jeff Crisman, Joel Crisman stands tall!

Kim Van Deest

Kim Van Deest was one of two women in the Charter Class of the Hall of Fame for her achievements in softball, golf, and basketball. She also had an outstanding basketball career at Iowa State.

Kim Van Deest and Kay Riek were the first two women selected for the Grundy Center Sports Hall of Fame in its Charter Class. In Kim, the Spartans had an athlete who could do it all! She played softball, golf and basketball and not only did them well, she excelled!

Kim was a four-year letter winner in girls golf, earned four more in basketball, and won five letters in softball, earning her first one while still in 8th grade in 1985.

Her freshman year, Kim was second team all-conference in basketball, first team all-conference in golf, and also all-conference in softball.

In her sophomore year of 1986-87, Kim continued to grow and improve. She was first team all-conference in basketball and softball and led the golf team to a conference championship while winning medalist honors in the conference tournament. She went on to win medalist at the sectional and regional tournaments and finished sixth in the State golf meet.

It got even better Kim's junior year of 1987-88. She was again first team all-conference in softball, but was also selected first team all-district and honorable mention all-state.

In the 1988 golf season, Kim led the team to a 6-1 dual meet record and another conference championship. For the second year in a row, Kim won medalist honors for the conference, sectional, and regional meets. Unfortunately, she had to withdraw from the State golf tournament due to an injury.

Sports Hall of Fame
Grundy Center, Iowa
Established 2004

It was the 1987-88 season where Kim helped the Lady Spartans basketball team step up from an average team to a State power. Kim and her teammates moved from a 10-13 record her sophomore year to 21-6 as a junior. They capped the season with an appearance at the Girls' State Basketball Tournament for the first time since 1935!

Kim was once again first team all-conference and also named Captain of the all-tournament team at the Girls' State Basketball Tournament where she set a record making 24 straight free throws. She finished her junior year with 1,291 points, an average of nearly 48 points per game!

Basketball continued to rise with a 22-1 record Kim's senior season of 1988-89. Once again the Lady Spartans won the conference championship and Sectionals. Personally, Kim was again first team all-conference and first team all-state capping an outstanding high school basketball career.

Moving into her last season in golf, Kim led the team to the Conference championship and was again named first team all-conference.

Wrapping up her softball career in the spring of 1989, the Spartans came together for one of Kim's most memorable high school moments. The team compiled a strong 25-7 season and Grundy's first Conference championship in the sport while qualifying for Regionals. Kim was again first team all-conference, conference Most Valuable Player, first team all-district, and first team all-state to wrap-up one of the greatest high school careers in Spartan history, boys or girls!
.
Kim carried her basketball success to Iowa State University where she was a three-point shooting specialist. Kim ranked third on the Lady Cyclones three-point percentage leaders when she graduated. She was also selected to the Big Eight All-Star team that played in Toronto, Canada in the summer of 1992.

With all her athletic success, Kim was also an outstanding scholar. She was an Academic All-Big Eight her senior year. Kim graduated from Iowa State with a Master's Degree and a 4.0 grade point in 1996.

After college, Kim went on to coach women's basketball two years at Indiana State as an assistant under none other than fellow Hall of Fame inductee Kay Riek! It is again, a small world for Spartan athletes.

Sports Hall of Fame
Grundy Center, Iowa
Established 2004

Class of 2005

Melvin Fritzel* 1926

Arnold Reynolds* 1939

Orville Allen* 1952

Dennis Dirks 1971

Paul Eberline 1972

Tim Clark 1977

Dave Smoldt 1980

Tracey Voss 1992

Bobbi Sealman 1992

Front row: Paul Eberline, Dorothy Reynolds (wife of Arnie), Tracey Voss, Bobbi Sealman, and Tim Clark. Back row: Orv Allen, Dennis Dirks and Dave Smoldt.

Melvin "Fritz" Fritzel

Melvin Fritzel is shown left in high school track, from college football, in a basketball pose and far right in baseball at Iowa State Teachers College, now the University of Northern Iowa. "Fritz" won four college letters each in football, basketball and baseball playing key positions in each. He was elected to the Hall of Fame for all three sports.

Melvin Fritzel is a great example of what the Grundy Center Sports Hall of Fame is all about and why we should preserve and share this legacy with future generations.

There is little information about Fritzel's high school sports career other than he played football, basketball and track. He graduated in 1926 and went on to Iowa State Teachers College, now the University of Northern Iowa, where an exemplary college sports career can be documented. If his college career is any indication, Melvin must have been a star for the Spartans in the early-to-mid 1920s.

It's hard to truly compare various eras in sports, but from 1926-1930, Melvin Fritzel established himself as one of UNI's greatest and most versatile athletes. He earned 12 letters in three major sports: football, basketball and baseball. He not only lettered all four years in each sport, but according to reports of the time, he played key positions in each one at an "all-conference" level of play. That's impressive in any era.

Playing fullback and linebacker on the gridiron, Fritzel earned all-conference honors as a junior and senior playing on championship caliber teams. It was noted in a UNI publication of the day that Fritz was, *"...one of the best all-around athletes that has ever represented Iowa State Teachers College."* The writer went on to say, *"Fritz was a battering ram at fullback and a hard, sure tackler."*

This further illustrates another difference in sports eras as Melvin played both offense and defense for the Panthers, something rarely seen at the collegiate level in today's

game.   A newspaper article from 1927, noted Fritz *"terrorized opponents with his fierce tackling."* in a game against DeKalb. It was further noted, *"This game was Fritzel's game.   The blocking half was on his toes at all times and his tackling was sensational!* You have to love the way they wrote stories in those days!

Following football, Fritz achieved even more success in basketball. Coached by the legendary Art Dickinson, the 1929 UNI yearbook states, *"Fritz was our Captain and the outstanding player on the team.   It was his job to guard the best man on the opposing team and keep his eye on the basket, always working."*   Another newspaper writer applauded Fritzel's defensive skills by suggesting opponents being guarded by Fritz would be just as effective sitting on the bench.

In fact, Fritz was the Panthers' captain both his junior and senior seasons. The 1930 UNI yearbook states, *"Captain Fritzel is one of the outstanding guards in the conference. Fritz inspired his teammates to the utmost."* The "Tutors", as UNI sports teams were often referred to in that era, compiled an impressive 25-4 record in basketball for the two years Fritz was captain. The Panthers won the conference championship with a record of 13-2 in 1929 and finished second in 1930 with the same 13-2 record. Much of that success on the court was due to the play and leadership of Melvin Fritzel.

As further testimony to his leadership, he was named the team's Most Valuable Player in 1930, following in the footsteps of Grundy Center Hall of Famer, Vernon Morrison, who also was accorded a similar honor a few years before.

The strong football and basketball teams at UNI during the late 1920s were also complemented by a strong baseball program and, once again, Melvin Fritzel was the heart of the team.   On the diamond, Fritz anchored the infield by playing the key position of shortstop. In one game in 1927, the college newspaper reported on a game with Fritz going five-for-five with a home run, two triples, and two doubles!

The UNI baseball team won a conference championship in 1929 with a record of 11-1, scoring over 10 runs in six of those games. Twice they scored 27 runs in a game! In the nine-game winning streak they had to end that season, the Panthers had a five-game run where they scored 14, 27, 27, 17, and 19 runs as they ran rough-shod over opponents.

Personal statistics for all sports in those days are sketchy at best, but clearly Melvin Fritzel, by winning four letters in each of UNI's three major sports of the day, was a superb athlete.

Melvin Fritzel's career as an athlete may have ended when he graduated from UNI, but he did do his share of coaching afterwards. He stayed around UNI for a few years as a graduate assistant coach and director of intramurals. But in researching information on Fritz, it turns out he was officially the head basketball coach for one season in 1932-33 while Coach Art Dickinson took a year sabbatical. The Panthers posted a 9-4 record. Although only head coach for one season, Fritzel has the second highest winning percentage of any UNI basketball coach.

Fritzel next coached football at William Penn College for a number of years and also served as Athletic Director. After moving back to Grundy Center in the 1940s, he even coached the Spartans football team for two seasons during World War II. Both were classic seasons and among the best in school history.

The 1943 Spartans under Fritz were a dominating team going undefeated and outscored opponents 242-13! They averaged of over 34 points per game led by Bud Peterson who scored 161 of those points himself. At the close of the season, Fritz challenged undefeated Marshalltown to a game, but they declined. The next season, Fritz's 1944 Spartan team went undefeated and unscored upon, although they opened the season with a 0-0 tie with Toledo.

Melvin lived out his retirement years in Grundy Center and passed away in 1985. He should long be remembered as one of the Spartans' greatest and most versatile athletes and the coach of two of the greatest football teams in Spartan history.

This 1930 article is a testament to Melvin Fritzel's abilities and success on the basketball court as he was named first team among college basketball players in Iowa. He is holding the ball in the first row of the UNI team photo.

Sports Hall of Fame
Grundy Center, Iowa
Established 2004

Arnold Reynolds

Arnie Reynolds is shown left around 1941 at spring training in Florida for potential major league baseball players. He was elected to the Hall of Fame for football, track, baseball, softball, and bowling. He is a member of the Iowa Bowling Hall of Fame.

One of the finest athletes Grundy Center produced during the 1930s was Arnie Reynolds. An all-around athlete, Arnie played football, basketball, and track in high school.

After graduating from high school in 1939, Arnie went on to Luther College for two years prior to World War II. In his short collegiate career, Arnie earned six total letters in football, track and baseball.

Certainly, Arnie was a gifted high school athlete in the Depression years of the late 1930s. He could do almost anything and do it very well. Besides football, basketball and track, Arnie gave tennis a shot one year in high school and placed 2nd in the conference tournament. However, he gave up tennis for track where he used his speed and quickness to excel in sprinting events, relay teams, and field events like the long jump, high jump and pole vault.

Oddly enough, Arnie was also an exceptional baseball player, but didn't play in high school because track and baseball were both spring sports and Arnie chose track. Somehow at Luther College, Reynolds was able to work around that issue and earned two letters each in those sports. In fact, Arnie was offered a contract to play

professional baseball at that time, but World War II started and ended his college athletic career.

Now a young adult after the war, Arnie renewed his sports career on the diamond playing as many as four times a week. His daughter, Jane, remembered how her dad would feed and milk cows, then race into the house to shower before driving off with wife, Dorothy, and the kids to Marshalltown to play in the Anson baseball games.

Arnie also played on Grundy Center's championship caliber softball teams in the 1950s with teammates including fellow Hall of Fame members Bud Bergman and Roger Peters and along with players like Alvin Harrenstein, Delbert Kell, Bud Pike, and Marv Ralston among others.

While the Grundy Center Sports Hall of Fame primarily features high school and college athletes, it is not limited to that. In the case of Arnie Reynolds, it was the sport of bowling where he made his biggest claim to fame.

Arnie eventually moved from outdoor sports to the indoor lanes of bowling. He not only had a Hall of Fame career as a bowler, but made it a business career with ownership of bowling alleys in Grundy Center and later Worland, Wyoming.

When Arnie and Dorothy moved back to Grundy Center in 1966, Arnie worked at Maple Lanes in Waterloo and had a bowling shop where he sold and drilled custom-fitted bowling balls. He was always very proud of the many "300 games" that were accomplished with balls he drilled.

For his success on the lanes, Arnie was honored by fellow bowlers with his induction into the Cedar Falls Bowling Hall of Fame and in 1978 with his election into the Iowa Bowlers Hall of Fame.

Arnie Reynolds was elected to the second class of the Grundy Center Sports Hall of Fame in 2005. He passed away in 1978 at the age of 57 and is buried in Rose Hill Cemetery in Grundy Center.

Sports Hall of Fame
Grundy Center, Iowa
Established 2004

Orville Allen

The late Orville Allen is shown left and center in 1952 and at right with long-time friend and teammate, John Doak in 2005 presenting Orv with his awards at the induction ceremony.

The 1950s are often described as the "Golden Years of Baseball". In Grundy Center, Iowa, a strong argument can be made about that same decade being the "*Golden Years of Spartan Sports!*"

The early 1950s started off for the Spartans with some powerhouse football and basketball teams that helped put Grundy Center on the map for Iowa high school sports. And Orville Allen was a key figure in getting that decade of sports off to a great start.

The Spartan football team in the fall of 1950 went undefeated during Orville's junior season. They were ranked highly in the state among small schools in the pre-playoff era.

As a two-year letterman on the gridiron, Allen played end on both offense and defense. While teams didn't throw passes like they do now, Orv caught a number of touchdown passes. Orville also took pride on the defensive side of the ball on how effectively he and linebacker and life-long friend, John Doak, would shut down opponents trying getting around their side of the field.

But basketball was Orville Allen's best sport. Orville was the team leader and a three-year letterman as the Spartans posted a record those years of 51-12. Fans in Grundy Center were very excited about those teams, especially the 1951-52 season when Orv was a senior.

Playing from the forward position, Allen was the only returning letterman his senior season. But with newcomers to the court like Hall of Famer Bud Bergman, Arnold Peterson, Jake Bergman, and Delbert Kell, the Spartans built on their two previous campaigns and put together a season to remember.

Orville long remembered how his older cousin, LuVerne Minnich, who lost his life in WW II, told him on more than one occasion that when Orv got to play in high school for the Spartans, they would go to State. And it happened!

Not only were the Spartans undefeated conference champions going into the State tournament series, they won the Sectionals, Districts, and sub-State championships to qualify for the State tournament for the first time in many years. They were also the only remaining undefeated team at 24-0 heading to Iowa City, which hosted the tournament at the Old Iowa Field House in 1952. Unfortunately, the Spartans lost to Glenwood in the first round of the tournament.

Looking back on it, what Orv remembered was their battle cry for the season was, "We're going to State!" That taught him a lesson to always set your goals as high as possible and "reach for the stars." After losing to Glenwood in the first game, he realized their battle cry should have been, "We're going to WIN State."

Interestingly, Orville won something else that senior season. He met a cheerleader from Traer who he married three years later, a marriage that lasted over 50 years.

Individually, Orville Allen was named to third team all-state and was recruited by several colleges to play basketball. He chose the University of Iowa and played one season there before enlisting in the Army. After his military service, Orv finished college at Northern Iowa, completed a Master's Degree, and moved on to Des Moines where he had a long and successful career with American Republic Insurance and Equity Dynamics.

Allen leveraged his lifelong interest in sports with many years of support for the YMCA, including serving on the Board of Directors. He even represented the YMCA organization in a delegation to the Soviet Union to establish a Youth Exchange program. He also served as the president of the Des Moines Golf & Country Club.

Several years after being inducted into the second class of the Grundy Center Sports Hall of Fame in 2005, Orville Allen passed away September 26, 2010 while living in retirement in Florida.

Sports Hall of Fame
Grundy Center, Iowa
Established 2004

Dennis Dirks

Dennis Dirks was inducted for basketball and baseball and also had a Hall of Fame coaching career as the Spartans Boys' golf coach for over 25 years. He is shown far left in high school basketball, next playing for Marshalltown Community College, then with daughters Trina and Kylie, and right accepting his awards in 2005.

Dennis Dirks was a unique blend of athletic ability, leadership by example, and performance under pressure. And he did it in three different sports at an all-conference level playing football, basketball and baseball.

On the gridiron, Dennis didn't get the glamour or headlines that came with the backfield and the receivers. He was in the trenches as a tackle on both offense and defense while lettering three years. Dirks was named all-conference as a senior and also handled punting and kicking chores for the Spartans.

When the Spartans of the early 1970s were looking for critical short yardage gains on the ground, they usually ran to Dirks' side. Likewise, opponents usually ran away from his tackle spot when running the ball where his quickness and toughness made him hard to block.

Basketball was an even better sport for Dennis. He earned three letters, started two years, was named all-conference both those years, and earned all-district honors as a senior and fourth team all-state.

On the court, Dennis dominated both offensively and defensively. Although not fast afoot, possessing superior jumping ability or gifted with great height, Dennis excelled through hard work, determination, and an exceptional feel for the game.

Dennis played in the middle of Hall of Fame Coach Harry Dole's full court press and often displayed an instinctive ability to intercept inbound passes by anticipating where the ball was going.

The 1971 Spartan basketball team was very similar to Orville Allen's 1952 Spartan team in many ways. Like the 1952 Grundy team, they went through the season undefeated at 23-0 often ranked #2 in the State, only to lose that first heartbreaking game in the State tournament just like the 1952 team.

Dirks was the Spartans' team leader and led them in nearly every statistical category playing with a strong contingent of players like Jerry Appel, Rod Ragsdale, and Hall of Famers Greg Goodman and Paul Eberline. Dennis was the consummate team player and helped mold good teams into great ones. And the 1971 team was one of the best.

As accomplished as Dennis was in basketball, his best sport was baseball where he again showcased his natural ability with his leadership skills on conference championship caliber teams coached again by Harry Dole. Dennis was an outstanding pitcher, a clean-up hitter with power, and a great glove man at third base. He played alongside Hall of Famers Mark and Paul Eberline, Rod Ragsdale, and Jerry Appel. As a hitter, Dennis could really turn on a fastball with his bat speed and power the ball deep into the outfield.

Pitching and playing third base requires a pretty strong arm and Dennis had one. To illustrate how strong his arm was, he could throw a softball from the back of the end zone on a football field beyond the opposite end zone. That takes a strong arm!

Dennis continued playing all three sports at Marshalltown Community College for two years and then went to the University of Northern Iowa where he concentrated on baseball. He continued to put up fine offensive numbers, but bursitis in his shoulder ended his pitching career by the time he got to UNI. However, it didn't affect his hitting as he played first base and designated hitter for the Panthers earning two letters.

Dirks returned to Grundy Center teaching business courses and driver's education. He also coached several sports including Boys' Golf for over 25 years. Dennis took the Spartan boys' team to State 16 times and won State championships in 2003 and 2005. All three of his children, Jordan, Trina, and Kylie Dirks, are also members of the Hall of Fame as golfers.

Sports Hall of Fame
Grundy Center, Iowa
Established 2004

Paul Eberline

Paul Eberline was a good all-around athlete and excelled at baseball in both high school and at Wartburg College. Right, John Doak presents Paul Eberline with his Hall of Fame awards in 2005.

When the freshman showed up for Hall of Fame Coach Harry Dole's baseball team the summer of 1969, he had no idea that the leading batting average for the team would come out of that freshman group. And that freshman was Paul Eberline, who played first base and pitched occasionally for the co-conference champion 1969 Spartans.

From that fast start, Paul Eberline started a baseball career that took him from Grundy Center all the way to the Orient as a member of a USA College All-Star team.

Paul was a lefty, both at the plate and on the mound. He certainly benefitted from a short right field fence, yet he didn't aim for that fence when he came to the plate. He aimed for the two-story house across the street! Not only did he occasionally hit the house, on one occasion he crushed the ball over the roof!

Paul did some pitching throughout his high school career and one of his most memorable games was on the mound against Dike. He had a "Sandy Koufax" type of game *before* Koufax found his control! Paul pitched a one-hit shutout that game and struck-out 16 batters. But as the legendary Paul Harvey used to say, "And here's the rest of the story." In that game, Paul also *walked or hit* 15 Dike batters!

Paul's twin brother, Mark, also a Hall of Famer, was an excellent ball player himself. He was catching Paul during this Dike game and Paul's many wild pitches were sending Mark running to the backstop too many times. Mark got so exasperated with

this wildness that on his last trip to the back-stop, he just rolled the ball back to Paul in frustration!

Following his outstanding high school career, Paul and twin brother Mark played baseball at Wartburg for Coach Ernie Opperman. Injuries kept Paul from playing as a freshman, so he went into his sophomore season untested and playing behind a senior first baseman.

In a Lou Gehrig-like manner, Paul got his chance to play when the coach got mad at his senior starter and put Paul into the line-up. For his first college at-bat, Paul doubled up the gap and never looked back. As Lou Gehrig did with his predecessor, Wartburg's senior first baseman never played that position again as Paul finished the Iowa Conference season hitting a red hot .618!

Paul remembered a couple of other college highlights. Upper Iowa boasted the conference's premier pitcher, a 6'6" fire-balling right-hander. In Paul's first at-bat against him, he hit a home run over the centerfield fence. In his second at-bat, he did it again sending the ball over the centerfield fence. In his third at-bat, he smashed a line-drive off the pitcher's shin that ricocheted into right field. Paul never faced that pitcher again. It's not hard to wonder why!

Paul also remembered a home run he blasted at a game against the University of Dubuque during a double header there. Paul went 7 for 9, but what stands out was a shot over the wall that was still going up as it left the stadium. It even went over a power line that was a good 100 feet behind the wall! He estimated it went 500 feet. So Paul could hit for power as well as average.

While baseball was Paul's ticket to the Hall of Fame, he was also a good basketball player and golfer for Coach Dole. Paul remembers Harry jumping into a rebounding drill and totally thrashing Paul for a few rounds and forcing him to take his game to the next level. He taught Paul up-close and personal how to make those rebounds his own.

Paul was elected to the Hall of Fame for baseball in 2005, the second class inducted.

Sports Hall of Fame
Grundy Center, Iowa
Established 2004

Tim Clark

Tim Clark was one of the Spartans' finest baseball and basketball players. He is shown left in action on the court, center as a Spartan basketball player in 1976, and right accepting his Hall of Fame awards in 2005 for both sports.

Tim Clark showed his natural athletic ability at a very early age, according to his little league baseball coach, Dave Pike. Even at 11 years old, Tim showed his athleticism in baseball with fielding skills, hitting, throwing, and that competitive drive and leadership which was soon paying dividends for the Spartans.

It was a great era for Grundy Center athletics when Tim was in high school. He played with other Spartan stand outs like Chris Hitchings and fellow Hall of Fame brothers Terry and Jeff Crisman. Tim earned 12 letters in baseball, basketball, cross country and golf.

The golf team was very respectable during the mid-1970s. During Tim's three years on varsity, they won the conference meet each year. They also won a Sectional championship and twice placed at State in the Top Ten. But Tim's forte was on the basketball court and the baseball diamond.

Building on those early skills from little league, Tim excelled in high school as a slick-fielding shortstop and pitcher. As a sophomore, Tim anchored the Spartans' infield that went all the way to the State finals in 1974 under Coach Don Kramer.

Tim's junior season, the Spartans again qualified for the State tournament and Tim was named first-team all-conference. One of his fondest memories was when he

played shortstop when Chris Hitchings pitched a perfect game against Beaman-Conrad!

During his senior campaign of 1977, the baseball team posted its best record going 14-3 and Tim was again selected first team all-conference.

As good as he was in baseball, Tim's high profile sport was basketball. As a starting guard his sophomore year in 1975, the Spartans went all the way to the State finals finishing runner-up in Class 1A where Tim was named first team All-tournament. He was also named first-team all-conference and honorable mention all-state as the Spartans finished the season 23-3 on one of the school's best-ever basketball teams.

It was more of the same for Tim as a junior as Coach Jim Brousard's hoopsters went 20-3 while winning the conference, Sectional and District tournaments. Tim was again named first team all-conference and conference Most Valuable Player. He was further named sixth team all-state by the *Des Moines Register.*

The 1976-77 season was another great one for the Spartans as Tim continued as the point guard and ball handler. The team posted a 21-2 record, winning the conference, sectionals, and districts once again.

During the regular season, Tim scored 36 points in a one point win over Waverly-Shell Rock, a team coached by Grundy Center native and Hall of Famer, Bud Bergman. Unfortunately, for the second year in a row, the season ended with a loss in the sub-State to Central Webster of Burnside in a heartbreaker.

Personally, Tim finished his high school basketball career earning first team all-conference and Most Valuable Player for the second consecutive year. He was named third team all-state and finished his Spartan career with 1,032 points.

After graduation, Tim played basketball and started for two years at North Iowa Area Community College where the team achieved a #1 ranking in the nation for a several weeks as they posted a 22-7 record in 1978 and a 23-8 record in 1979.

Tim gave a lot of credit to his coaches for their guidance, but he was most appreciative for the support received from his parents, Bob and Dorothy Clark, during his entire sports career. They never missed one of his games and were privileged to see one of the best basketball and baseball players in Spartan history.

Dave Smoldt

Dave Smoldt is shown in his days of playing football for Iowa State and right accepting his Hall of Fame award. He was a gridiron standout the Cyclones as a tight end and joined the Hall of Fame for football.

One of the first football memories, or maybe it was a nightmare, that Dave Smoldt remembered from high school football was with upperclassman Dave Ehrig, a Hall of Fame football player and wrestler. Smoldt was the underclassman and vividly remembered his indoctrination to Grundy Center football by getting knocked around in practice by Ehrig on a regular basis.

It must have done some good, because Dave Smoldt developed into an all-state football player himself and went on to distinguish himself as a starter for the Iowa State Cyclones.

Tim Hager coached the Spartans through the 1979 season which featured a strong cast of gridiron greats going 8-1 for the season. Their only loss was to Hudson, who made the State football finals that year.

Besides a solid group of linemen and running backs, the Spartans had a powerful passing game with Mike Plaehn at quarterback throwing to Todd Stumberg at wide receiver and Dave Smoldt at tight end. Additionally, the Spartans had a bone-crushing defense where Dave played linebacker.

One of the things that stood out in Dave's memory was Coach Hager's film sessions after each game. Mistakes did not go unnoticed by his team. When Coach Hager played and replayed a mistake, the ensuing heckling from teammates were great incentives to not make that mistake again and to avoid making others as well.

Dave gave a lot of credit to Coach Hager and the way he could motivate players and how well he related to them. Smoldt considered him a real "players coach."

Dave was a three year letterman in football and was named an Elite Team all-state linebacker and participated in the Shrine Bowl after graduating. He went on that fall to Iowa State where he played tight end and lettered three years earning honorable mention All-Big Eight in 1983.

His senior year in 1984, Dave was a team captain and named the Most Valuable Lineman for the Cyclones from his tight end position, yet he actually did catch 40 passes and was honored at the end of the season by being named first team All-Big Eight.

After graduating from Iowa State, Dave signed as a free agent with the Atlanta Falcons for his shot at professional football in the NFL. While that didn't pan out, Dave completed one of the most successful college football careers in Spartan history.

Sports Hall of Fame
Grundy Center, Iowa
Established 2004

Tracey Voss

Tracey Voss was an outstanding golfer who earned 13 letters while also playing softball, basketball and volleyball for the Spartans and went on to become an All American golfer for Simpson College.

It seemed obvious that great things were destined for Tracey Voss as a golfer when she made a hole-in-one at the age of 12! And so it was.

While Tracey's ticket to the Hall of Fame was golf, she was also a great all-around athlete earning 13 total letters for the Spartans in basketball, softball, volleyball and golf.

Tracey combined academics and athletics by graduating in 1992 as the class Valedictorian. She made numerous all-academic teams in her sports and also garnered a number of academic and citizenship awards as a senior. She was selected to the National Honor Society as a junior.

Her best sport, no doubt inspired by the hole-in-one as a youth, was golf. She was a four-year letterman for the Spartans, was named all-conference those four years, and twice named to the all-conference academic team.

Girls golf coach Rick Schupbach and his teams from the early 1990s put the Grundy Center golfers on the map winning the Class A State Championship in both 1991 and 1992. In fact, the 1992 team tied for the best overall team score with the Class 3A champions. Tracey teamed up with Jill Ahlberg, Marilyn Dellit, Monica Greany, Staci Kruger and Sue Meester to win those titles.

After playing her best two 18-hole golf rounds in high school at the State tournament, Tracey vividly remembers the trip home where she broke down and sobbed because she had just graduated from high school and golf was over and done! As it turned out, her golf career was far from over.

Tracey went to Simpson College where she golfed for Coach Bob Darrah and earned another four letters. Just like high school, Tracey was all-conference those four years and earned NCAA All-American honors as a sophomore! The Simpson women's golfers dominated the Iowa Conference winning the conference championship her freshman, sophomore, and junior years and only losing it by one stroke her senior season.

Simpson qualified for the National tournament each of her four seasons and finished second each year behind the same North Carolina team. Tracey earned All-American honors by finishing third in the Division III tournament, an accomplishment she is rightly proud of.

But one national tournament always triggered a vivid memory and the word, "shank." Tracey rarely played a round of "all fairways and greens." But as a freshman playing in her first National tournament, Tracey had to avoid her wedge like the plague because it just wasn't working. She got a lot of practice that day with "pitch & run" shots!

Tracey also remembers that her parents, Ron and Candi Voss, were there to support and cheer for her throughout her college career. They made trips to Massachusetts, Michigan, and Indiana in addition to her Iowa Conference play around the Hawkeye State. If they gave "All-American Fan" designations, Tracey felt strongly that her parents deserved it, even if she did hear a few gasping "sighs" from her mom when she landed in the rough or the bunkers.

Tracey was named to the GTE Academic All-American golf team her junior and senior seasons at Simpson before graduating Summa Cum Laude in 1996. But her golf life was not over.

Tracey and her husband lived in Colorado where she worked at a golf club in Highland Ranch, a PGA tour stop. She loved being around the sport so much that she even caddied for her husband in Colorado state amateur tournaments.

Bobbi Sealman

Bobbi Sealman was an outstanding all-around athlete for the Spartans who earned 16 letters while excelling in softball, basketball and volleyball.

Bobbi Sealman came from some pretty good Spartan sporting stock. Her dad, Bob "Goldie" Sealman, was an outstanding football lineman in the early 1960s and he Grundy Center's first heavyweight and winningest wrestler on John Doak's initial wrestling team in 1962.

Young Bobbi Sealman began her sports career at the tender age of five when she started tumbling lessons in Jane Jansen's basement. By the time she finished her gymnastics career to concentrate on high school athletics, she had won over 75 ribbons, trophies and medals at local, regional, state and even national levels!

Her gymnastics accomplishments included winning the balance beam title and the All-Around competition for the state of Iowa as well as being named the "Outstanding AAU Gymnast" for the State. She also spent two years on the National Junior Elite Development team. It turned out, Bobbi was merely giving Spartan sports fans a preview of things to come.

With no formal gymnastics program at the high school level, Grundy Center benefitted from one of the most talented athletes in the school's history. She earned 16 sports letters for the Spartans, won 10 all-conference awards, and four all-state honors.

Looking first at her softball record, Bobbi earned five letters where she played short-stop. She hit .358 as a freshman and led the conference champion Spartans in RBIs as they reached the Regionals. As a sophomore, Bobbi hit .425, led the team in in doubles and triples, and was second in both RBIs and total hits on another Regional qualifying team.

As a junior, Bobbi hit at amazing .510 and led the team in almost every hitting category. She had the sixth highest batting average in the State, was fourth in the State for home runs, and eighth in the State for RBIs.

Bobbi finished her softball career as a senior batting .391 leading the team in batting average, doubles, home runs, and second in RBIs and runs scored. She was named to numerous all-conference, all-district, and all-state teams. Any all-time Spartan girls softball team wouldn't be complete without including Bobbi Sealman.

Moving from the softball diamond to the basketball court, Bobbi once again excelled lettering all four years in high school and earning all-conference honors three years. She scored a career high 53 points her junior season against Dike and 49 points in a game against Beaman-Conrad as a senior. Bobbi ended her basketball career with a total 1,377 points including 77 three-pointers. She certainly knew how to put the ball through the hoop!

Bobbi earned three more letters in volleyball along with all-conference honors as a senior when she led the Spartans in kill shots, attack average and a serving efficiency of 96%. Bobbi was also named all-conference twice in tennis and lettered one year in track. She could do it all and do it very well. But high school wasn't the end of her career. Bobbi went on to earn six more letters at Ellsworth Junior College playing volleyball, basketball and softball.

During her Ellsworth basketball career, she was a two-year captain of the team and set three Ellsworth records. First, she set the two-year free throw shooting percentage with 81%. Second, she set the two-year three-point shooting percentage record with 75%. And third, she set the two-year record for most three-point baskets made with 77. Bobbi was named all-conference and earned all-tournament team honors as well.

Back to the softball diamond, Bobbi played third base and was all-conference both years. As a freshman she batted .425 and followed that with a .376 average the following season while leading Ellsworth in nearly every hitting category.

Before graduating from Ellsworth, Bobbi was named in the "*Who's Who*" in Junior College athletics and received the "Outstanding Female Athlete Award" from Ellsworth for her career achievements.

A truly gifted athlete, Bobbi will be long remembered for her many outstanding sports accomplishments.

Class of 2006

Harold Engelkes* 1943-1978

Max Appel* 1943

John Doak 1961-1974

Dave Pike 1969

Lance Van Deest 1982

Mike Stumberg 1985

Tim Baker 1986

Scott Yoder 1993

Front row: David Pike, John Doak, Lillian Appel (wife of Max), Maxine Engelkes, Carol Engelkes Brobst and Wilma Engelkes (representing Harold Engelkes). Back row: Mike Stumberg, Tim Baker, Lance Van Deest, and Scott Yoder.

Sports Hall of Fame
Grundy Center, Iowa
Established 2004

Harold Engelkes

Harold Engelkes, a popular area funeral director, was an ever-present figure at Grundy Center sporting events during a thirty-five year period announcing for football and basketball games. Harold's daughters Maxine and Carol are shown with Harold's wife, Wilma, following the 2006 induction ceremony.

When you look for contributors to honor with a place in the Grundy Center Sports Hall of Fame, the very first inductee in that category is perfect example of what type of person and activities qualify for the honor.

The late Harold Engelkes, long-time Grundy Center funeral director, was not only a highly respected businessman, he was a mainstay behind the scorer's table at any basketball game or in the press box at any football game from 1943 until 1978.

It was 1943 when Harold heard that the school needed a new scorekeeper for the basketball games. Having had about six years' experience prior to coming back to Grundy Center, he applied for the job and was accepted. His family thought this was a good job for Harold as he would have to "sit down and keep his mouth shut".

At both the football games and basketball games, Deke Behrens (former industrial arts teacher at the school) was usually the official timer and they worked together for thirty-three years, a relationship Harold valued and enjoyed.

In his scorekeeper's role, Harold's strong, low, gravelly voice resonated foul calls and substitutions with confidence and authority. And with all the chaos that goes hand-in-

hand with a high school game, he was always cool under pressure. Bad calls or good calls, exciting moments or not, Harold always maintained his poise.

But that doesn't mean he was infallible. One gaffe that Harold laughed about was when he called substitutions at a Spartan football game in the mid-1960s when Bob DeVries and Hall of Fame coach Randy Peters substituted for each other. DeVries had to come out of the game and Peters went in to play defensive end for him. Harold, as usual, kept up with substitutions and announced, "That's Peters going in for DeVries on the Spartan defense." But he would have liked to have his call back when they switched again the next play and Harold announced, "That's DeVries in and Peter's out."

Harold had a lot of fond memories of Spartan sports. He remembered the 1944 football team was undefeated, scored 185 points and shut-out every opponent. That team was coached by Melvin Fritzel, inducted into this Hall of Fame in 2005. Harold recalled that games were sometimes stopped by the officials if a player lost a contact lens. But, in 1947 a football game was stopped to help Bill Wilson find a gold tooth that he lost!

Harold was proud of the 1952 basketball team, led by Hall of Famer Orville Allen that made the State tournament field. That Spartan team played an undefeated regular season winning over such teams as Grinnell and Oelwein. But after winning Sectionals, Districts and sub-State, Grundy lost their only game of the season in the first round of State.

Harold also remembered the team of 1971 that went to the State basketball tournament by winning a sub-State game over United of Boone in one of the best played games he had ever seen. Harold always felt very close to that '71 team as those boys like Hall of Famers Dennis Dirks, Greg Goodman, and coach Harry Dole made him a part of their group. Harold was even sitting on the bench with them at Vets Auditorium in Des Moines, just as he had done with the 1952 team at the old Field House in Iowa City.

Other highlights during Harold's years of scoring included these memorable events. Roger Stachour made a basket sitting on the floor at the free-throw line with his back to the basket. Tim Ralston didn't get to play much during the 1973 season, but his last-second shot at Traer from beyond the center line gave Grundy Center a 47-46 victory.

Many other players Harold specifically remembered have been chosen for the Hall of Fame: Melvin Fritzel, Norm "Bud" Bergman, Arnold Reynolds, Rick Kriz, Tim Clark, and Kay Riek.

Harold Engelkes passed away in 1995, but it brings to mind a quote from an article by John Claassen in the *Spartan News* many years ago. Claassen said*, "Old sports heroes never die— they just turn into scorekeepers."* Harold Engelkes was certainly one of those. And he was one of the best.

At Harold's induction, his awards were received by his two daughters, Carol Brobst, and Maxine Engelkes, who also brought their mother, Wilma, to the induction ceremony.

Harold Engelkes
Contributor Award
2006
Contributor 1943-1978

The late Harold Engelkes was not only a highly respected Grundy Center businessman, he was a mainstay behind the scorer's table at basketball games or in the press box at football games from 1943 until 1978. In his scorekeeper's role, Harold's strong, low, gravelly voice resonated foul calls and substitutions with authority. With all the chaos in a competitive high school game, he was cool under pressure. Bad calls or good calls, exciting moments or not, Harold was always poised. Harold witnessed many great athletes and sports moments in Spartan history but he was particularly proud that the 1971 basketball team made him a part of their group ... sitting on the bench with them at Vets Auditorium in Des Moines just as he had done with the 1952 team at the old Field House in Iowa City. Harold passed away in 1995.

Above is the HOF plaque for Harold Engelkes on the Hall of Fame wall at the high school.

Sports Hall of Fame
Grundy Center, Iowa
Established 2004

Max Appel

Max Appel was part of the State Champion American Legion team of 1947. Right, members of the Max Appel family receiving his awards at the 2006 induction ceremony. Left to right are Max's wife Lillian, and children Maxine, Jerry, and Larry.

Max Appel represented the first athlete from the decade of the 1940s to be elected to the Grundy Center Sports Hall of Fame. This was a decade that spawned so many significant world events from the bombing of Pearl Harbor in 1941, the war with the Empire of Japan, the defeat of Nazi Germany, the dropping of atomic bombs in 1945, to the rise in world communism that started the Cold War. Max served his country in World War II and was part of the "Greatest Generation" that national news anchor Tom Brokaw wrote about so passionately.

In sports, Army was a national football powerhouse that had Heisman trophy winners Doc Blanchard and Glenn Davis as Mr. Inside and Mr. Outside. In 1941, Ted Williams was the last baseball player to hit .400 and Joe DiMaggio hit safely in 56 straight games as they sparkled on the baseball diamond.

In Grundy Center, Max Appel was a local star on the football field as an end and playing center on the basketball court. The games were different then. They were lower scoring and play was more conservative. Max and other Spartan athletes had no off-season camps to improve their skills. But in that era, Max Appel carved out an outstanding high school career and then went on to play on the best Legion teams the State of Iowa had to offer.

Max didn't move to Grundy Center with his parents until he started his freshman year in high school. He played both football and basketball, but basketball was his first love.

Sports Hall of Fame
Grundy Center, Iowa
Established 2004

Max and his parents lived four miles southwest of town and Max would tell his kids how he would have to walk home after practices and games. One winter evening, the weather was so bad, he got lost in a snow storm and barely found his way home.

On the football field, Max was an end and lettered three years for the Spartans. Their best season was Max's sophomore year in 1940 when Grundy won the North Iowa Cedar League championship and had a 7-2 record. As with many of our great athletes from earlier decades, statistics are hard to come by, but Max was impressive enough on the gridiron that he was recruited by and had the opportunity to play football at the University of Iowa.

As noted earlier, Max's first love was basketball and Grundy Center was exceptionally strong with Max standing at 6' 5". He was a foreboding figure leading the team as the center as well as the Spartans' leading scorer. During the three years that Max lettered, the Spartans had a combined record of 57-8.

During the 1940-41 season when Max was a sophomore, Grundy finished the year 16-3 winning the NICL and the county tournament.

The following season, as the nation plunged into World War II, Max led the Spartans to a 21-4 season repeating as conference champions. The also won the league playoff championship, repeated as county champions, and ram-rodded their way through the State playoffs wining Sectionals and Districts before losing in the finals of sub-State. They were just one game from the State tournament, which in those days had no class sizes.

That set the stage for a great senior campaign in 1942-43 when Max once again led the Spartans to one of their best seasons ever. Grundy went through the regular season undefeated and repeated as the NICL and county champions. But after winning all 20 of their games to that date, they felt the agony of defeat with a two point loss in the Sectional championships. It was a bitter disappointment and a hard way to end Max's high school basketball career.

Even though Max turned down a chance to play football at Iowa and to play basketball at the University of Colorado, his basketball career did not end. While staying home to farm with his brother, Raymond, Max played forward for Grundy's Legion ball team.

Those Legion teams Max played on were so good that fans around Grundy were saving up their gas stamps in 1946 to see them when they went to the State Legion

championships. The Grundy team didn't quite make it that year, but they came back the following year and were State champions in 1947!

One of the highlights of Legion basketball was playing against the Van Dyke House of David, a traveling black team of the era. Grundy defeated them once in Grundy Center 42-32 and the David's wanted a return game on a neutral floor in hopes of avenging the loss. They played the second game in the old Marshalltown Coliseum. Grundy won that game in even more dominating fashion 46-23 led by Max Appel with eighteen points. He nearly outscored the whole House of David's team!

This is Grundy Center's State championship Legion basketball team from 1947. Max Appel (#13) is the, the tallest person in the back row. Hall of Famers Roger Peters (#10 and next to Max) and Leon Bockes (#12) were also a part of the team.

Max Appel passed away about three weeks before his induction in 2006. However it brought the Appel family some comfort because Max was informed about this honor during the last month of his life. His wife, Lillian, accepted his awards with daughter Maxine and sons Jerry and Larry at her side.

Sports Hall of Fame
Grundy Center, Iowa
Established 2004

John Doak

Coach John Doak, left, started the wrestling program in Grundy Center. The photo to the center shows him in 1966 with Hall of Famer Steve Ehlers and right John is leading the "Parade of Champions" at the State wrestling tournament in 1976. Doak was elected to the Hall of Fame as both a coach and contributor.

John Doak was a good all-round athlete for Grundy Center in the early 1950s. He played football, basketball, and track in high school. While earning three letters in football, John was a team co-captain as a senior and named a second team All-Territory halfback by the *Marshalltown Times Republican* newspaper. On defense, he played linebacker behind defensive end and fellow Hall of Famer Orville Allen. John also lettered three years in track and one in basketball.

Going to school at Iowa State Teachers College, now the University of Northern Iowa, John was told he was too small for the football team, so he decided to try wrestling even though he'd never wrestled before. With his typical tenacity and ability to learn quickly, John made the team and secured the background in wrestling that would help lead to his Hall of Fame coaching career.

After a short teaching and coaching stint in Osage, Iowa, Doak was hired as a guidance counselor in Grundy Center in 1961. He then started the wrestling program from scratch where senior Bob "Goldie" Sealman was the program's first heavyweight and the Spartans' most successful wrestler in their inaugural season. With Goldie's strength and toughness, Coach Doak would have liked to have seen him as a four year wrestler. It was only a few years later when Hall of Famers Charlie Peters at 145# and Wayne Wrage at 133# led the 1965 Spartans to its first District championship with Wayne, Charlie and Larry McClanathon qualifying for State tournament. Wrage became Grundy's first State place winner finishing third.

.
Coach Doak built a solid program with a reputation for well-conditioned and fundamentally-sound wrestlers. The Spartans won a high percentage of their matches over John's 12 years of coaching. His teams won three Sectional titles, one

District title and qualified three wrestlers for State in the days of a two class system where only eight wrestlers to a weight class qualified for the State tournament.

There's a strong contingency of ex-Grundy Center wrestlers who still talk about running the stairs in the old elementary building. Not that they liked it, but Coach Doak made them do it! He sent his wrestlers up three flights, across the hallways, and down three flights over and over. The stairs weren't just for conditioning, but for putting a mental edge in his wrestlers' minds. This helped win matches when they thought they were tired and couldn't go on. The wrestlers still take great pride in the fact that they survived "the stairs."

John's most successful wrestlers included Hall of Famers Wayne Wrage, Charlie Peters, and Dave Pike along with Larry McClanathon, Gary Schroeder, and Doug Van Gelder. Two of John's wrestlers, Charlie Peters and Dave Pike, won conference championships in college. Charlie won his at Wayne State University and Dave at Northern Iowa. John also coached Pike to a second place finish in the 1969 State AAU freestyle tournament when freestyle wrestling in Iowa was in its infancy. As a great organizer, innovator, and promoter, Doak initiated the Spartan Invitational Wrestling Tournament which Grundy hosted for many years.

Coach Doak also revitalized boys tennis and played a key role in beginning Grundy Center's excellent tennis tradition that produced some of the state's best boys tennis players. This included two State champions in Bob Stock and Norm Riek as well as Steve Ehlers, Ed Palmer, and Dave Ralston, who all qualified for State in a one class tournament field. All of these players went on to play collegiate tennis and all have been elected to this Hall of Fame. It's hard telling how many State championships those teams and individuals would have won in today's multi-class system.

In the 14 years John was the Spartans tennis coach, his teams won 12 District tournaments and qualified 17 individuals for the State tournament. There were only two of those 14 years that a Spartan tennis player did not qualify for the State tournament. Four of Doak's players eventually became teaching tennis pros. John also came out of retirement to assist with the high school's girls' and boys' tennis teams in the early 2000s.

John Doak's wrestling influence went beyond his coaching career. In addition to refereeing high school and college wrestling meets and tournaments, he and his assistant high school wrestling coach, Dennis Highland, launched the very first-in-the-nation statewide newspaper devoted exclusively to high school and collegiate wrestling in 1970, covering the state of Iowa. They called it *"The Predicament."*

John Doak and Dennis Highland started the first state-wide newspaper in the country to focus exclusively on high school and college wrestling. The first issue is shown above.

"The Predicament" remained the leading wrestling publication in the state with several succeeding owners of the newspaper carrying on the tradition. John received a national award from Amateur Wrestling News as the "Writer of the Year" in 1972. He was further honored by being named the Grand Marshall of the Parade of Champions at the 1976 State wrestling tournament, the same year he was awarded the IHSAA wrestling coaches "Outstanding Contributors" award.   John was the first coach elected to the Hall of Fame with the additional category of "Contributor".

Coach John Doak with four of his Hall of Fame athletes in 2015: L-R: Dave Pike, John Doak, Charlie Peters, Wayne Wrage, and Steve Ehlers. Doak also coached Hall of Fame tennis players Bob Stock, Ed Palmer, Norm Riek, and Dave Ralston, not pictured.

Dave Pike

Dave Pike is shown left and center left wrestling in high school in 1969, center right in a 1972 Northern Iowa press photo and right at UNI in 1971 where he was a conference champion. Pike earned 15 letters for the Spartans and lettered all four years at UNI.

Dave Pike's wrestling career started inauspiciously as a freshman in November of 1965. As the Spartans came bursting out of the locker room toward the mat, the cheerleaders were holding a paper hoop for them to charge through, but held it right in front of the team chairs. Breaking through the paper, Dave and several teammates went tumbling over the metal folding chairs sprawling with embarrassment on the floor but fortunately uninjured. Minutes later, Pike avenged the only loss from his junior high career and started a stellar high school campaign.

The Spartan wrestling team of 1965-66 was Coach John Doak's best dual meet team and featured nine seniors. They posted an 11-1 dual meet record and won the Sectional title. Five Spartans won Sectional championships (Wrage, Mast, Schroeder, McClanathon, and Pike) and all nine seniors finished second or better in qualifying for Districts. Pike is circled along with team captain and fellow Hall of Famer, Wayne Wrage and Coach Doak.

Pike was the only freshman on the 1965-66 varsity team and posted a solid 14-6 record along with a sectional championship. The line-up featured nine seniors for John Doak's most successful dual meet team. As defending District champions, the Spartans were highly ranked in the State. Pike remembered the toughness of Hall of Famer Wayne Wrage and Gary Schroeder as team leaders along with other rugged seniors like Tom Van Gelder, Dennis Augustine, Marvin Groote, Roger Holeman, Darl Mast, Al Rewerts and State qualifier Larry McClanathon. Wrage and Schroeder instilled a hard work ethic Dave credited for a lot of his victories where conditioning could win out over talent and experience.

By the time Pike graduated from high school, he owned most of the individual career wrestling records such as most career wins, most pins, most team points, and most tournament championships. Pike was a lifetime 12-1 in sectionals while winning three titles. He finished his last two years with a 44-6 record, including a 15-0 record in five invitational tournaments as he chalked up five championships against heady competition.

Dave was proud to be the first Spartan, along with Tim Wrage and Doug Van Gelder, to win a tournament held in Grundy Center. That tough trio won championships in the 1968 class 1A sectional in Pike's junior season. He was also proud to be the first Grundy Center wrestler to win the hometown Spartan Invitational as a senior in its inaugural year. Dave shared team captain honors as a senior for the 1968-69 season with teammate Tim Wrage, whom he admired for his dedication, toughness, and determination on the mat.

Back in the late 1960s, only eight wrestlers qualified for State tournament at each weight class and it was a major disappointment to Dave that he never accomplished that feat. He had the misfortune of having both the State champion and the third place winners come out of his District as a junior and senior. However, he finished second in the Iowa's state AAU freestyle championship the summer of 1969 beating some Class 3A place winners. He was a member of the Iowa contingent representing the state of Iowa at the National AAU tournament in Wyoming.

While wrestling was his forte, Pike engaged in other sports and earned a total of 15 high school letters. Besides four letters in wrestling, Dave earned four more in baseball where he was Coach Harry Dole's first catcher on the 1968 and 1969 Spartan teams. He loved baseball and has great memories catching pitchers Rod Wolthoff and Jim Clark during those years. He also won three letters in football and track plus one in tennis. Pike was presented the Jordan Larson Athletic Citizenship Award in 1969.

Next, it was off to the University of Northern Iowa where Dave wrestled for UNI Hall of Fame coach Chuck Patten. He lettered all four years and saw significant varsity action. It was often Dave's lot at UNI to fill-in the line-up where needed and that's what happened in 1971 during his sophomore season.

UNI's senior 134 pounder was injured late in the season. Pike came down to his regular weight for the North Central Conference wrestling tournament, a conference that boasted four of the top ten Division II teams in the nation, including the Panthers. Coach Patten felt if Dave wrestled well at the tournament, he could potentially get a second place finish, conceding that Ken Stockdale, the defending conference champion and league MVP from Mankato State, was a lock to repeat his title.

However, in one of the tournament's major upsets, Pike not only made it to the finals, he beat Stockdale in a very exciting match that had the crowd on their feet as Dave held on for a 7-5 win. Just one week later, Stockdale went on to win the Division II national championship at 134#.

Dave Pike provided one of the biggest upsets in the 1971 North Central Conference championships when he unexpectedly beat the 1971 NCAA Division II national champion.

Pike also went to the 1971 NCAA Division II national tournament and won two matches to get into the quarterfinals. There he lost to the 1972 NCAA champion. His regret is that the rules in 1971 didn't give him a chance to wrestle-back for a top-8 finish and All-American status. The rules then required a wrestler to get beat by a finalist to get to wrestle-back. Those rules changed in 1972 to allow all wresters to wrestle-back after their first loss regardless of when it happened, but it worked against Dave in 1971.

Pike finished a solid career at UNI as a junior and senior wrestling winning nearly 70% of his career matches and chalking-up over 60 total victories. His career culminated with selection by UNI for recognition in Outstanding Athletes of America in 1973 and at graduation Dave received UNI's Purple and Old Gold Award for Conspicuous Achievement in Athletics.

Sports Hall of Fame
Grundy Center, Iowa
Established 2004

Lance Van Deest

Lance Van Deest was an all-around athlete for the Spartans earning 13 letters in football, basketball, baseball and golf. He went on to a strong college career at Wartburg for Coach Buzz Levick. At right, Rollie Ackerman presents Lance with his awards in 2006.

Many of our Hall of Fame inductees were great all-around athletes who have excelled at one or two sports, but played others, as well. Lance Van Deest certainly falls into that category. He excelled at basketball, but in earning 13 high school letters, he also played football, baseball and golf.

It would be "par for the course" to start with golf and Lance did a lot of "pars" in his four letter-winning years on the golf team. As an all-conference golfer for Hall of Fame Coach Dennis Dirks, Lance was part of the boys golf teams that were successful in winning the conference three times, the sectional title three times and placing in the top seven of districts three times.

On the gridiron, Lance was an All-North Iowa Cedar League defensive back and lettered three years on Spartan teams that went 20-7. Grundy Center finished second in the conference twice including an 8-1 season in 1979.

But Lance's ticket to the Hall of Fame was basketball. During his three letter-winning seasons, Lance was also awarded the Father John Connell team Most Valuable Player award, which tells us what Van Deest meant to the success of those teams.

Spartan teams from the 1979-80 season, when Lance was a sophomore, through his senior season of 1981-82 had a combined record of 47-16. They went undefeated in the conference Lance's junior year while winning the conference championship.

They finished runner-up in the conference the other two seasons. Lance was first team all-conference as a junior and senior and named an all-state first team player by the IPDA and he was a Dr. Pepper all-state participant as a senior. At graduation, Lance was awarded the Jordon Larson Athletic Citizenship award.

FRONT ROW (l-r): Jeff Curren, Robbie Fogt, John Venenga, Rick Ragsdale, Ron Ragsdale, Jeff Ryan, and Jeff Dole BACK ROW (l-r): Coach Huber, Dennis Porter, Mark Lebeda, Lance VanDeest, Mike DeBerg, Lowell Ware Randy Hinders, Larry Appel, Steve Jungling, and Coach Monke

The 1981-82 Spartan basketball team features two future Hall of Famers. Lance Van Deest is #41 and Jeff Dole is #15.

Following high school, Van Deest took his talents to Wartburg College where he earned another four letters in basketball. As a freshman, he was named "Most Promising Player". Lance fulfilled that promise and then some. As a sophomore, he earned honorable mention all-conference and was named the team's best defensive player, which he also won as a junior and senior.

Unfortunately, Lance suffered through some injuries throughout his athletic career. As a senior in high school, he broke his neck playing football and missed half his senior season of basketball. He also missed the majority of his junior and senior seasons of basketball at Wartburg with stress fractures in his left foot. The life lesson he learned was, *"You never know when you may have played your last game, so practice and play and live each day as if it's your last."* That is sound advice to all athletes and for life in general.

Lance had many fond memories of his sports career in Grundy Center and even some good memories from childhood that related to his sports career.

He remembered looking up to and trying to emulate the high school players when he was in grade school. His parents, Jim and Shirley Van Deest, would have a high school girl baby-sit Lance and his sister when they would go out for dinner on a Saturday night. Some of those times when the babysitter was there, three or four high school boys would come and shoot baskets with Lance in the drive way. Naively, he thought they were there to shoot baskets with him! It was years later before he realized they weren't there to shoot baskets with him, but rather to see the babysitter. In hindsight, *"I felt so used!"* he said with a smile.

Lance also had a lot of support and encouragement from the community as he developed his basketball skills. He remembers going up to the high school gym at 6:00/ a.m. and playing two-on-two or three-on-three with some of the adults in town, like Kevin Swalley and Brent Wilson. After those morning work-outs, they would go to work and Lance would go to school.

Van Deest also credited the great coaches he had throughout high school and college. They included Dennis Dirks, Lowell Monke, Bruce Huber, Tim Hager, Don Knock, Bob Schmadeke, and Wartburg's Buzz Levick.

In fact, Coach Dirks knew Lance was bound for greatness when he was still a sophomore playing junior varsity level games with dreams of reaching and playing at the varsity. When Lance suited for his first varsity contest against Iowa Falls, Coach Dirks waited until the fourth quarter before entering him into the game. As Dennis recalls, Lance's performance went something like this:

- 4 total minutes played before fouling out with his 5th foul
- 4 for 4 from the field
- 3 for 3 from the free throw line
- 11 total points

Not too bad for only four minutes of play. Coach Dirks noted that if Lance could have played the entire game like that, he could of scored 88 points! Of course he probably would have had over 20 fouls!

Mike Stumberg

Mike Stumberg had an outstanding Spartan football career and also earned All-American honors at Central College as a defensive tackle. He then became a football referee working up to games at the Division I college level in the BIG 10 Conference.

The Stumberg families in Grundy Center have long produced great athletes that have participated in various sports for the Spartans over the past 40+ years. And the first of the clan to be inducted into the Hall of Fame was Mike Stumberg. Mike excelled in the trenches of the football field as a defensive lineman earning All-American honors in college and even reaching the NFL.

Mike was a good all-around athlete in high school and participated in a variety of sports including golf, track, wrestling, baseball and football. On the baseball diamond, Mike anchored the infield at first base where he was all-conference and the team co-captain.

But football is where Mike was an unmovable force from his defensive end position on the State tournament teams coached by Don Knock. As a junior, the 1983 team won the North Iowa Cedar League title and made it to the State semi-finals with Mike and Hall of Fame teammates Jeff Dole and Tim Baker.

In the fall of 1984, the Spartans went all the way to win the State championship capping an undefeated 12-0 season. Mike was named first team all-conference and first team all-state by the *Des Moines Register* at defensive end.

After graduation, Mike moved on to the outstanding football program at Division III powerhouse Central College in Pella under Coach Ron Schipper, where Mike lettered all four years. In his first season in 1985, he won the freshman Most Valuable Player award while still playing defensive end.

Moving to the defensive tackle position as a sophomore, Mike earned first team All-Iowa Conference with 76 tackles, 24 of them unassisted, 21 for losses, and 13 sacks of the quarterback. He also won the team's award for the outstanding underclassman player.

Mike continued to improve the following season at his defensive tackle position and chalked up 102 total tackles, of which 41 were unassisted, 37 were for losses, with 28 sacks as he once again earned first team all-conference honors.

Topping off his career at Central as a team co-captain, Mike dominated the conference and pushed his total tackles to 109, with 40 unassisted, 26 for losses and 24 sacks. For the third straight year, he was named first team All-Iowa Conference and he was additionally named conference Most Valuable Player. He was further named to four All-American teams, including the Associated Press and American Football Coaches Association. Mike was also a nominee for Domino's NCAA Division III "Player of the Year."

Mike Stumberg was an All-American defensive lineman for Central College and team captain. He was named first team All-Iowa Conference three times and he was additionally named conference Most Valuable Player as a senior. Mike was further named to four All-American teams, including the Associated Press and American Football Coaches Association. He was also a nominee for Domino's NCAA Division III "Player of the Year."

Sports Hall of Fame
Grundy Center, Iowa
Established 2004

Interestingly, Mike said the hardest hit he ever took on the gridiron came from Central College teammate and Grundy Center graduate, Ron Saak, who played middle linebacker. One play, Mike made a stop at the line of scrimmage and Ron piled on at full speed, ear-holing Mike knocking him out for a few seconds.

From a team perspective, Central College reflected the success that Mike enjoyed individually. In Mike's four years, Central was 44-5 with NCAA Division III playoff appearances each year and a second place finish in 1988.

Mike held at least six Central records including most sacks in a game (5), most sacks in a season and most sacks in a career (an astounding 64!). Just to put this in perspective, the NCAA only started tracking this statistic since 2000 and the recent NCAA record for all classes was 49. Similarly, Mike held the Central records for most tackles for losses in a game (7), season and career.

Mike took it to the next level by signing a free agent contract with the Seattle Seahawks and played in four games before a knee injury ended his pro career.

Football remains in Mike's blood. After moving back to Grundy Center, he took up football officiating and is currently on staff with the BIG 10 Conference. Mike has been honored with the following post-season bowl assignments: the BIG 10 championship game, the Orange Bowl, the Russell Athletic Bowl, the Heart of Dallas Bowl and the Texas Bowl.

Tim Baker

Tim Baker was a talented athlete for the Spartans who excelled at football and went on to play varsity for the Iowa State Cyclones as a defensive back. Right, Tim is receiving his awards from Rollie Ackerman at the 2006 induction ceremony.

It will be hard to find another tandem where two Grundy Center Spartan athletes and high school teammates, started together in the backfield of a major college football team. But it happened at least once.

In this case, it was the defensive backfield for the Iowa State Cyclones and the tandem are two of the best Spartan athletes seen in the 1980s. Those Spartan athletes are Charter Class Hall of Famer Jeff Dole and 2006 inductee, Tim Baker.

Grundy Center was blessed with some outstanding athletes in the mid-1980s and Tim Baker was one of those great talents. He had success in more than just football, where he lettered four years in high school. He also lettered three years in track, three in basketball, and one more in baseball for a total of 11 letters.

In basketball Tim played on teams that had a combined record for three seasons of 60-13, won two conference titles, three sectional championships, three district championships, two sub-State championships, two State tournament appearances, and a second place finish in the Class 2A tournament. Individually, Tim earned all-conference honors and all-state honorable mention as a forward.

Track was another outstanding sport for Tim. He literally hit stride as a senior by qualifying for the State long jump and finished runner-up in the State finals for the 400 meter low hurdles. He also set a school record in the 100 meter high hurdles. Tim was awarded the A.V. Dieken Award as Most Valuable Player on the track team.

But Tim's best sport was football and he played in a great era for Coach Don Knock. In his four years on varsity, the Spartans went 36-5, winning the conference three times and qualifying for State twice. As a junior, Tim quarterbacked the Spartans all the way to the top with a State championship!

Tim Baker #11 is running the option in the Spartans victory in the State championship game in the fall of 1984.

For Tim individually, he won honors as the Most Valuable Back in the conference as a senior and received all-state recognition from the *Des Moines Register* and IDPA. He also won the Deke Behrens Award for the team Most Valuable Player as a senior and also the Jordan Larsen Athletic Citizenship Award. Then it was on to Iowa State where he reunited with Spartan teammate, Jeff Dole.

Although noted for his offensive abilities in high school, Tim turned his talents to defense in college. While attending an Iowa State football camp, Tim captured the

attention of one of the Cyclone coaches for his defensive skills. They followed his high school career and convinced Tim that he had a future in Iowa State's defensive back field. And they were right. Tim excelled for the Cyclones in winning four letters as a safety.

While the memories of winning the State championship in football and finishing runner-up in basketball his junior year will always be at the top of Tim's high school memories, the transition from high school football to Division I football was an experience he'll never forget.

Tim learned quickly that he was playing in a much higher level of competition. He secured a couple of spots on special teams for the first game against Iowa and was feeling pretty good about it.

In one of the last practices before the Hawkeye game, the coaches decided the Cyclones needed to "go live" with the kickoff team. Well, one of their All-American linebackers was declared ineligible for the Iowa game, so in order to keep him "fresh" they put the linebacker on the "meat squad" kick-off return team in practice.

As Tim went flying down the field at full speed trying to make an impression on the coaches, that 250 pound All-American Cyclone linebacker came out of nowhere and "ear-holed" him. Next thing Tim knew, the bottom of his feet were pointing skyward and he landed flat on his back as a chorus of *"OOOHH's"* echoed from around the field. He managed to survive that hit and keep his place on special teams for the Iowa game. The coaches must have figured if Tim could survive a hit like that, he was a "keeper".

Game time against Iowa finally came and Tim was all excited to hit the field for the first time. His initial chance on the field was on the punt coverage team. They lined-up and as soon as the ball was snapped, Tim started to release to go down field. But, the Iowa player across from him gave him a forearm shiver through his face mask right to the nose. When he ran back to the sidelines after the play, with blood gushing from nose, he looked like he'd been on the wrong end of a Joe Frazier left hook! Tim quickly realized the speed of the game was a little different from his days of running the belly option against Hudson, Dike and North Tama.

Despite being on the receiving end of a hard hitting start, Tim went on to finish a great career with the Cyclones. Among his accomplishments were being named Big Eight Defensive Player of the Week, being awarded the Cyclone Defensive Player of the Year in 1989, being named honorable mention all-conference and being named a team captain his senior season. It was a great way to top off a great career.

Scott Yoder

Another outstanding all-around athlete, Scott Yoder earned 14 letters for the Spartans. He went on to play football at the University of Iowa as a linebacker. Right, Scott received his Hall of Fame awards from Rollie Ackerman in 2006.

Scott Yoder freely admitted his biggest inspiration was his brother, Kevin, who was two years older. Scott remembers when they were growing up, Kevin would let him tag along everywhere he went to play pick-up games. Kevin took Scott with him to play in every sport with the older kids and never told him to stay home. And one of Scott's fondest sports memories was playing football with him during Kevin's senior season.

The "older kids" must have taught him well because Scott earned 14 letters in his high school career with four in football, four in tennis, three in basketball and three more in baseball. It didn't matter what ball he used, Scott was adept at all of them.

The tennis teams of the late 1980s and early 1990s continued the strong Grundy boys' tennis tradition started by Bob Stock over 30 years before. Scott Yoder played on three consecutive conference championship tennis teams, won two conference singles titles and earned all-conference honors in the North Iowa Cedar League. Scott's quite proud of that accomplishment because during his freshman year, he doesn't remember winning one match!

On the basketball court, Scott started his junior and senior seasons and helped lead the team to its first State appearance since 1985. He was all-conference NICL averaging 10 points a game and leading the league in rebounding.

Sports Hall of Fame
Grundy Center, Iowa
Established 2004

An even better sport for Scott was baseball, where he was a solid first baseman during the three years he started and lettered for Hall of Fame Coach Phil Lebo. Scott was first team all-conference and second team all-district as a junior and honorable mention all-state as he led the team in home runs and RBIs.

His senior season, Scott batted over .400 and again led the team in home runs and RBIs leading the Spartans to their first State tournament appearance in over 20 years where they reached the semi-finals. He was particularly proud to have been co-captain of this team and scoring the winning run in the sub-State final against four-time defending State champions Kee High of Lansing.

Yoder was first team all-conference, first team all-district and second team all-state in wrapping up his baseball career for the Spartans.

But it was the gridiron where Scott truly excelled as one of the best running backs to ever don a Spartan football uniform. He was a starter for three years and finished his career as one of the top rushers not only Spartan history, but in the North Iowa Cedar League as well, compiling over 2,800 yards rushing and 40 touchdowns. He was also an exceptional linebacker with 270 career tackles and a great punter, too.

As a sophomore, Scott was an all-conference running back and the NICL punter of the year. As a junior, he led the Spartans back to the playoffs as they won the conference where he was again all-NICL and first team all-district as a linebacker. Scott was the NICL punter of the year again and was named first team all-state in that role.

In his senior season, Scott and the Spartans continued their winning ways qualifying for the playoffs again. He was named first team all-district as a linebacker again and first team all-state as well. He is one of only a select few Grundy Center football players to participate in the Iowa Shrine Bowl.

Showing he had brains as well as brawn, Scott graduated with a 4.0 grade point and was Valedictorian of his class making him one of the best student athletes Grundy Center ever had.

Moving on to college, Scott was a walk-on in Iowa City for the Hawkeyes and by his senior year had earned a full-ride scholarship. He was one of only two of the 20 walk-ons his freshman year that made it through five seasons. He spent much of his career on special teams, but as a senior was a contributing linebacker helping the Hawks reach a bowl game four of his five years on the team.

Scott was part of a Hawkeye defense that ended the year ranked fourth in the country in total defense and he personally earned Defensive Hustle MVP awards against both Northwestern and Minnesota.

Scott may also own the Hall of Fame record for most "*boos*" on a play. During that Northwestern game, he was playing man-to-man coverage on the tight end. Scott was on him like a glove and broke up the pass. Every partisan Northwestern fan in the stadium thought it was pass interference and Yoder immediately received a resounding chorus of boos from 35,000 Wildcat fans! But it certainly didn't hurt Scott's feelings or his coaches!

Scott also played in the National College All-Star football game before graduating and moving to Colorado Springs where he was the linebacker coach for Division III Colorado College. While there, he played a year of Arena football with the Rocky Mountain Thunder.

Scott Yoder goes down in Spartan sports history as one of its greatest all-around athletes.

Class of 2007

Vernon Morrison* 1921

Leon Bockes* 1945

Glen Van Fossen 1954

Al Harberts 1957

Ivan Miller 1966

Norm Riek 1972

The Class of 2007 front row: Glen Van Fossen, Chad Bockes and Mabel Bockes (grandson and wife of Leon Bockes), and Clare Morrison (son of Vernon Morrison). Back row: Norm Riek, Ivan Miller, and Al Harberts.

Vernon Morrison

Vernon Morrison was elected to the Hall of Fame as a Coach and Administrator. He is a member of four other Hall of Fames in Minnesota. His son, Clare (right photo) accepted his dad's awards on Vern's behalf in 2007 from John Doak.

The people who know anything about Grundy Center athletes who pre-date World War II are few and far between. But those few would remember the Morrison brothers from the early 1920s. One of those brothers was Vernon Morrison.

Vernon made his mark on athletics as a competitor in both high school and college, but left his true legacy in the state of Minnesota as a coach and administrator. In fact, Morrison's already a member of four separate hall of fames in Minnesota: the Minnesota High School Football Coaches Association, the Minnesota High School Coaches Association, the Minnesota Athletic Directors Association, and the Tech High School Hall of Fame in St. Cloud, Minnesota. The Grundy Center Sports Hall of Fame makes five!

Morrison's status in the Gopher state is legendary, but he got his start as a 1921 graduate of Grundy Center High School. His success as a Spartan athlete and then at nearby Iowa State Teachers College (now Northern Iowa) laid the foundation for many future successes as a coach and athletic director.

Not surprisingly, there is very little information available on Vern's high school days. But while playing at age 19 on an amateur basketball team called the Grundy Center "Reds", Vern, along with twin brothers Lloyd and Floyd, took the hoopsters to the finals of the Iowa Amateur Basketball Tournament. The "Reds" finished the season 29-3. Another teammate on the "Reds" was Hall of Famer, Forrest Meyers, who along with Lloyd Morrison and Vernon were the team's leading scorers.

At times during the 1923 season, this basketball team played four Morrison brothers. That was Vern, his older and identical twin brothers Lloyd and Floyd, and Vern's

oldest brother, Ray. Incidentally, Lloyd and Floyd occasionally switched jerseys to fool opponents since nobody could tell the difference!

Considering Vern made his reputation as a football coach, he never played a down competitively. He either didn't play in high school or there wasn't a Spartan team at that time. Morrison went out for football at Iowa State Teachers College (UNI), but sustained season ending injuries both years he tried to play. As a result, his focus turned to basketball and baseball and he played both of those in high school and college.

Vern initially went to Cornell College for a year and then transferred to Iowa State Teachers College (UNI), where he had to sit out a year of competition. As a two-year starter on the Panthers' basketball team, Vern Morrison established a reputation for his two-hand set-shot. He was so consistent on the basketball court that his son, Clare, said Vern was recognized with a plaque on a wall in the Old Men's Gym honoring Panther student athletes for scholarship and sportsmanship where he was known as "*Steady Eddie Morry*".

On a trip back to UNI while Clare was growing up, Vern took his son and showed him that plaque. Clare wondered if it's still in the Men's Gym today and this author found it in the summer of 2016, worn and hard to read, but Vern was the first recipient.

On the baseball field, Vern was a third baseman and shortstop and did play for UNI, although Clare is not aware if he was a letter winner or not. Chances are he was because his picture was featured prominently in his college yearbooks for baseball and Vern also played a couple years of Class A baseball.

Following college, Vern headed north to start his coaching career. He coached football, basketball and track at Ortonville, Minnesota where his five-year gridiron

record was 24-2-2. He then moved on to Hutchinson where his four-season record was 21-3-5.

Next, Vern went on to St. Cloud Tech where he cemented his coaching reputation as one of the best-ever in the Gopher state, going 121-25-9 from 1935-1954. In the early 1940s, Vern's St. Cloud Tech teams set a State record of 32 straight wins in football that stood for decades. Another great accomplishment was the 1946 team that went undefeated at 7-0 and outscored all opponents by 157-0, a season of shutouts, just like the Spartans did in 1944.

Vern always felt that the key to success was not so much what the coach knew, but what his players could learn. He was a great psychologist and had a way of convincing his players they could win. If students had some ability along with the desire, dedication and willingness to work hard, Coach Morrison had a place for them on his teams.

It was a successful formula as Vern retired from coaching in 1954 with a career record of 166-30-16 over 29 seasons. That's an average of only 1 loss per season and an 85% win ratio. Beside coaching football, Morrison also served as Tech High's Athletic Director for many years where he proved he could administrate every bit as well as he could coach.

When talking to Clare about his dad's accomplishments, he felt Vern's most outstanding achievement was building the Minnesota State High School Coaches Association from a fledgling group to one of the best coaches associations in the country. Vern served as Executive Director of that organization from the 1950s until his retirement in 1975. Membership soared from just a few hundred to over a thousand during his tenure. Morrison was also the first president of the National High School Football Coaches Association illustrating his reputation went well beyond the borders of Minnesota.

If being a coach, a history teacher, an athletic director, and everything else he did for education and his schools weren't enough, Vern was also active in his community serving as a Scoutmaster, St. Cloud City Charter Commission, county draft board, Kiwanis, and the Chamber of Commerce. His was a life well lived in the service of others and his influence was wide-spread in St. Cloud and the state of Minnesota.

Vernon Morrison passed away in 1981 and is buried in St. Cloud, Minnesota. He was inducted into the Grundy Center Sports Hall of Fame in 2007 as a coach and administrator and was represented at his induction by his son, Clare Morrison. Vern was the first administrator elected to the Hall of Fame.

Sports Hall of Fame
Grundy Center, Iowa
Established 2004

Leon Bockes

Leon Bockes was a standout in both football and basketball for the Spartans. He was represented at his induction by his wife, Mabel, and grandson, Chad.

Leon Bockes passed away a week or two before his induction into the Hall of Fame. He was a strong all-around athlete in football, basketball, baseball and track. Dave Pike had the pleasure of calling Leon a month prior to his passing to get the background for his induction biography and said Leon had fun reminiscing about his career. Pike noted Bockes was truly humbled and honored to be elected to the Hall of Fame.

A 1945 Grundy graduate, Leon was an end on defense and offense for those memorable Melvin Fritzel-coached teams in the mid-1940s. At a time when most male teachers were off to WW II, there was a real shortage of coaches. Leon remembers Melvin Fritzel, a Hall of Famer himself, had recently retired from coaching in college and was coaxed out of retirement to coach the Spartans in those war years. And he produced back-to-back undefeated seasons in 1943 and 1944 where the Spartans were 14-0-1.

The Grundy gridiron team of those years featured players in addition to Bockes like Hall of Famer Max Appel, Bud Peterson, Kay Reynolds, Max Smith, Lyle Heltibridle, Harry Borne, Hank Mol, Beverage Nickerson, Bill Kuhlman, and Vernon Feisner to mention a few.

In 1943, Spartans only gave up two touchdowns, both in lopsided wins, while going 7-0 in their games. They played at the former football field next to the old junior high school, which was the high school back then. They outscored opponents 242-13, an average of over 34 points a game to less than two points a game for their victims. The Spartans had a strong offense led by Bud Peterson to go along with a stingy defense and Leon was a key part of both. Peterson personally scored 161 of the team's 242 points.

The next year, the fall of 1944, the Spartans held their opponents scoreless for the entire season. No team crossed their goal line. They were tied once that season in a scoreless first game of the year against Tama. And they had some tough games from Nevada and Teachers High School, but for the season, Coach Fritzel's team outscored the opposition 186-0! Of course, Leon Bockes was in the middle of it both seasons as one of the defensive and offensive ends.

Leon specifically remembers one tough game against Ackley his junior year with game still scoreless and the ball on the 40 yard line. Bud Peterson was calling signals in the huddle. They had a pass play called 17-L, but in the huddle, Peterson just said to Leon, "*Go straight down and cut left. Be down by the English Room window and I'll throw it to you.*" Leon did what he was told and saw the ball soar toward him while being closely covered. As it came down, he wasn't sure he could reach it. But Bockes jumped and caught the ball while being immediately hit by the Ackley defender in the end zone. Leon held onto the ball to score the winning points on a 40 yard touchdown pass reception.

Coach Fritzel must have been pretty confident with the teams those two years because Leon remembers that Fritz loved to duck hunt. One time on opening day of the duck season, Melvin announced that if he wasn't back in time for the beginning of practice, to go ahead and start without him. And they did. They just finished calisthenics when Fritz showed up.

Leon also noted another thing that made them good was they were allowed to scrimmage against alumni. This was good since in 1944, they only had 17 guys on the squad. When the alumni weren't around, they would have to scrimmage on just one side of the ball during practices.

Grundy Center also had some strong basketball teams during Leon's era. As a freshman, Leon credits Deke Behrens for teaching him a lot about the game. As a three-year basketball letterman, Leon played forward as well as some center. As a sophomore with Max Appel leading the way, the team went 21-1 where Leon played

with Max, Bud Peterson, and Roy and Russell Thoren. They lost their only game in the State tournament sectional.

As a junior, the Spartans were 11-1 with many of the same players, but weren't able to advance in the State tournament qualifying games. Leon's senior season wasn't quite as successful finishing 9-14. But Bockes also played Legion ball on a very strong Grundy team that won the State in 1947. In fact, in a game on the night before he reported for duty to the Army, Leon scored 30 points.

Grundy's Legion teams were very good in those years. Leon played on those teams which featured guys like fellow Hall of Famers Roger Peters and Max Appel along with Bob Grabinski and Doug Arends.

The following story was also captured in Max Appel's biography about how the Grundy Legion team beat a traveling team called the House of David by 20 points in a game in Grundy. The "David's" wanted a rematch on a neutral site, so they played again in Marshalltown and beat them even worse. Well, Leon Bockes was on that team, too, and here, as Paul Harvey would say, is the rest of the story.

During the rematch, Leon dived after a ball going out of bounds early in the second quarter. In that effort, he ripped his basketball shorts in the crotch all the way up the back side, "*stem-to-stern*" Leon said. In order to finish the game, he had to use a pair of white boxer shorts belonging to Bob Grabinski for the remainder of the game.

Leon was offered two scholarships coming out of high school, but instead went into the Army and married his wife, Mabel. He played both basketball and baseball in the Army. On the diamond, Leon played centerfield and was a decent power hitter and carried a pretty fair average. But what he really remembers is playing in wool uniforms, typical of the day even in the major leagues. The uniforms were very hot and became quite heavy with perspiration.

Although he didn't quite live until his induction ceremony, Leon was well represented at the event by his wife Mabel and grandson, Chad.

The offensive line of the undefeated and unscored upon 1944 Spartans. Bockes is circled.

Sports Hall of Fame
Grundy Center, Iowa
Established 2004

Glen Van Fossen

Glen Van Fossen is shown in high school basketball and baseball. In the mid-1950s he played baseball for the Iowa Hawkeyes as a third baseman and pitcher. He is shown right in 2007 at his induction getting his awards from John Doak.

The 1950s may have been the golden age of baseball, but it was also a golden age of Spartan athletics. Putting out great teams on the gridiron, basketball court, baseball diamond and the cinder track, Grundy Center sported great individual athletes like Hall of Famers Orville Allen, Bud Bergman, Bill Smith, and Glen Van Fossen, who graduated in 1954.

An all-around athlete, Glen played beside Hall of Fame athletes like Orv Allen, Bud Bergman and Hall of Fame coach John Doak during his Spartan career, complementing the talent on those teams of the 1950s decade.

Glen did not start his high school career in Grundy Center. He had already lettered in basketball and baseball as a freshman at Thornburg High School in the southeast part of Iowa. After relocating to Grundy, Glen proceeded to earn three more letters in each of those sports plus an additional three in football for the Spartans.

Fellow Hall of Famer Bud Bergman and Glen Van Fossen were classmates. Army football had the famous duo of Glen Davis and Doc Blanchard in their backfield in the 1940s. In the 1950s, Grundy Center had Glen Van Fossen and Bud Bergman. Not only did opponents have to deal with them on the football field, they had to deal with this pair on the basketball court and the baseball diamond.

On the football field, Glen played the single wing swing back who got to throw the ball and run it, too. He also played end when Bud Bergman had the swing back duties

and was surrounded with other talented teammates like Jerry Smith, Jim Wells, Gene Grimmius, and Don Niehaus. The Spartan team of 1953 ended highly ranked in the State during Don Abney's first year as the Spartans' coach.

Van Fossen climaxed a great high school football career in the fall of 1953 with a team that went undefeated at 8-0, winning the North Iowa Cedar League championship. Glen earned third team all-state honors from the *Des Moines Register* and fourth team all-state by the IDPA during an era before there were classes or football playoffs.

The most memorable game in Glen's career was the last game of the 1953 season. Both Grundy Center and Reinbeck were undefeated and the Spartans had to travel to Reinbeck for the game. Glen remembers there was a huge crowd on hand with over 3000 people that all but shut down the town. Grundy Center won the game with a 12-0 shutout. Glen scored a 30 yard touchdown on an end-around that helped turn the tide in favor of the Spartans.

Glen was also very successful on the basketball court during his three years as a Spartan. He was the sixth man on the 1952 team led by Orville Allen that went undefeated in the regular season and into the State tournament before losing their only game. It was a team that the long time Spartan scorekeeper Harold Engelkes said was one of his two favorite basketball teams of all time.

While the Spartans of 1953 and 1954 did not make it back to State where there were no classes to separate the big schools from the smaller ones, they produced excellent teams wining the NICL, county and Sectional championships. Glen played guard and his teammates in addition to Bergman included Jerry Smith, John Doak, Arnold Peterson, and Chuck Smoldt. The three-year combined record of those Spartan teams Glen played on was 63-6. If you take out the State tournament series losses, they were 63-3.

Glen was a good hustler on the court and earned all-state honorable mention as a junior and senior. He fondly remembers when the Grundy coach thought the Spartans could help sharpen their game by scrimmaging a tough team from East Waterloo. And they beat them!

As good as Glen was in football and basketball, his best sport was probably baseball where he was a successful pitcher and infielder. Glen was a right-handed pitcher with a good fastball and left-handed batter who, while he didn't hit for power, could be counted on for putting the bat-on-the-ball chalking up singles and doubles at the plate.

Glen shared pitching duties with Bud Bergman. As a senior, the Spartans only lost one game when both Bud and Glen came up with sore arms at the same time. Jimmy Wells was the catcher and when Glen was pitching, Wells would stuff his catcher's mitt with a bra pad. Glen doesn't know where Jimmy got it, but it took the sting out of his fastball.

The 1954 Spartan baseball team features two Hall of Fame members.

In addition to his Spartan exploits, Glen went on to the University of Iowa and lettered three years on the Hawkeye baseball team in the late 1950s. He was on campus pitching and playing third base during the same era as the Hawkeyes legendary Rose Bowl winning football teams of 1957 and 1959.

Glen also played semi-pro baseball for Anson's in Marshalltown from 1954-1960. He remembered that Bill Welp, a catcher in Dodgers organization, caught him. Another memory was a game when the coach asked Glen to pitch the first three innings against an All-Star team from the Quad Cities. Glen struck out 7 of 9 hitters and that was really about as long as he could throw hard in those days. But the coach asked him to stay in the game and he got shellacked the next few innings. Another season with Anson's, Glen was hitting over .400 and then had to go to ROTC camp. When he came back, Glen said he couldn't hit a thing!

Glen was inducted into the Grundy Center Sports Hall of Fame in 2007 as a baseball player.

Al Harberts

Al Harberts owned the Spartan record for the mile run for over 50 years and was part of State record relay teams from the late 1950s. Right, Al is receiving his Hall of Fame awards from John Doak in 2007.

For most of his life, Al Harberts lived right in Grundy Center where he worked and raised a family. He was a common sight downtown or at Spartan sporting events. What most people didn't know or remember is that Al held the school's record for the mile run for a half a century. It was 50 years before it was finally broken 2006 by Hall of Famer Dana Schmidt. Al's 4:31 mile stood the test of time making it a true Hall of Fame achievement.

It is interesting to note that the previous mile record was held by Hall of Famer Don Purvis, who held the record 25 years before Al broke it. The mile run wasn't the only school or State record that Al was a part of, but it should be noted that Al was also a good basketball and football player in his high school days.

Al was an end on the football team all four years in high school, lettering twice. He lettered as a sophomore on a mediocre Spartan that was 2-6 for the season. Then, as a junior, Al hurt his knee and was unable to play in the fall of 1955. But his senior season, Al was back on the gridiron for the 1956 Spartans playing both offense and defense on a team which went undefeated going 8-0 and winning the North Iowa Cedar League Conference championship behind the running of Hall of Famer, Bill Smith. Perhaps Al's favorite football memory was sealing a victory over Eldora with a 63 yard return of an intercepted pass for a touchdown. Al was recognized as an all-area end by the *Marshalltown Times Republican*.

Basketball was Al's third sport and he earned three letters on the court. While lettering his sophomore year, the Spartans tied for the conference championship with

a 9-3 record and 14-7 overall. As a junior and coming off his knee injury, the team wasn't as good, reversing the previous year's record to 7-14. However, Al had his best individual game that year by scoring 39 points, falling just short of Hall of Famer Bud Bergman's single game school record of 41 points. Al also chalked up games where he scored 27 and 22 points that season. As a senior, the basketball team turned things back around and finished with a respectable 13-7 record as Al earned his third letter.

Returning to the old cinder tracks of the 1950s, Al excelled as a distance runner. He earned three letters in track participating in distance events, relays, the long jump, and even the high hurdles.

Harberts has the distinction of being a part of several State track records set either by Al or as part of a relay team. In 1955, he broke the 24 year old conference record for the mile by over two seconds with a time of 4:44. He also anchored the Mile Medley relay team at the State meet that set a new State record of 3:53. His relay mates were Jay Keen, Dicky Van Deest, and Tom Terrell. Then Al turned around and was part of the two-mile relay team that broke the 25 year old State record anchoring a team of Donavan Heltibridle, Larry Hickman, and Art Henze.

During the 1956 track season, his last year of track competition, Al broke school records for the high hurdles and the half mile. After winning the NICL conference meet in the mile, Al went on to State and won the indoor mile. He then set the State and Spartan school record at 4:31.1 while winning the State outdoor mile event.

Al remembered that race clearly. His typical race strategy was to let someone else set the pace while he would settle in close to the leader in second, third or fourth place. By the final lap, Al would position himself by the leader and then make his move on the final turn and sprint to the finish. In winning the outdoor mile, Al followed his strategy trailing a good miler from Tama Toledo into the bell lap. True to form, Al blew by him on the last corner and won the race and State mile championship by 20 yards as he set the State mile record. His Grundy school record lasted a half century. In total, Al actually set and broke the school record for the mile four times!

Following high school, Al was recruited by Northern Iowa, Drake, Wartburg and Luther to run while UNI and Wartburg also wanted him as a two-sport athlete for basketball and track. However, Al went into the Army and actually played a little basketball overseas in the early 1960s on an Army basketball team in Germany to wrap up his athletic career.

Sports Hall of Fame

Grundy Center, Iowa

Established 2004

Ivan Miller

Ivan Miller was the Spartans' first golfing standout and went on to a great amateur career in the state of Iowa. He was the first male golfer inducted into the Hall of Fame. Ivan is shown right receiving his Hall of Fame awards from John Doak.

In the recent annals of Grundy Center sports, golf has been the game where the Spartans have had outstanding success with both girls and boys golf programs. But Ivan Miller was the first Grundy Center native to put an imprint on Iowa golfing and it's one that's yet to be surpassed.

Golf didn't make an appearance in Grundy Center athletics until the late 1960s, shortly before Grundy Center built its own golf course. It's pretty tough to generate a lot of interest in golf when the closest courses were in Reinbeck and Eldora. But a young student named Ivan Miller, son of long-time high school chemistry teacher Clarence Miller and elementary teacher Ruth Miller, managed to give Ivan his start in golf back in the late 1950s. By the time Grundy fielded their first golf teams, Ivan Miller stepped right up to the tee.

Ivan's interest in golf started at age nine in Norman, Oklahoma where he took lessons while his family was attending a National Science Foundation summer school. In subsequent years, Ivan gained golf experience and took lessons during other summer school programs his parents attended in New Mexico and South Dakota. One course he practiced on in South Dakota even had sand greens!

In those early days, Ivan acquired most of his clubs through garage sales and hand-me-downs and used them until they broke. Growing up near the high school, Miller

found areas of pasture where he would create his own little golf course and play and practice for hours.

Naturally, Ivan went out for golf in high school even though Grundy Center did not have a course at the time. The Spartans played their meets at Reinbeck and Ivan was a four-year letter winner and top player on the team for Coach Arnie Schager. When Grundy finally built its own course around 1966, Ivan actually helped with the construction. He also remembers the encouragement he received from several of the early members, like Roy Vanderwicken, Ralph Anderson, Merritt Pitcher and others.

In this 1967 team photo, Coach Arnie Schager (kneeling in the middle of the front row) was Ivan Miller's high school golf coach. He is flanked by Chuck Goodman (left) and Ken Halstead (right). Back row is Gary Heronimus, Daryl Meyer, Jerry Greany, Ivan Miller (cirlcled), Steve Arends, John Storey, and Ed Reedholm.

Moving to the next level, Ivan spent a year at Marshalltown Community College, made the golf team, and qualified for the National Junior College tournament in New Mexico.

Ivan's next stop was Peru State College in Nebraska where he lettered all three years he was there. His senior season in 1970, he went undefeated in matches and

won the Nebraska College Golf Championships. He also qualified and played in the NAIA Collegiate Golf Tournament that season.

About this time, Ivan began working diligently on his game playing in small tournaments around the Grundy County area. He practiced almost all day long when he wasn't competing. And soon, he began winning a few of them.

The next few years were very exciting as Ivan began winning small tournaments one after another while his placing at major championships in the State continued to improve. He'd just load his golf cart into his van and head to a tournament somewhere. With all his victories in these small tournaments around Iowa, Ivan picked up a couple nicknames. One was the "*Iowa Minnow King*" and another was "*The Drifter*" because he would just drift into almost any small town where there was a tournament. His favorite slogan was "*Have Golf Will Travel*".

Miller's play continued to improve and in 1977, he was runner-up for the Iowa Amateur Player of the Year before winning it twice in 1978 and 1980, an accomplishment that tops his list of many career highlights.

Ivan was runner-up in almost all of the Iowa majors and won his first major in 1980 at the Iowa Masters. He followed it up with two other State majors in Spencer and Ft. Dodge. He was also a two-time winner of the State two-man. In total, Ivan won over 130 tournaments.

One of his other great experiences was playing the courses of Ireland in 2006. Ivan just happened to have a friend who belonged to the exclusive RNA, which allowed him to play many of these very private courses. They also have a museum of golf history that was a very moving to experience. He topped it off by playing most of the British Open courses.

Ivan Miller lived in Eldora where he was a teacher and golf coach for 35 years. Although he lived in the next county, Ivan always credited Grundy Center as a great place to grow up and he truly appreciated the encouragement he received from his parents and other Grundy golf enthusiasts.

Ivan Miller stood as Grundy Center's most successful golfer with his career from high school to college and into the top of the State's amateur golfers. For Ivan, it was "par for the course."

Sports Hall of Fame
Grundy Center, Iowa
Established 2004

Norm Riek

Norm Riek was a State champion tennis player for the Spartans in 1972 and went on to a successful college and adult tennis career. He is pictured left in the 1972 State tournament, center with his State championship trophy, and at right in 2012. Norm and his sister Kay Riek were the first "brother / sister" combination in the Hall of Fame.

One can imagine Charlie Riek was a pretty proud father with the election of his son, Norm, to the Grundy Center Sports Hall of Fame. Norm's selection created the distinction of the first brother / sister combination in this Hall of Fame. That other half is Kay Riek, a charter member of the Hall of Fame.

Norm Riek provided another in a line of highly successful tennis players for Hall of Fame Coach John Doak's coaching career for the Spartans. Doak had a State champion on the front end of it with Hall of Famer Bob Stock winning the State singles championship in 1962. And Norm Riek duplicated that feat with his State singles championship ten years later in 1972 while still playing in the era when there was only one class in high school tennis.

Norm is the oldest of the Riek children born to Charlie and his wife, Pat. Like many other boys growing up in Grundy Center in the 1960s, he participated in a variety of sports including basketball, cross country, and of course, tennis. Norm credits his parents for raising them in a sports-oriented environment and setting the great foundation for the success all the Riek children had at Grundy Center.

It's probably forgotten in lieu of all his tennis success, but Norm played basketball and ran cross country for Hall of Fame coach, Harry Dole. He was a letter winner on

the great Grundy basketball team of 1971 led by Hall of Famer Dennis Dirks. Then the following season, Norm was a starting guard averaging 15 points a game on a Spartan team that posted an excellent 16-2 record.

Already a noted tennis power for over a decade, the Spartans welcomed a young freshman to their storied franchise in 1969, a history that started with Bob Stock then produced State caliber players like Steve Eilers, Jim Stevens, Ed Palmer, Dave Ralston and also Hall of Famer Beth Stock from the girls' side of the court. In fact, it was Beth Stock who had a big influence on Norm's early career.

At age 12, Norm started playing tennis and found he had an affinity for the sport. He began taking summer tennis lessons from Beth, herself a two-time state runner-up and sister to Bob Stock. She saw that he had a lot of potential and began taking Norm along to area tennis tournaments. Norm proudly remembered the first tournament he ever won when he and fellow Hall of Famer, Dave Ralston, won doubles at the Waterloo Open at age 12. Norm also benefitted from hitting on a daily basis with quality players like Beth, Ed Palmer, and Dave Ralston. All of this support fueled Norm's desire to succeed at tennis.

Norm immediately made his presence known as a freshman on John Doak's high school team when he captured the #2 singles spot behind senior and 3-time state qualifier, Ed Palmer. Norm never lost a dual match that first season. And after ascending to the #1 spot, he held it for the next three years. Norm never lost a singles dual match during his entire high school career!

Riek qualified for State as a sophomore, junior and senior and capped his 1972 senior season with a State championship. In fact, nobody even challenged Norm in the State tournament as he won his crown very impressively 6-1, 6-2.

Moving on to college, Norm went south to Northwest Missouri State University in Maryville, Missouri, where he was a four-time conference champion in both singles and doubles. He qualified for the Division II Nationals three times. His college accomplishments were recognized by Northwest Missouri State when they elected Norm to their Sports Hall of Fame in 1999.

One of his fondest memories from college was Norm's freshman year. He was matched against another freshman from Oklahoma State, who was the Minnesota State singles champion the year before. They were matched up in this dual meet and everyone was making a big deal about the two state champions playing against each other, which added additional pressure to the match-up. However, Norm

stepped up and won the match 6-4, 6-4 and helped Northwest Missouri State beat Oklahoma State 6-3.

One humorous note from college was that Northwest Missouri State featured a lot of foreign players on their tennis team. At the time, Norm played with long blonde hair during his career and most people assumed he was from Sweden.

Norm Riek is shown circled with his college teammates in the mid-1970s while playing for Northwest Missouri State team with a strong international presence. With his long blond hair and the foreign players on the team, opponents thought he was from Sweden instead of Grundy Center!

Norm's college career may have ended in 1976, but his competitive tennis continued. In the 1980s and through the 1990s, Norm was a very successful adult singles player in Iowa, often carrying the top USTA ranking in the State for 35-45 year olds. He was ranked as high as #30 in the entire country in 1999 in the 45 year-old age group. Apparently, he just didn't know when to quit! In his long career, Norm collected around 200 singles and doubles titles.

Norm's outstanding tennis career was recognized by the tennis community of the State of Iowa when he was elected to the Iowa Tennis Hall of Fame in 2000 making him a three-time Hall of Fame recipient and one of the greatest tennis players in Grundy Center tennis history!

Class of 2008

Don Purvis* 1935

Wayne Wrage, Jr. 1966

Kevin Ralston 1975

Molly Thoren 1989

Trina Dirks 1998

Class of 2008 front row: Kevin Ralston, Wayne Wrage, and Jim Purvis representing his father, Don Purvis. Back row: Trina Dirks and Molly Thoren.

Sports Hall of Fame
Grundy Center, Iowa
Established 2004

Don Purvis

The late Don Purvis (left) was the Spartans first great distance runner. He was a State champion miler and held the school record for many years until Al Harberts broke it in 1957. Don went on to run track for the University of Iowa. He loved to golf and twice scored a hole-in-one. His son, Jim (shown right at the ceremony), accepted the awards for his dad.

One of the great things about establishing the Grundy Center Sports Hall of Fame is the preservation of the heritage of Spartan sports and the individuals who those many decades ago set the foundation for the success Grundy Center continues to build today. And that is certainly true with the late Donald Lee Purvis.

Although Don passed away in 2003, many people from his youth and high school days called him "Bill". According to son, Jim, an old Grundy Civil War veteran named Jack Hefflefinger (he was the father of Mrs. Art Briggs) started calling Don by the name "Bill" and soon the name just sort of stuck. Half the people around Grundy Center called him "Bill" throughout high school.

A 1935 graduate from high school, Don Purvis made his mark beyond the arena of sports. He was president of his class and Valedictorian before going on to the University of Iowa on an academic scholarship. But it is sports that paved the way for Don Purvis to be elected in the Class of 2008.

Don played football, basketball and tennis in high school, but he was a pretty small guy only weighing about 120 pounds when he graduated. So he was a bit small for some of those team sports. However, he did play a fair amount of basketball as the sixth man in the line-up. Don was a pretty quick runner. He noted to his family that back when economic times were tough, he used to catch rabbits in the snow with his bare hands!

However, it was track where Don excelled as a distance runner. Yet it wasn't until Don was a senior that his track coach, Mr. Wells, encouraged him to run the mile. And run he did, right into the Grundy Center record books.

Al Harberts held the school's mile record for nearly 50 years when he set the record in 1957. The runner who held the record for 22 years before that was Don Purvis. Like Harberts, Don won the mile at the State high school track meet and set the school record with a time in the low 4:40s to cap off his brilliant high school career.

Moving on to the University of Iowa, Don participated in both track and cross county. He won three letters in both sports and set a new university track record for the mile with a time of 4:27. Don also had the distinction of being a "pace runner" for the legendary Kansas miler, Glenn Cunningham, on at least one occasion. Pacers would go out to the front of the pack and lead the way for the first half or three-quarters of a race as part of the strategy for the faster runners like Cunningham. So once again, a Grundy athlete crossed greatness in his career.

Don Purvis (circled) also lettered in cross country for the Hawkeyes.

Following college, Don taught for one year then joined the service as a Lieutenant in the Army during WW II. He served mostly in Asia with assignments in Nepal, India, Burma, China and Australia. He met his wife, Evelyn Ross, from Wellsburg, on a blind date in college. It was arranged by Don's friend, Harold Kluver in 1941. Evelyn and Don eventually married forming a union that lasted 62 years. He also loved to golf and twice scored a hole-in-one.

After serving his country, Don went into business with his father-in-law and established Ross & Purvis Implement in Wellsburg. He retired at age 57 and moved to Florida in 1975. At a 1991 Hawkeye football game, Don was among the former Iowa track and cross country athletes recognized for achievements from 50 years ago. Don passed away in September of 2003 at age 86. His plaque and certificate for induction into the Hall of Fame were accepted by his son, Jim Purvis.

Sports Hall of Fame
Grundy Center, Iowa
Established 2004

Wayne Wrage, Jr.

Wayne Wrage, Jr. was a standout football player and wrestler. He was the first ever Spartan wrestler to place at the State wrestling tournament placing 3rd in 1965. He was also known for the use of his sharp chin (center). He is shown at right in 2015.

Tenacious. That's a great word to describe Wayne Wrage, Jr. Whether it was football or wrestling, Wayne embodied the word "tenacious". Tackles or takedowns, Wayne brought an uncommon determination and desire to the gridiron and the wrestling mat that made him one of the most respected and successful athletes of the 1960s.

Football tends to single out the "skill" positions like quarterback, running back, and receiver, the ones that score the touchdowns. But it's the guys in the trenches that open the holes for the runners, protect the passers, and give them time to deliver the ball downfield to the receivers. Wayne Wrage was one of those guys in the "trenches". He wasn't big, but he was a tough, hard-nosed center on offense and played linebacker and interior line on defense.

Wayne remembers the first game he played as a freshman. Coach Greg Bice sent him to play outside linebacker late in a game when the Spartans had a big lead. Hall of Fame charter member, Jim Basye, was the senior middle linebacker. Wayne looked frantically over to Jim and asked, "What am I supposed to do?" The big veteran just said, "All you have to do is follow me". And that's what Wayne did and it worked!

Spartan football coach, Marv Ott, singled out Wayne in his senior season as "the best player on the team". Wayne's 117 tackles and being chosen as Grundy's only first team all-conference selection in 1965 supports that. And his leadership was also recognized when he was named the team's captain. Wayne demanded a lot from his teammates, but he demanded even more of himself.

Wayne's Hall of Fame wrestling coach, John Doak, always preached about giving "180%". In both football and wrestling, Wayne did exactly that. And it was on the wrestling mat where Wayne's tenacity was most apparent. He led by example and set the standard for his teammates like Gary Schroeder, Larry McClanathon, Darl Mast, Tom Van Gelder, Roger Holeman, Al Rewerts, Jim Hulne, Marvin Groote, and Dennis Augustine. But it didn't come easy.

As a freshman and only in the second year of the Spartan wrestling program, Wayne paid his dues on the mat. He called that his "character building season." Wayne's determination brought him a winning record as a sophomore and set the stage for his final two years where he compiled a very impressive 45-3-1 record, winning several tournaments in the process.

As a junior, Wayne posted a 24-2-1 record, won two invitational tournaments, plus Sectionals and Districts. He was the first Spartan wrestler to ever win four tournaments in a season. Wayne joined Hall of Fame teammate Charlie Peters and fellow junior Larry McClanathon as the Spartans' first-ever State qualifiers. They led the team to its only District championship for Coach Doak. Wayne won two of three matches at State to become Grundy's first wrestler to win a match at State and place at State. After winning that historic first match, Wayne went into overtime in the semi-finals before losing to the State champion, but came back to soundly beat Joe Carstensen of Camanche for third place. Carstensen became an All-American wrestler at Iowa and a NCAA runner-up. Wayne also set the school's season scoring record for the Doak era and graduated in 1966 as the highest career point leader.

As team captain for his senior campaign, Wayne waltzed through the regular season undefeated, winning two more invitational tournaments plus Sectionals before having that one bad match at Districts that left him with no opportunity to wrestle back. His senior record was 21-1. But while that ended his wrestling career, Wayne never lost his love for the sport as he continued to support Grundy Center wrestling, football and other sports for more than four decades.

Wayne was a referee, helped coach the Little Spartan Wrestling program, and he continued to be part of the "chain gang" at home football games. His support of Spartan athletics was recognized when he and wife, Doris, were given the "Spartan Booster" award. Wayne continued to be a positive, productive role model in the Grundy Center community.

Sports Hall of Fame
Grundy Center, Iowa
Established 2004

Kevin Ralston

Kevin Ralston was one of only two Spartan wrestlers to reach the State tournament finals twice. He won a State championship in 1974 and finished runner-up in 1975. The middle photo shows Kevin on the State champion's podium in 1974 and right during his induction ceremony in 2008.

Grundy Center wrestling got its foundation from guys like Wayne Wrage under the coaching of John Doak. But it was the next era in Spartan wrestling under Hall of Fame Coach Clint Young where Spartan wrestling peaked with four state champions and all of them are in this Hall of Fame. Mike Draper was the first ever State champ along with two-time State champ Dave Ehrig, Rick Ruebel, and Kevin Ralston.

Although Kevin excelled in wrestling, it's worth noting Kevin was the second baseman on Grundy's 1975 State runner-up baseball team And one of Kevin's best memories from high school is making a couple of good defensive plays during a perfect game pitched by Chris Hitchings that season.

But Kevin, the son of Marv (one of the Spartans most loyal wrestling fans) and Rosie Ralston, earned his ticket to the Hall of Fame in wrestling. His quiet and friendly demeanor masked a fierce competitiveness that brought him great success on the mat. Wrestling the lowest weight classes, Kevin's record during his junior and senior seasons was 54-7-2. He won a State championship at 98# as a junior in 1974 and made the finals as a senior at 105# when he finished second in the State to cap his great wrestling career.

Looking back on those years, Kevin remembered his coach, Clint Young. Clint knew how to motivate his wrestlers and adapt his motivational techniques based on what worked best for each wrestler. With Kevin, Young put challenges in front of him. He would tell Kevin to *"show me what you've got"* and *"we didn't come here to get second,"* or sometimes, he just tried to make Kevin angry. And when he got angry, Kevin would also get very focused producing very positive results.

Naturally, Kevin is very proud of his State championship and being Grundy's first two-time State finalist. Dave Ehrig was the only other wrestler to accomplish that. However, one of Kevin's proudest moments was actually his semi-final match at State his senior year. He was wrestling a tough kid from Riceville who had already beaten him in close matches three times before. But the fourth time was the charm as Kevin pulled off the upset that moved him into his second consecutive State finals match.

Ralston was an excellent tournament performer and always wrestled his best at invitationals and especially in the State tournament series of Sectionals, Districts, and State. He won four invitational championships, two Sectional championships, along with two District runner-up finishes in qualifying for State. Of course his State championship and second place finishes rounded out his outstanding tournament record.

Kevin earned other accolades for his wrestling. He was a first-team all-conference wrestler, winner of the Ralph Schmidt Outstanding Wrestler Award, and a leader on Clint Young's teams that finished 8th and 15th in the State.

Kevin also did a little summer wrestling and in one tournament was matched up against a high school freshman from Ames by the name of Gibbons: Jim Gibbons. And Kevin, going into his senior year, built up a comfortable lead before pinning the future Cyclone NCAA champion and Iowa State wrestling coach. Good thing he got Gibbons when he was young!

Kevin settled in Grundy Center and continued to stay active with young people and sports activities. He spent a couple years as an assistant wrestling coach at the high school, head coach of the junior high team, and also coached little league baseball.

Sports Hall of Fame

Grundy Center, Iowa

Established 2004

Molly Thoren

Molly Thoren was a great all-around athlete for the Spartans earning 15 high school letters. She went on to Wartburg College and excelled in volleyball.

Molly Thoren's high school athletic career actually started while she was still in eighth grade. She earned a letter that year in softball and started a high school sports career that earned her a total of 15 letters.

The daughter of Chuck and Ruth Thoren, Molly earned five letters in softball during her career. She was an all-conference player three times and helped the Spartans win the North Iowa Cedar League championship her senior year. Besides softball, Molly also helped set school track records on two relay teams. But her strongest sports were volleyball and basketball.

When Molly graduated from high school in 1989, she was the third highest scorer in the history of Grundy girls basketball during the six-on-six era. She was part of that remarkable Spartan team of 1989 that went undefeated through the regular season for Coach Chuck Bredlow and won the NICL conference championship. Molly was part of a great cast of players including fellow Hall of Famers Kim Van Deest and Sarah Lynch as well as Sara Baker, Amy Harken, and Stacie Meester. For most of the season, they were ranked #1 in the State.

One of the most memorable things in Molly's career happened her junior season of 1987-88 in basketball. The Spartans had qualified for State and won their first round game. During the second game, Molly made the clutch basket that tied the game

with five seconds left. However, their opponents got off one more shot to win the game. After the loss, Molly remembers how disappointed the girls were on the way home. But then something happened that made a life-time memory.

As the team drove home and approached Grundy Center, a caravan of cars accompanied them to the high school where family, friends and fans held a pep rally showing the love, support and appreciation for the team's accomplishments. Molly said they were treated like queens and it really meant a lot to them to walk into the gym in front of a cheering crowd that was so proud of them, even though they came up short in their last game.

Molly won a variety of accolades during her hoops career. She was an all-conference player and all-tournament at the Waverly Invitational as a freshman. She participated on the Spartans' state tournament team in 1988 that finished 21-6, and showed her grit and determination by winning the one-on-one and three-on-three competitions at the University of Iowa Sports Camp.

Molly also left a strong impression on the conference and the State in her other sport: volleyball. Molly was the Spartans' Most Valuable Player for three consecutive years, all-conference for two, and she was chosen to play in the East-West All-Star volleyball game in 1988. Yet it was while attending Wartburg College where Molly took her game to the next level in this sport.

As a three-year starter for the Lady Knights, Molly made a strong impression her sophomore year. On a team with six seniors and where she started in the front row, but didn't play the back row, her teammates voted her "Most Improved" and "Most Inspirational" player. As a junior and senior, she won numerous All-Tournament team awards and was voted the team's Most Valuable Player as well as best offensive player both years.

After graduating from Wartburg with a degree in Fitness Management, Molly continued to compete in volleyball at various levels: sand volleyball, indoor women's and coed volleyball, reverse coed 6's, and she was also active in the U.S. Volleyball Association competitions.

Molly Thoren ranks among the greatest all-around athletes in Spartan history.

Trina Dirks

Trina Dirks was a two-time girls' State golf champion and runner-up twice while leading the Spartans to three State team titles. She is one of three Dirks siblings in the Hall of Fame along with their father, Dennis Dirks.

The selection of Trina Dirks to the Grundy Center Sports Hall of Fame captured a couple of milestones. First, she became the youngest member to join this elite group in 2008. Second, her election also made her the first father-daughter combination in the Hall of Fame. She joined her dad, Dennis Dirks, an outstanding Spartan basketball and baseball player from the early 1970s who was inducted in 2005 and was also a very successful Spartan coach for boys golf.

There must have been something that transferred from Dennis' baseball swing to Trina, her sister Kylie, and older brother, Jordan, who were all three elected to the Hall of Fame on their own merits. In fact, Trina and Kylie were teammates and helped mold one of the most successful Grundy Center teams in any sport in any era.

During Trina's four years of high school, the Spartans' girls golf teams won three State Class A championships and finished runner-up the other time. In two of those State championship years, they outscored all of the larger classes as well, becoming the first Iowa small school to accomplish that feat. In fact, the 1997 team achieved the second lowest score in State girls golf history! Those young ladies were outstanding on a team that included Abby Oglesby, and another sister combination with Hall of Famer Carla Iverson and her sister, Sarah.

By the time Trina graduated in 1998, she added many individual achievements to the great team accomplishments. She was a four-year letterman, a four-time all-

conference player, and additionally, an all-conference player in basketball and volleyball, earning five letters in those two sports.

Back to golf, Trina was a two-time State individual runner-up, a two-time State individual champion, and she held three of the top six scoring averages in Spartan school history. Her career included the best season average of 39.1 stokes and Trina also shares the best career average shared with her sister, Kylie.

Trina remembered a critical and lucky moment of her career during the final round of the State championship her senior year in 1998. She laid-up beside the huge 15th green on the course, leaving a long chip shot. She intended to chip with her seven iron, but as she hit the ball, it came out harder than expected. This had the potential of leaving a long putt after going past the hole, but luckily, the ball hit the pin dead-on and dropped in! As Trina breathed a sigh of relief, she looked down and realized she had actually hit the shot with her five iron.

In 1997, Trina was named Iowa Golf Association Player of the year and played on the Iowa Four State Team in 1997 and 1998. And just to show how good a golfer Trina was, she scored two holes-in-one during tournament play within eight days of each other at two separate courses in Waterloo and Iowa City.

Trina teamed up with her younger sister, Kylie, to make one of the most decorated sister combinations in the history of high school golf in the state of Iowa. The sisters, coached by Rick Schupbach, won two team championships together before Kylie continued with two more consecutive State championship titles during her career.

Trina fondly remembers the great fan support the team enjoyed with a Grundy gallery that followed the girls religiously at every meet. The fan support was there regardless of whether it was the State tournament or a dual meet at home or away.

After graduation, Trina went on the University of Northern Iowa where she competed for the Panthers in their top five for two years before concentrating on academics. She graduated from Northern Iowa in 2003 and went on to earn her doctorate in Physical Therapy from the University of Iowa in 2005.

Sports Hall of Fame
Grundy Center, Iowa
Established 2004

Class of 2009

Dale Smith* 1929

Bob Smoldt 1963

Harry Dole 1967-1995

Doug Stumberg 1983

Andy Lebo 1995

Todd Haupt 2003

Hall of Fame Class of 2009 front row. Todd Haupt, Harry Dole and Doug Stumberg. Back row. Bob Smoldt, Bob Smith (son of Dale Smith) and Andy Lebo.

Dale Smith

The late Dale Smith was one of Grundy Center's great athletes from the 1920s and 1930s playing football, track (left photo), basketball, (second photo) and baseball. He was represented by his sons, Jerry, Bob, and Merle at his 2009 induction, shown on the right in a photo provided by grandson, Doug Smith.

Those who grew up in Grundy Center in the late 1950s or 1960s probably knew Dale Smith as the owner and operator of Smitty's Drive-In next to the old swimming pool. But long-time Spartan sports fans knew Dale Smith as a great multi-sport athlete in high school, college and even beyond.

Born to Clyde and Lilly Smith in 1911, Dale attended high school back in the *"Roaring' Twenties"* graduating in 1929. Dale made a big impact in the early years of Spartan sports history following in the footsteps of fellow Hall of Famers Vernon Morrison and Melvin Fritzel.

An all-around athlete, "Smitty" excelled in football and baseball, but was also an outstanding track athlete and basketball player. He won letters all four years in football, basketball and track. Had Grundy played baseball at that time, Dale probably would have won four more letters. Instead, he played baseball for the Conrad town team.

Playing football in leather helmets, Smitty was a *"triple threat"* player in the backfield who could kick, pass, or run with equal ease. His high school yearbook attests to his passing by saying, *"The success of Grundy's aerial attack was made possible by Smith's bullet-like passes."*

In fact, the Spartan team during the fall of 1928, Dale's senior season, was one of the best in Spartan history. They finished 8-0 and were technically unscored upon. That's technically, because the Spartans actually lost a game 7-6 to the Teachers

College High School. However, it was later discovered they used an ineligible player and had to forfeit the game negating the one score against the Spartans. Dale's teammates included Dwight Dickson, Wayne Newton, Charles Kerr, Sid Greany, Bruce Brockway, Delbert Clark, Donovan Baldwin, John Graves and Ralph Heltibridle.

To illustrate how dominating that team was, among the football scores that year, Grundy beat Ackley 69-0, Tama 37-0, and Iowa Falls 20-0 in winning the conference championship.

Dale also excelled at track and was team captain. He was a consistent point winner and held school records in the pole vault and javelin throw. He also competed in running events and relays, but the javelin was his specialty. Dale set school and county records with his strong-armed throws and also won several invitational meets. He may have even held the State record, although his sons couldn't substantiate that.

After graduating from high school in 1929, Dale attended Coe College in Cedar Rapids and was an outstanding athlete in football, basketball, baseball and track. He was honorable mention All-American in football as their quarterback, a starting guard on the basketball team, a starting pitcher on the baseball team, and record-holder on the track team. His Coe College record for the javelin throw remained unbroken for many years. Dale also pole vaulted and ran sprints.

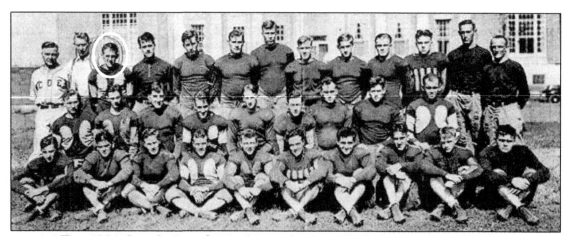

The 1931 Coe College football team featured Dale Smith, circled above.

Dale left Coe to sign a minor league baseball contract with the Washington Senators. He pitched in the Triple-A league in Topeka, Kansas and even pitched against the legendary Satchel Paige. His contract was bought out in 1934 by the St. Louis

116

Cardinals and Dale attended their spring training camp. During this era, St. Louis was laden with talent like Dizzy Dean and brother Daffy, Leo Durocher, Pepper Martin, and the rest of the "*Gas House Gang*". Smith's family doesn't think Dale made the final cut after spring training due to an injury to his pitching hand, so afterwards, he gave up baseball and returned to Grundy Center because he was now married and had a family to support.

Dale Smith is shown circled in this 1933 team photo with the Triple A minor league baseball team the Topeka Senators.

When World War II erupted, Dale was drafted into the Army. With some ROTC training while at Coe, Smitty became a Master Sergeant in an armored tank division. After the war, he bought an ice cream parlor, added a Maid-Rite franchise, and eventually built Smitty's Drive-in, which continued to operate under several other owners after Dale retired in 1966.

Smitty was a unique man. He seemed tough and temperamental to some. He would yell at the rowdy kids hanging around his drive-in restaurant, but turn around and offer the same kids (the author was one of them) the chance to eat the scraps of his wonderful home-made curly french fries for free. To his family, he was loving and caring to his wife Hazel and three sons Merle, Jerry and Bob.

Dale passed away in 1996 and is buried at Rose Hill Cemetery in Grundy Center. He was inducted into the Grundy Center Sports Hall of Fame in 2009 represented by his son Bob.

Bob Smoldt

Bob Smoldt is shown in a high school basketball photo from 1963, at Iowa State in 1964, and at his induction in 2009. He was elected for basketball in 2009 and was known in high school for dropping jump shots from deep in the corner.

One of the pleasures of watching Spartan basketball in the early 1960s was the emergence of a slender, blonde-headed kid with a flat-top who became the premier basketball player of the North Iowa Cedar League with his smooth, effortless jump shot. That was Bob Smoldt. And if asked, he would likely say he developed that shot playing one-on-one games against his mentor and big brother, Chuck, eight years older, who would give him uncontested long shots.

Bob Smoldt was a three-year letterman playing on talented Spartan basketball teams. In today's era with multiple class sizes, one or more would have certainly been State qualifying teams. But back in the early 1960s, Iowa basketball only had one class and it took large city schools to keep them out of Vets Auditorium.

The Spartans won the conference all three years Bob was a starter. Hall of Fame track star Dick Lynch was a teammate of Bob's and clearly remembers what a great team player he was. Bob was always making great passes to open teammates with perfect anticipation. He was outstanding on defense as well and developed a great skill of sensing where opponents' passes were going and stepping in for a steal. Bob also had a knack for anticipating where a ball was going to come off the rim on missed shots and put himself in position for a rebound.

Yet most people who saw Bob play remember his jump shot. It was deadly accurate and often launched from the corner with no back-board behind it. *"Number 30"* could pump those corner shots all game long. Bob would have loved a chance to play with a three-point line!

There are a lot of relatives within the Grundy Center Sports Hall of Fame, including Bob and his nephew, former Iowa State football player, Dave Smoldt. But Bob also played basketball in high school with two other relatives on those stellar teams of 1962 and 1963. Chris DenOuden and Dave Willoughby were both cousins. The team also featured two charter members of the Grundy Center Sports Hall of Fame, in Jim Basye and Bob Stock, along with Dean Myers, Arlen Kruger and the aforementioned Hall of Famer Dick Lynch.

While not terribly tall teams, these Spartans under Coach Marv Ott were a tough, well coach, cohesive team that battled to a 45-5 regular season record over three seasons while winning back-to-back-to-back conference championships. Interestingly, all the starters of the 1963 team went on to college athletic careers, although not necessarily in basketball. They were clearly talented athletes.

Looking back on his first year as a starter in 1961 under Coach Arnie Gaarde, Bob said their only senior starter was John Dieken. LaPorte City was favored to win the conference, but the Spartans pulled an upset and beat LaPorte on their own court to steal the conference championship and finish with a 14-3 record. That built confidence for their junior season in 1962 where, under new coach Marv Ott, the Spartans were favored to win the conference. And so they did, finishing the year 17-1 highlighted by a game against Iowa Falls where Bob pumped in his career-high 32 points for a single game.

Again, playing in the era before class sizes, the road to the 1962 State tournament went through Marshalltown, who had a strong basketball heritage of their own. Grundy met Marshalltown in the district finals at the Coliseum playing to a packed house and a very noisy environment. The Spartans took an early lead and kept it most of the game before it slipped away at the end. It was a bitter defeat that stayed with team and motivated them for the 1963 season.

As fate would have it, Grundy Center again won the NICL and again cruised into the district final in Marshalltown. It seemed like *"déjà vu all over again"*. But this year, Bob led the Spartans to a hard-fought win over the Bobcats and moved on to the sub-State game against East Waterloo, which they unexpectedly lost. Bob laments they were so focused on beating Marshalltown that they let down for East Waterloo and missed their chance for the State tournament.

Bob attributes the success of those basketball teams to great coaching, a strong work ethic, and playing together as a team. Bob was among many Grundy kids who could often be found playing pick-up basketball games in Preach Basye's driveway in

the off-season or playing one-on-one or two-on-two games after practice against Coach Ott and football coach Greg Bice, great athletes themselves.

Bob Stock, Dean Meyer, Bob Davis, Jim Basye, Bob Smoldt, Gene Krenz, David Willoughby.

This 1963 Spartan basketball team was one of the best in school history and features three Hall of Famers in Bob Stock (tennis), Jim Basye (football & track), and Bob Smoldt (basketball).

After high school, Bob was recruited heavily by Norm Stewart at Northern Iowa, along with Northern Illinois, New Mexico, and Iowa State. He chose Iowa State to play at the Division I level and still be close to home. Freshmen could not play varsity in those days, but Bob was the leading scorer on the freshman team. He played one more season as a sophomore, but seeing how his role was playing out, he gave up basketball and concentrated on his studies.

Grundy Center fans will long remember those deadly corner shots from one of its finest basketball players, Bob Smoldt.

Sports Hall of Fame

Grundy Center, Iowa

Established 2004

Harry Dole

Harry Dole coached both baseball and basketball for the Spartans and never had a losing season. He also served for years as the Athletic Director and joined the Hall of Fame as both a coach and administrator.

Anyone who's been around Grundy Center from the 1960s into the mid-1990s knows that the name "Harry Dole" is synonymous with sports in Grundy Center High School. First as a coach, later as Athletic Director and Principal, Harry Dole set the foundation for successful sports teams until his retirement from education in 1995.

Harry grew up not too far from Grundy Center, between Hubbard and Eldora. He attended his first two years of high school in Eldora and the last two in Hubbard, where he played basketball and baseball.

Interestingly, one of Harry's first sports highlights was against Grundy Center as a freshman in 1948. Harry pitched a no-hitter against the Spartans! While that sounds pretty impressive, as the legendary radio commentator Paul Harvey would say, "Now here's the rest of the story." The rest of the story is Eldora won the game by a score of 9-6. Harry struck out about ten Spartan batters, but he walked 13 batters and hit three more!

After a strong high school basketball and baseball career, Harry worked for two years on the family farm, then enlisted in the Marine Corps for another three years. Using the G.I. Bill, Harry then went to Ellsworth College and compiled a very successful basketball and baseball career. He was named Ellsworth's Athlete of the Year in 1958 and was also student body president. Harry was elected to the Ellsworth College Sports Hall of Fame.

From Ellsworth, Harry did a year at Northwest Missouri State and played football and basketball. He finished college at Iowa State and started his teaching and coaching career in 1961 at Denver, Iowa. During his six years in Denver, Harry coached baseball, basketball, and started the Denver junior high football program. He was always proud of the 28-2 record they compiled.

While Harry liked Denver, he was looking into jobs in Charles City and Brookfield, Illinois near Chicago when his wife, Jean, suggested he look into a job in Grundy Center. It just so happened that Jean's twin sister, JoAnn Rouse, taught there. So Jean filled out an application for a teaching and coaching job in Grundy Center to replace Marv Ott. Harry interviewed, liked what he saw, and the rest is history.

In all his years of coaching baseball, basketball, golf and cross country, Harry never had a losing record, although he did get close once! Harry had some exceptional basketball teams including his conference champion 1969 team that went 18-2 led by Al Everts and Hall of Famer Ed Palmer. Harry also had a conference championship team in 1972 that went 16-2 and set a school record of 111 points in a game! But his favorite was the 1971 team lead by Hall of Famer Dennis Dirks and featuring other stars like Jerry Apple, Jerry Moeller, Rod Ragsdale, Darrel Dirks, and Hall of Fame twins, Mark and Paul Eberline and Hall of Famer Greg Goodman.

The 1971 team went undefeated in the regular season, won the conference and qualified for the State tournament. They had regular season wins over Waverly-Shellrock (coached by Spartan Hall of Famer Bud Bergman), Iowa Falls, and the fourth ranked 4A school East Waterloo. Much like the 1952 Grundy team led by Orville Allen, the Spartans sputtered in their one bad game of the season at the State tournament and finished the year 23-1. That loss was Harry's biggest disappointment, one he took responsibility for as the coach.

Harry finished his basketball coaching career with a 78-23 record. His Spartan teams were noted for tenacious defense with a full court press that made other teams dread playing against them. Harry's teams were always in shape, which often showed in the fourth quarter when other teams were running out of steam.

In baseball, Harry won several conference championships, but actually thought one of his best coaching jobs was in relief of his replacement, Don Kramer. When Don had to fulfill a military commitment during the summer of 1975, he had a talented team struggling on the field and playing below .500 ball when Harry took the helm. With players like Hall of Famer Tim Clark, Danny Szegda, Scott Voss, Hall of Fame wrestler Kevin Ralston, and the Hitchings brothers, the Spartans went on a roll and qualified for the State tournament and finished second in the 2A division.

After coaching, Harry continued to have a strong influence on the Spartan sporting scene. As athletic director, Harry hired two great coaches in Jim Brousard for basketball and Don Knock for football, who took Grundy teams to State tournaments and State championships.

Harry was also instrumental in planning and building the new sports complex east of town and building a good track program with a very popular 18 team invitational track event back when Grundy Center had a very well-packed and fast cinder track.

Much of Grundy Center's recent athletic heritage and success was built on what Harry Dole did as a coach, athletic director, and high school principal from 1967 to 1995. Spartan sports fans should thank his wife, Jean, for pointing Harry towards Grundy Center back in 1967, where they remained in retirement.

Harry Dole, shown coaching his 1969 conference champion basketball team, taught his players strong teamwork and tenacious defense which produced great results for the Spartans.

Doug Stumberg

Doug Stumberg shown left as a high school wrestler and right at his induction ceremony in 2009 receiving his awards from John Doak. Doug was one of the most successful wrestlers in Spartan history and qualified for State all four years in high school.

When you hear the name "Stumberg" in conjunction with Grundy Center sports, you're either talking football or wrestling. In the case of Doug Stumberg, it's both! Doug is cousin to Hall of Fame football player Mike Stumberg and is the last of five sons born to Porky and Arlene Stumberg.

Certainly having four older brothers had a major impact on Doug's sports outlook. Oldest brother Norm set the stage for the rest of the kids, so it's fortunate that he picked wrestling. Brothers Todd and Curt were both State place-winning wrestlers for Coach Clint Young, but Doug remembers when brother Bryan went out for basketball one year. He thought the world was going to come to an end! Apparently, Bryan quickly saw the light and got back to wrestling to keep the family tradition intact. And little brother Doug took it to new heights. In fact, by the time Doug graduated, he held nearly every career record and many season records.

In Doug's four-year high school wrestling career, he set school records for most wins with 114, most pins with 49, most tournament place winnings with 25 (and 19 of those were championships and also a record), and most team points scored with 760. Hall of Famer Dave Ehrig is second in points scored with 611 and no one else has over 500 career points.

Interestingly, Doug said his career could have been derailed early in his freshman season by just charging by out of the locker room and running through a paper hoop. Charlie Evans, the team's 98 pounder, was followed by Doug, at 105 pounds, then brother Curt at 112 and the rest of the team as they approached the hoop. But Charlie failed to break through the paper and Doug, Curt and the rest of the Spartans all crashed into each other like an accordion! They barely kept their balance while pushing Charlie though the paper barrier. Doug said his wrestling career could have been over before it started had he taken a nose dive and been trampled by teammates!

That freshman year of wrestling, coached by Hall of Fame coach Clint Young and assisted by Dwayne Cross, was very special for Doug because he wrestled with brothers Todd and Curt on a very strong Spartan team. Twice during Doug's freshman year, he and his brothers all scored falls in the same meet. The first was against in a dual meets against LaPorte and then they repeated the feat at the first round of districts!

They competed for team championships in every weekend tournament, went 10-1 in dual meets, and eventually qualified seven wrestlers for the State tournament, including all three Stumberg brothers. While wrestling is often viewed as an individual sport, Doug valued the spirit and camaraderie of that Spartan team.

Doug also remembered how he could always hear his mom's voice above everyone else in the crowd and how his dad, Porky, would watch from the stands and lean with this body like he was making his own moves in the bleachers.

Stumberg's 1979-80 record of 28-2 was the best ever for a freshman and beat brother Norm's old freshman record of 17-5 from 1969. His sophomore season, Doug posted a 30-3 record, the most wins by a sophomore, and placed fourth in the State. As a junior, Doug posted another stellar year with a 26-4 record and placed second in the State tournament. He then finished out his career as a senior going undefeated at 30-0 through the District tournament. He was ranked #1 before suffering a devastating ankle injury in practice right before the State tournament. Doug valiantly tried to wrestle on one leg at State, but was unable to overcome the injury and lost his only match of the season while someone he beat earlier in the year went on to win the State title at his weight.

Despite that disappointing end, Doug left his mark on Grundy Center as the most successful high school wrestler in Spartan history and its only four-time State qualifier. He was four times first team all-conference, a three-time winner of the

Ralph Schmidt Award and two-time winner of the Wayne Wrage, Sr. pinner's award. Doug was also selected to the Iowa All-Star team after his senior season.

In addition to Doug's great success on the wrestling mat, he was also an accomplished running back on the football team in the early 1980s. Fans remember that Doug was part of the *"Mr. Inside / Mr. Outside"* combination that had Larry Appel handling the chores up the middle while Doug would run the ball out and around the ends. Stumberg also remembered and admired how teammates like Travis Noble, Larry Appel, and Todd Phelps played the game so physically making big play after big play.

Doug won the first of three football letters as a sophomore, but really broke through his junior and senior seasons making all-conference as a junior and first team all-conference his senior season of 1982 when he led the league in rushing with over 800 yards and scoring nine touchdowns. Notably, he scored four of those touchdowns in a game against Reinbeck. Doug also achieved honorable mention all-state that senior season on Coach Don Knock's 8-1 team.

Doug Stumberg (left) and Tim Stanley (right) represented the Spartans at the 1983 State wrestling tournament. Doug qualified for State all four years he was in high school and finished a State runner-up in 1982. He carried a top ranking in his weight class to the 1983 tournament before being sidelined by a severe ankle injury.

Andy Lebo

Andy Lebo was an outstanding all-around athlete for the Spartans earning 15 letters in baseball, basketball, football and track. He was one of the Spartans' greatest catchers and one of the best hitters in team history.

Andy Lebo was another in a long line of great athletes in Spartan history who left their mark in the record books. Andy was an all-around athlete and earned 15 letters in high school and all-state honors in three sports: baseball, football and track.

Andy was a right-handed hitting catcher who followed a legacy of strong Grundy catchers including Jim Wells in the 1950s, Jim Hulne in the 1960s, Mark Eberline in the 1970s, and Jeff Crisman in the 1980s. Looking at Andy's baseball career, a case could be made for him as the Spartans' "all-time" catcher and one of our best-ever baseball players at any position.

Andy won five letters in baseball. In 129 games he had 163 hits, 104 RBIs, stole 64 bases, hit 14 home runs, and had a career batting average of .382. As a junior, Lebo hit .433 and as a senior he upped his average to .451. Andy holds the Spartan single season records for home runs with seven, runs scored with 35, doubles with 14, at-bats with 101 and sacrifices with 12.

But Andy wasn't just a hitter. He was also a great defensive catcher. He once threw out four runners in one game in eighth grade playing Legion baseball against Ames. Andy could catch a pitch and get it down to second base in less than two seconds. With his strong arm, teams rarely tried to run on him. Since they didn't run on him, it wasn't uncommon that Andy would pick runners off first and second base

from behind the plate!   He loved to throw and was clocked with a velocity on his throws at 90 mph.

Andy's play earned him first team all-conference honors for three years and he was voted Most Valuable Player as a senior.   Lebo was named first-team all-district for three years, first team all-state as a junior and again as a senior. Andy was named to the Elite All-State Super Team as catcher by the Coaches Association and played in their all-star series.   He was also on the select Iowa AAU team that toured Japan his junior year in 1994.

One of Andy's baseball highlights was playing in the State baseball tournament for his dad, Phil, who coached the team and was himself elected to the Hall of Fame in 2016 as a baseball coach.

In 1993, the Spartans faced perennial baseball power Kee High of Lansing for a place in the semi-finals of Class 2A.   While Andy had two hits and two RBIs in that game, he remembered the team effort of coming back in the last inning, trailing by two runs.   The Spartans loaded the bases with two outs before Ryan Block hit a deep line drive to center field.   The Kee High outfielder made a valiant attempt to catch the ball and end the game, but he missed it, letting the ball get past him and allowing three Spartans to score and win the game for Grundy Center.

Another baseball highlight for Andy came after graduation playing in the Junior College World Series for Indian Hills, where he spent two seasons.   He also went on to earn letters at Grand View and Wartburg before ending his college baseball career.

Baseball wasn't the only sport Andy excelled at.   He played quarterback and defensive back for Grundy Center in winning three letters in football.   The Spartans qualified for the playoffs all four years he was in high school.   Andy was all-conference and all-district as a junior and senior and all-state as a senior defensive back.   Andy's proud to say that he only got sacked once in his entire career as a quarterback, but he's quick to add that playing behind guys like all-state guard Brad Harms, another Hall of Famer, made it pretty easy on him.

Andy's most poignant memory of football was the playoff game against Madrid his junior year in 1993.   Things weren't clicking and the Spartans were down 28-7 at halftime.   But the Spartans rallied in the second half and brought the score within eight points with 40 seconds left and the ball on their own 30 yard line.   On the first play, Andy launched a long pass to Jarod Wilson who laid out for a fantastic catch and a 55 yard gain.   The next play, Andy hit Ryan Westerman for a touchdown

bringing the Spartans within two points with just eight seconds left. However, their try for the tying two-point conversion failed and their valiant comeback effort came up just a little short.

Andy's third all-state sport was track, where he ran the sprint events and relays. A four-year letter winner, Andy was all-conference as a junior in two events and all-conference as a senior in three events. He was part of the school record for the 4x200 meter relay team that finished second in the State meet and the 4x100 meter relay team that placed fourth. Andy received the A.V. Dieken Award as Grundy's most outstanding track athlete as a senior.

Andy continued to support athletics in Grundy Center coaching and umpiring baseball and playing on semi-pro teams around the area. He also earned Most Valuable Player honors one year with the Grundy Center Gamecocks in the Iowa Valley League. Lebo was a high school football official for eight years and also an NCAA College football official.

Sports Hall of Fame
Grundy Center, Iowa
Established 2004

Todd Haupt

Todd Haupt was a four-year letterman for Coach Rollie Ackerman and finished his Spartan career as the boys' all-time leading scorer and first team all-state honors.

Grundy Center's boys basketball heritage is legendary. The Grundy Center Sports Hall of Fame has inducted Forrest Meyers from the 1910s, Melvin Fritzel and Vernon Morrison from the 1920s; Max Appel and Leon Bockes from the 1940s; Orville Allen and Bud Bergman from the 1950s; Bob Smoldt and Ed Palmer from the 1960s; Dennis Dirks and Greg Goodman from the 1970s; and Lance Van Deest from the 1980s.

In 2009, the Hall of Fame inducted Todd Haupt, the career scoring leader for Spartan boys basketball and also the first inductee graduating from the 21st century.

Todd grew up in the Wellsburg-Steamboat Rock area and didn't move to Grundy Center until he was a freshman. During his formative years, Todd was influenced strongly by his parents, Ray and Cheryl, who always supported him but were never "pushy". He was also a big Michael Jordan fan.

As he was preparing to enter high school, Todd played with the Spartan first-team high school players during Coach Rollie Ackerman's summer camp. Todd attributes that experience as great preparation for playing at the varsity level. Not many freshman start on varsity at any school, but Rollie told Todd that he would be starting in his first varsity game a week before their first game.

When the game was played, Todd made the first points of an illustrious career with a three-pointer. Although he made another one later, the Spartans lost that game by

two points as Todd missed a potential game winning three-pointer at the buzzer. Still, it was a good beginning for the rookie starter who was named a second team all-conference selection.

Although tall at 6' 5", Todd played the three-guard wingman in Coach Ackerman's offense. He averaged 21 points per game as a sophomore, 25 as a junior and 21 as a senior while compiling the boys' career scoring record with 1,914 points. He was first team all-conference and first team all-district those three years. Todd was honorable mention all-state as a sophomore, second-team all-state as a junior, and first-team all-state as a senior. He also received the school's Father John Connell Most Valuable Player Award three times, the first to ever accomplish that honor.

Todd's proudest achievements at Grundy Center were making it to the State tournament twice as a junior and senior playing with teammates like Doug Shuey, Joe Hoskins, Tyler Burmester, and Scott Spiers. As juniors, the team was only 15-11, but qualified for the State tournament only to lose a close game to top-ranked Danville in the first round.

Todd remembered the Danville contest as a real up-and-down struggle. He scored 15 points with 15 rebounds in the game. With the score tied and under ten seconds on the clock, Todd drilled a three-pointer, which appeared to be a game winner. But Danville took the ball out of bounds with three seconds left and made a desperation half-court shot to send the game into overtime where the Spartans lost.

Next season, the boys played inspired ball and went 23-3 for the year, losing only twice in the regular season as the Spartans again qualified for State. Todd remembered playing Northeast of Goose Lake in the first round and having a terrible first half where he went scoreless. But the Spartans battled back to win with a big fourth quarter. The next game, Grundy played and lost to Wapsie Valley and finished the tournament in fourth place.

Following high school, Todd went on to play at Kirkwood College, but sat out his first season with a knee injury. His second season, he led Kirkwood in scoring with a 17 points-per-game average and took them to the Junior College nationals where they finished second. Todd was also among the top five in the nation for three-point field goal percentage capping an amazing basketball career.

Sports Hall of Fame
Grundy Center, Iowa
Established 2004

Class of 2010

Ed Palmer 1969

Mark Eberline 1972

Orrin Brown 1975

Sarah Lynch 1990

Brad Harms 1996

The Hall of Fame Class of 2010: Brad Harms, Sarah Lynch, Orrin Brown, Mark Eberline, and Ed Palmer.

Ed Palmer

Ed Palmer was third in a legacy of Coach John Doak's boys tennis players and also an excellent basketball player. He went on to a very successful tennis career at Luther College and was selected to the Hall of Fame for tennis and basketball.

Ed Palmer brought excellence in two sports to the Spartans in the late 1960s. A good all-around athlete, Ed was fast, quick, and savvy. The son of Carl and Kathryn Palmer, Ed grew up in Grundy Center in the late 1950s and early 1960s playing various sports with the neighborhood kids. By the time Ed got to high school in the mid-1960s, he focused on basketball and tennis.

Palmer quickly proved himself at the high school ranks earning a varsity spot as a guard in basketball his sophomore season for Coach Marv Ott. Showing he had quickness and speed, Ed also displayed his insight and feel for the game. He was a very unselfish player throughout his career and a leader in assists, although he could score when he needed to. Ed also used his quickness to play tenacious defense.

Harry Dole, Hall of Fame coach and administrator, came to Grundy Center during the 1967-68 school year. Palmer stepped into the point-guard role for his new coach and brought the ball down the court calling the plays Harry signaled from the bench. This first Spartan team of Harry's finished with an 11-6 record and placed second in the conference as Ed earned first-team all-conference honors.

Heading into his senior season, Palmer captained a team of fellow seniors Al Everts, Steve DeVries, Gale Stock, Doug Hess and junior Doug Sietsema to the conference championship, losing only once in the regular season campaign. The Spartans took

their one-loss record to the State tournament series that culminated winning the sectionals and scoring a decisive district game victory over fourth-ranked LeGrand.

Unfortunately, the Spartans were upset the very next game by South Hamilton in the district finals to end a great season at 18-2. It was also the end of Palmer's basketball career. He was once again named first-team all-conference and earned honorable mention all-state while leading the team in assists and steals.

As good as he was in basketball, Ed's real passion was tennis, one that took him through high school, college, and to a career in adult tennis that spanned 27 years. Ed was quick as a cat, had unbelievable hand-to-eye coordination, great concentration, and stroked the ball like a pro. He blended the mechanics, finesse, and strategies of tennis into a life-long joy that continued for decades.

In high school, Ed learned from the newly-established Spartan tennis tradition that strongly influenced his development under Hall of Fame Coach John Doak, who thought of him as "Steady Eddie". Besides Coach Doak, these influences included State champion and Hall of Famer Bob Stock and carried on with Hall of Famer Steve Ehlers, Jim Stevens, and Ed's older brother Ron. Another influence was Beth Stock, Bob's little sister and herself a Hall of Famer, who made her own mark on Grundy Center tennis.

In Ed's early playing years with Beth, they often practiced doubles against older players like Steve Ehlers and Jim Stevens, a very talented tandem in their own right. Ehlers and Stevens were both older and more experienced, plus, as Ed tells it, Beth loved to lob the ball! Unfortunately many of Beth's lobs ended up short and Steve and Jim reveled in taking target practice on Ed with overhead smashes. He remembered having *"Wilson"* tattooed on his back long before tattoos became popular.

Ed spent a lot of time in those early years with Beth Stock, who was a year younger, and they played a lot of summer tournaments together over the years. Coincidentally, Beth later married another tennis player named "Palmer" and a lot of the statewide tennis circle thought Beth and Ed got married.

Competing under the single-class system for tennis, Ed earned four letters in tennis and made it to the State tournament three times. He led the Spartans to outstanding team records playing both #1 singles and #1 doubles from his sophomore year through graduation. Then it was on to college.

Row 1: Palmer, Wolthoff, Bee, Shoemaker, Row 2: Riek, Barg, Hess, Meester, Coach Doak.

The 1969 Spartan tennis team, led by Ed Palmer, featured two other future Hall of Famers in Norm Riek and Coach John Doak.

Luther College attracted Palmer because of their highly regarded tennis program. Under Coach Ed Gordon, the Norsemen built powerful teams and dominated the Iowa Conference. Outside of their conference, Northern Iowa was their biggest rival. Building on his high school success, Palmer achieved some milestones at Luther that still showed on the record books at his induction. As of 2010 as a singles player, Ed was one of only four Luther tennis players to be a four-time conference champion. He also picked up three conference titles playing doubles.

Ed and his doubles partner qualified for Division II Nationals twice, first in 1971 and again in 1973. In their first nationals, they made it to the third round before losing with Luther finishing 10th in the nation that year.

After his college career, Ed consistently played successful adult tennis in tournaments throughout Iowa and the Midwest for 27 years. Although he retired from active competition, Ed still played tennis twice a week in Des Moines as of his 2010 induction and was many times the club singles champion at the Des Moines Golf & Country Club.

Sports Hall of Fame
Grundy Center, Iowa
Established 2004

Mark Eberline

Mark Eberline was a good all-around athlete who excelled at baseball. He was part of the long legacy of outstanding catchers in Spartan baseball history. He went on to a strong baseball career at Wartburg College with twin brother, Paul.

When Mark Eberline was notified of his selection to the Hall of Fame, one of the things the Hall of Fame committee tried to confirm is whether he would be able to attend their induction ceremony. While Mark affirmed he could attend, he also added that if something came up and he couldn't make it, his twin brother Paul could fill in for him and we probably wouldn't notice the difference.

The Hall of Fame has a good number of siblings inducted: Kay and Norm Riek, Trina, Kylie and Jordon Dirks, and the Crisman brothers of Terry, Jeff and Joel. But Mark Eberline's selection made Paul and him the first and only twin brother combination in the Hall of Fame as of 2016.

Mark was a good all-around athlete in high school earning 13 letters in football, golf, and basketball. But his best sport was baseball where he lettered all four years under Hall of Fame Coach Harry Dole. Mark was known for both a strong bat and strong arm, but he was also very adept at handling pitchers like his brother Paul, Rod Ragsdale, and later the Warburg pitching staff. He had a solid Spartan batting average as a junior of .349 and then jumped it all the way to .485 as a senior.

While he appreciated all-conference and all-state recognition during his high school career, the thing Mark really enjoyed was picking off runners from his catcher position.

It started with the close relationship he had with his brother Paul playing first base when Paul wasn't pitching. Mark had a signal for Paul when he was going to try to pick off the runner at first and Paul knew he had to be there for the throw to slap on the tag. They were very successful usually picking off a runner at least every third game. That helped keep the opponents' runners honest the rest of the time as their pick off reputation grew.

Expanding on that, Rod Ragsdale played shortstop when he wasn't pitching and Mark soon pulled him into the scheme throwing out runners at second base as well. It was also something Mark carried over into college with Paul and his Wartburg teammates.

Mark has fond memories of the lessons Coach Dole taught the team. One time, Mark took a hard hit blocking the plate while tagging out the runner. Coach Dole told him next time to *"give a little"* as the runner comes into him. Mark took the lesson to heart and added his own little twist. As a runner bore down on him, Mark gave a little, but also dropped low and let the runner flip over his back as he applied the tag.

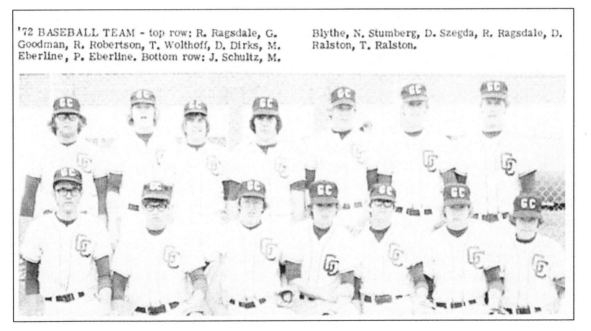

'72 BASEBALL TEAM - top row: R. Ragsdale, G. Goodman, R. Robertson, T. Wolthoff, D. Dirks, M. Eberline, P. Eberline. Bottom row: J. Schultz, M. Blythe, N. Stumberg, D. Szegda, R. Ragsdale, D. Ralston, T. Ralston.

The 1972 Spartan baseball team featured four future Hall of Fame members, including the Eberline brothers shown in the back row far right.

Eberline also laughed about playing with Paul, who besides being an outstanding first baseman, was also a left-handed pitcher with a powerful fastball and sometimes erratic control. As Mark remembered it, when Paul missed, he didn't miss close. Of

course this made batters very, very nervous at the plate! One game, Paul was particularly wild, throwing balls in the dirt and to the screen and yet pitching a one-hitter. It was a hot and dusty game and Mark was getting very irritated from getting beat up by balls in the dirt. Finally, after one more ball in the dirt, Mark just slowly rolled the ball back to Paul to the amusement of all the fans, but not Paul, at least at the time.

Following his successful high school career, Mark and brother, Paul, went to Wartburg College and continued playing baseball together at the next level. Mark broke into the line-up as a freshman splitting duties with the Knights' senior catcher. Mark played under a coach who didn't like using freshmen, not to mention a freshman catcher! But he made an exception when Mark batted .357 overall, and over .400 within the Iowa Conference. Mark was named honorable mention all-conference that freshman year.

One game memory Mark had was a double-header against Northern Iowa. The first game came down to the bottom of the last inning with Wartburg trailing by a run. Mark was up to bat against a tough Panther relief pitcher with two runners in scoring position. A hit would tie and possibly win the game. But Mark struck out. In the second game, the same situation presented itself. It was the bottom of the last inning, runners in scoring position with Wartburg trailing by a run when UNI brought in the same tough reliever to close out the game. This time, Mark jacked a 400-foot home run deep over the centerfield fence to win the game for the Knights.

From his freshman year at Wartburg until graduation, Mark developed into a leader on the team and was formally named team captain as a junior and senior while earning first team all-conference honors his junior year. He continued to build on his strong defensive skills, management of pitchers and field direction. The pro scouting report on Mark was *"Major league bat, major league arm, minor league speed."* As Mark noted, he ran too long in one place.

Mark did have a couple regrets in a great baseball career. His junior year at Wartburg was their best season and tops in the conference, but due to weather they failed to play enough games to qualify for the NAIA post-season tournament. He also regretted that with their talent in high school the Spartans never made it to State during his four years. Regardless, it was a great run and a great career for Mark.

Orrin Brown

Orrin Brown is shown as a senior for the Spartans in 1975 and receiving All-Tournament honors at State (#25). He was selected for the Hall of Fame as a basketball player and had a successful college basketball career at Grandview College and Winona State.

Over the years, Grundy Center has developed some outstanding basketball teams. Hall of Famer Orville Allen led the 1952 squad to an undefeated regular season and took them to the State tournament where they were upset in the first round. In 1971, Harry Dole's squad with Hall of Famers Dennis Dirks and Greg Goodman once again took their #1 ranked team to the State tournament only to fall victim of an upset in the first round.

Then, just four years later, the 1975 Spartans took it all the way to Vets Auditorium in Des Moines and the State finals game. Leading the way for the Spartans was a tall, six-foot-six inch lanky blonde-haired senior by the name of Orrin Brown.

Orrin broke into the starting line-up at the end of his sophomore season of 1972-73 due to an injury on the varsity team. Coach Dole brought young Orrin off the junior varsity and introduced him to competition at the varsity level as the Spartans started Sectional play. Orrin quickly showed the potential for the next two seasons to come as he scored his share of points and grabbed more than a few rebounds at the end of the 1973 season.

The 1973-74 basketball campaign started off with a new coach, Jim Brousard. The Spartans finished the season 13-8, but laid the ground work for the season ahead playing a fast-and-fun style of ball. Orrin, along with senior teammates Jerry Voss, Randy Ragsdale, and Bob Riek, learned about playing together in high school competition.

Sports Hall of Fame
Grundy Center, Iowa
Established 2004

Actually, these seniors had already been playing together for a long time with pick-up games of basketball for years. They even played outdoors with snow on the ground. Orrin remembers how mentors like Darrel Dirks and Greg Goodman took him under their wing. They would pick up Orrin and practice with him and let him play in their pick-up games, providing a very positive influence on his practice habits and development.

Orrin's junior year was very successful as he led the team in scoring and rebounding. He was named Spartan Most Valuable Player, first team all-conference, second team all-area, and honorable mention all-state in spite of missing six weeks of the season to injury. He was hurt getting undercut on a lay-up and breaking his right arm in a home game against Eldora. But the Spartans' taste of success in 1974 only whet their appetite for their senior season in 1975.

VARSITY BASKETBALL TEAM - Scott Vos, Chris Hitchings, Mark Everts, Rod Curren, Dale Grimmius, Terry Crisman, Orrin Brown, Bob Riek, Jerry Voss, Randy Ragsdale, Tim Haverkamp, Tim Clark, Coach Brousard.

The 1975 State runner-up Spartan basketball team was coached by Jim Brousard.

With the addition of future Hall of Famer, then sophomore, Tim Clark to the starting line-up, the Spartans put it all together as one of the greatest Grundy Center basketball teams of all-time. They finished the season leading to the State tournament 21-2. Once again, Orrin led the team in scoring and rebounds averaging 18 points per game and 11 boards. He was again team Most Valuable Player, first

team all-conference, first team, and was named to two all-state teams. He also earned the Rev. John P. Connell Award for basketball.

Heading into the State tournament, the Spartans avoided the first round upset and dispatched both Tripoli and Alta with relative ease and headed into the State finals against Clinton St. Mary's. Orrin remembers that St. Mary's had two 6' 6" guys on the inside that the Spartans needed to stop in order to the win the game. And they accomplished that goal, but unfortunately, the Clinton guards, not normally known as scorers, got hot. Both players put up over 20 points from the perimeter. Despite a heated battle, the Spartans came up a little short on the scoreboard, but left the Grundy Center fans with a great season full of memories from one of the Spartans' greatest basketball teams.

For Orrin, he made a mark for himself at the State tournament by being named captain of the All-Tournament team. His 18 rebounds in the State finals game was also a record that stood for many years.

After graduation, Orrin played basketball at Grandview College for two years and then finished his career at Winona State University. He noted it was a tough transition going from small town high school ball to college. It was a big step up in style and aggressiveness where his teammates and opponents were bigger, faster and quicker. Orrin said he had more shots blocked in his first month at Grandview than in his entire high school career.

Despite the learning curve, he figured it out and went on to average 10 points a game starting for a Grandview team that was fourth in the nation. As a starter for Winona State, Orrin led the team in rebounds as a senior and was second in points-per-game when he graduated in 1980.

Orrin stayed in the Winona area and did a lot of work as an alumnus for the Winona State basketball program. The program was one of the best in Division II basketball winning two national titles in the four years prior to his Hall of Fame induction in 2010. Over the years, Orrin continued to play recreational basketball until his knees said "enough" at age 50.

Sports Hall of Fame
Grundy Center, Iowa
Established 2004

Sarah Lynch

Sarah Lynch scored the winning run for Central College in the Division III NCAA semi-final softball game against the tournament favorites. She earned 15 letters for the Spartans in high school.

Sarah Lynch was the seventh female athlete to be inducted into the Grundy Center Sports Hall of Fame in 2010 joining Kay Riek, Bobbi Sealman, Tracey Voss, Trina Dirks, Molly Thoren, and Kim Van Deest. Like all of these gifted athletes, Sarah starred in multiple sports earning fifteen high school letters in volleyball, basketball, track and softball. And she set some school records in the process.

Sarah took to sports naturally with older brothers Tom and Rob leading the way with their own sports careers and her dad, Hall of Famer Dick Lynch, himself a multi-sport athlete in the early 1960s. She also got a lot of support from her mom, Jo. Sarah's sports career got off to an early start while still in elementary school. She won both the local and district free-throw contest sponsored by the Elks Club. She went on to finish third in the State competition, a signal of good things to come.

Sarah's basketball exploits grew. She attended the Vivian Stringer basketball camp at the University of Iowa along with Molly Thoren. Together, they won the three-on-three camp championship. Sarah was also proud of the Spartan girls winning their sub-State game her sophomore year in 1988 and qualifying for the State tournament. With fellow offensive court players and Hall of Famers Kim Van Deest and Molly Thoren, the threesome foreshadowed things to come while achieving a 21-6 record for the season.

In the 1988-89 campaign, the Spartan girls went through an undefeated regular season and achieved the #1 ranking in the State. However, one of the most disappointing things in Sarah's sports career was when Dike, who they beat twice in

conference competition, upset the Spartans by one point in the Districts to end their season at 22-1.

Another great memory was something that would probably make "*YouTube*" today. Sarah went scrambling for a loose ball and got control of it while lying on the court. Seeing nobody open she could pass to, Sarah launched a shot from the floor and it dropped in the hoop! ESPN would have loved showing that one!

Sarah finished her basketball career as the seventh all-time scorer with 1,116 points and as one of the top-assist players in program history.

Yet basketball wasn't even Lynch's best sport. That was softball, where Sarah earned five letters and posted a career pitching record of 47-14. Spartan softball struggled up until the 1989 season when Sarah, as a junior, took over the pitching chores and pitched every game her last two years. As a junior, Sarah was 25-7 overall and 15-3 in the North Iowa Cedar League. She was really proud of her batting average of .446 without striking out once during the season as they won the NICL conference championship! Her senior year, Sarah was 22-7 and 14-4 in the conference with an ERA of 1.58 and 119 strikeouts. Although the Spartans finished second in the NICL, Sarah was named conference Most Valuable Player.

The 1989 Spartan softball team featured four future Hall of Fame members, including Sarah (circled).

Another memory from softball came when Sarah felt compelled to retake her ACT test to get a higher score. For the record, Sarah was co-valedictorian in her class and graduated with a 4.0 average. But there was a softball tournament that weekend

and she was torn about what to do. Brothers Tom and Rob said her grades were fine, she wouldn't have any trouble getting into any college, and encouraged her to play ball. And she did. Sarah went 9 for 12, hit three triples, and pitched all three games as the Spartans won the tournament.

After graduation, Sarah went to Central College and into an excellent softball program. She didn't play much in the field or at bat except in junior varsity games, but she caught the coach's attention with her speed and quickness on the bases. This got her promoted to varsity as a situational base runner and she did it very well. In fact, Central made it to the NCAA Division III tournament and finished as National Champion!

Sarah played a key role in getting Central into the finals. Toward the end of the semi-final game against the tournament favorite out of New Jersey, Sarah went in to pinch-run on first base with the game tied 1-1. Central sacrifice bunted her to second base and then the coach signaled for a hit-and-run. The batter hit the ball just over the shortstop's head and Sarah sprinted for third and got the "green light" from the coach to go for home. In a close play at the plate, Sarah slid head first to one side and brushed her hand under the tag on home plate scoring what turned out to be the game-winning run.

Sarah also excelled at track in high school where her speed and quickness helped her earn three letters. By the time she graduated in 1990, Sarah held five school records: four in sprint relay events with some pretty fast teammates, and individually in the 100 meter hurdles.

Sarah also just missed another school record in the long jump, an event in which her dad excelled. She pulled off her best jump of the year of 16' 7½" in the 1990 Districts to win it, but fell one inch short of the school record held by Robin Venenga. Sarah went on to finish fifth at State in the long jump. Ironically, just a few weeks earlier, she had actually exceeded the long jump record, but barely scratched on the jump. Clearly, Sarah was a special athlete.

Sarah finished college at Central graduating Summa Cum Laude and ranked #1 in a class of 331 graduates. She went on to get her Master's degree and turned her talents to teaching.

Sports Hall of Fame
Grundy Center, Iowa
Established 2004

Brad Harms

Brad Harms earned All-American honors as an offensive lineman for the University of Northern Iowa. He is shown at right during the 2010 induction ceremonies. He also made the first grandfather-grandson combination in the Hall of Fame joining his maternal grandfather, Max Appel.

The youngest inductee of the Class of 2010 joined a prestigious group of football players who ground it out in the trenches with strength, ability, determination, and toughness. Brad Harms was a fitting addition to the tradition of Spartan linemen who battled at the point of attack on both sides of the ball.

Brad Harms joined other outstanding linemen in the Grundy Center Sports Hall of Fame like Jim Basye, Charlie Peters, Wayne Wrage, Terry Crisman, Dave Ehrig, Mike Stumberg and Joel Crisman. Like Basye and Ehrig, Harms also excelled in field events in track.

Brad Harms also entered the Hall of Fame with some existing heritage. His grandfather, Max Appel (Grundy Center High School Class of 1943) was a Spartan football and basketball star who was inducted in 2006. With Brad's election, they made the first grandfather-grandson combination in the list of Hall of Fame relatives.

Brad lettered all four years as a high school football player for Coach Bob Meyers. As a freshman, he started in the defensive line, but didn't play on offense for the 1992 State qualifying Spartan team. The following year, Brad became a two-way player as a defensive tackle and offensive guard, positions he continued to play throughout his high school career.

Brad credits his line coach, Bill Itzen, for making him the player he was. Itzen, a former Spartan lineman himself, not only taught Harms a strong work ethic and the basic fundamentals, he also showed Brad techniques that few linemen in the state learned. This paid handsome dividends to Brad, especially when he transitioned from high school to college ball.

One memory that Brad laughed about was when the coach was ejected from a game at Hudson. Meyers was no longer on the sideline, but he took his head-set with him to the team bus overlooking the field and coached the game remotely from there.

Brad is also proud of his accomplishments as a punter. He was recognized his senior year by being named all-district Most Valuable Punter and being named to the Des Moines Register Elite team for that position by averaging over 47 yards per punt.

Brad further showed his versatility by playing fullback on goal-line situations, even scoring a few touchdowns in his high school career. At 275 pounds in high school, not too many defenses relished seeing Harms lined up at fullback whether it was to lead block for teammates like Brian Lynch or run it himself! They were literally putting themselves *"in Harms' Way."*

One interesting note about Brad was that he started his high school career wearing jersey #71. But somehow that freshman year, his white jersey got washed with the maroon jerseys and came out pink! So he had to pick another number for the next game and got #60. From that point forward, Brad was #60 through both high school and college.

By the time he finished his Spartan career, Brad earned a mountain of accolades and awards. He was named first team all-district three years. As a junior, he was also named all-district Most Valuable Player for offensive linemen, Iowa Prep Illustrated All-Elite Team, Des Moines Register first team all-state offensive line, and second team all-state by the Iowa Newspaper Association.

His senior year, the fall of 1995, Brad was both the all-district Most Valuable Player as an offensive lineman and punter. He made the previously mentioned Des Moines Register All-Elite Team as a punter, and was designated as *"Blue Chip"* All-Big Ten Region and participated in the 1996 Shrine Bowl.

For fun, Brad also threw the discus and shot put in high school. While his primary interest was in football, he set the Spartan school record for the discus. He placed fourth as a junior and sixth as a senior in that event at the State track meet, and also sixth in the shot put. Brad also set numerous meet records in those events.

The University of Iowa was Brad's first choice for college and he completed his redshirt freshman year as a Hawkeye walk-on. However, he had a scholarship offer at the University of Northern Iowa and chose to transfer and play for UNI coach Mike Dunbar. By his sophomore year at UNI, he was a 300-pound starting guard playing next to ex-Parkersburg star and UNI center Brad Meester, who went on to become the center for the NFL's Jacksonville Jaguars for over a decade. Meester served as a good mentor for Harms. When asked what he like about playing with Meester, Brad noted, *"He covered up for all my mistakes!"*

Following Meester's graduation, Brad moved from his guard spot to center for his senior year filling in for his mentor. It was a good move as Brad earned Gateway Conference first team all-conference honors and the UNI Best Blocker Award. He was also named third team All-American by the Sports Network and Honorable Mention All-American on another team.

Sports Hall of Fame
Grundy Center, Iowa
Established 2004

Class of 2011

Melvin Heckt 1942

Jack Basye 1960

Tim Williamson 1971

Carla Iverson 1998

HOF Class of 2011: Carla Iverson, Jack Basye, Tim Williamson, & Melvin Heckt.

Sports Hall of Fame
Grundy Center, Iowa
Established 2004

Melvin Heckt

Mel Heckt was a football and basketball standout for the Spartans from 1938-1942. He's shown right accepting his awards at his 2011 induction ceremony as a football player.

Melvin Heckt was born in the Roaring Twenties, grew up through the terrible Depression of the 1930s and was part of the "Greatest Generation" of Americans who fought in World War II in the 1940s. He made his mark on Spartan sports as a football and basketball player.

Mel, the only child of Wes and Ada Heckt, like most kids his age, played pick up games of football and basketball with the other kids his age. Mel remembered fondly that they often played football on his front yard next to the German Lutheran Church along Main Street while basketball games frequently took place in the Boren's barn.

Starting his football career in high school, Mel was a guard on the offensive line as a freshman and sophomore and remembers playing next to center, Carroll Broderick, who Mel described as an outstanding lineman who started at that position for three years. Mel played the next two years as fullback and on defense, he normally played linebacker. His coach was Cliff Hansen, a former NFL player for the Chicago Bears.

The Spartans of the late 1930s and early 1940s were very competitive under Hansen's leadership. They included players like Doug Arends, Ed Klosterboer, and Hall of Famer Max Appel. As a senior, Mel was named captain of the team and though playing fullback, he called the signals in the huddle. Mel would often line up as a wingback, then come in motion from the right side and take a pitch running to the left where he would have the option to run or pass. Mel was not afraid to throw

the ball and frequently passed taking advantage of being left-handed and running to the left side.

At 6' 1" and 185 pounds, Mel helped the Spartans amass some strong team records and two conference championships. The Spartans even beat Des Moines Dowling 14-0 in 1940, a feat Mel recalled with great pride. They finished both his freshman and junior seasons undefeated in the North Central Conference. Mel was all-conference and honorable mention all-state in an era where it was hard for players in small schools to get that all-state recognition.

One memory Mel had from his football career resulted in him getting kicked out of a game. Normally a linebacker on defense, the coach put him at defensive back against Ackley, who featured a good passing quarterback. On one play late in the game, the referee flagged Mel for pass interference with Grundy leading 7-0. Mel ran up to him not understanding what the ref had called. Unfortunately, his blurted question was loaded with saliva and inadvertently hit the ref in both eyes! For this accident, Mel was not only flagged for another penalty, but he was kicked out of the game! If he'd only known at that time he would become a trial lawyer, he might have been able to plead his own case. Despite the penalties on Mel, the Spartans managed to hold on for a 7-6 win.

On the hardcourt, Mel played guard and was once again surrounded by good talent. He usually only scored a few points per game in an era where most games were fairly low scoring anyway. Their senior season, Mel was co-captain of the team along with LuVerne Minnich, who later lost his life in combat during World War II. Other teammates on that 1942 team were Doug Arends, Ed Klosterboer, Tom Robbins, Roy Thoren, and Max Appel, who saw limited action from a broken leg that happened during football.

Besides winning the conference, the Spartans won the County tournament, won Districts, and beat Gilbert in the first game of sub-State. Mel remembers that game well as he scored 17 points, very unusual given his normal role on that team. The next game was the sub-State final to qualify for the State tournament. But the scrappy Spartan team came up short against Neveda to end their run and their season. Besides his four letters in football and three in basketball, Mel also chalked up three more letters in track for a total of ten in his high school career.

While World War II was now in full swing, Mel went to the University of Iowa on a football scholarship. As a freshman, Mel vividly remembered living that first summer in the old Field House with other football players. One of their jobs to help pay for things was to mow the grass at the university using the old push mowers of the day.

Mel recalled the interesting sight of seeing a long line of Hawkeye football players pushing their mowers around campus in a staggered procession.

Mel won a freshman letter playing quarterback for the Hawks, but his career was interrupted when he enlisted in the Marines and became a Marine Raider. The horrors of war quickly came upon him when he was part of a group of 53 machine gunners storming the beaches of Okinawa. He was one of only four who were not killed or wounded in the bloody battle.

After the war, Mel returned to Iowa weighing 195 pounds and became a center on the football team. Although never a starter, Mel was on the travel team and was there for all the Hawkeye games. He said his downfall as a center was he couldn't snap the ball accurately to the kickers. Mel acknowledged he was a great long-snapper, but he was just too long, too often.

After football, Mel obtained his law degree starting a long and illustrious career in Minnesota. Among his many accomplishments, he did great pioneering work in estate planning for parents of disabled children.

Terry Haren presented Mel Hecht with his Hall of Fame award in 2011.

Sports Hall of Fame
Grundy Center, Iowa
Established 2004

Jack Basye

Jack Basye is shown left in 1958 shooting a jump shot in high school. Center shows him in a University of North Dakota press photo where he was captain of their greatest-ever team of 1965. Right, Jack is receiving his Hall of Fame awards from Terry Haren in 2011.

Rarely will you find, even among all our great Spartan Hall of Famers, an athlete who has combined all-around athletic ability with the longevity of active competition of Jack Basye. Jack, older brother of fellow Hall of Famer Jim Basye, made his mark primarily for his basketball career, but his athletic talents extended far beyond the court.

Jack Basye played at a high level in football, baseball (he was a starting pitcher for the Spartans for 3 years), softball, tennis, racquetball, 5K runs, and golf over a period of 45 years!

Jack and wife, Jeanne, played all 388 golf courses in Iowa between 1990 and 1993. He scored four holes-in-one!. Jack took up racquetball while living in Sioux City and won two city championships, then moved to Scottsdale where he won another eight tittles, usually against men 20 years younger.

Basye also officiated high school and college basketball for 30 years and baseball and softball for 10. Clearly, Basye was an exceptional athlete even before touching on his Hall of Fame basketball career.

When Preach Basye and his wife, Mary, first moved from Dysart to Grundy Center in the mid-1950s to be the minister of the Methodist Church, the parsonage was next door to the church and it had a large driveway and a double car garage in the back.

One of the first things Preach did was attach a basketball hoop to the garage. It quickly became a focal point for pick-up basketball games for the high school kids of this town during his tenure as Methodist minister.

Jack hosted the likes of Bill Clark, Bill Stock, Daryl Connell, Ken Dirks, Dan DenOuden, and Buster Lowry as they honed their competitive basketball skills in spirited play. During summers, Bud Bergman would come home from Iowa State and play with the kids. Even little brother Jim played with Jack and his friends who were three years older. Of course, by that time, little brother Jim wasn't so little anymore and could hang in there with the older boys!

The high school was brand new in 1957 when Jack was a sophomore and he broke into the starting basketball line up as a guard. The first home game was against Iowa Falls and Jack is proud of the fact that he was the leading scorer in that initial contest on the new court. They had an excellent team going undefeated into district play where the Spartans lost to Waverly, a team that went on to finish second in the State tournament.

Jack led the Spartans in scoring as both a junior and senior averaging around 16 points a game and scoring often from long-range before there was a "three-point" line. They lost in the Sectional finals to Marshalltown St. Mary's his junior season.

Jack was also a good football player, and one game is worth noting. He played wingback and receiver for the Spartans which had excellent teams going undefeated in the fall of 1958 and 7-1 the following season in 1959. In his first game as a senior against Nevada, Jack intercepted three passes, including one of them for a "pick-six." He also scored another touchdown on a run, and third one on a pass! That was quite a game for Jack.

On the court for his senior season, the Spartans got off to a good start, but at the very end of the season, Jack became ill. The Spartans won all three of their sectional games by a grand total of just seven points as Jack, was already feeling the oncoming effects of what turned out to be mono, Yet he scored 69 points in those three games. But the illness and the doctors benched him before Districts and he wasn't able to play as Grundy Center lost to Waverly again. Jack was selected first-team all-conference and honorable mention all-state both his junior and senior seasons.

After high school, Bill Fitch, a colorful basketball coach of the era, recruited Jack to play for him at Coe College. Basye led the freshman team in scoring averaging 20

points per game. As a sophomore, he started at shooting guard and averaged 10 points a game and led Coe in free throw shooting percentage with 82%.

Jack transferred to the University of North Dakota when Bill Fitch took over the head coaching job. Basye red-shirted one year due to the transfer rules of the time. As a junior and senior, Jack was co-captain of the team. He averaged 10 points per game and five rebounds as a junior and led the team in scoring six games that season.

Basye's senior season in 1964-1965, UND went undefeated in North Central Conference play at 12-0, a feat never again accomplished in the old conference. Jack's biggest thrill as an athlete was making the Final Eight and placing third in the Division II NCAA championships that season. They lost in the semi-finals and a guy named Walt Frazier, later an NBA Hall of Famer, guarded Jack and led Southern Illinois to the finals. North Dakota's overall record was 26-5 for the season.

Jack Basye (white uniform) is scrambling for the ball while playing for the University of North Dakota in 1965. He was captain of the team that finished 3rd in the NCAA Division-II tournament.

In 2003, the University of North Dakota inducted the 1965 basketball team into their Hall of Fame and named them the greatest basketball team in the school's history. As an interesting side note, the legendary Los Angeles Lakers basketball coach, Phil Jackson, was a teammate of Jack's that year and remained a friend.

After college, Jack continued to play full-court recreation league basketball until age 55. He was elected to the Hall of Fame in 2011 for basketball and racquetball.

Sports Hall of Fame
Grundy Center, Iowa
Established 2004

Tim Williamson

Tim Williamson is part of the legacy of great Spartan distance runners over the years. He also excelled in track and cross country at Luther College earning eight letters. He is shown left as a two-time winner of the L.M. Thompson Mile at the Spartan Relays in 1971, center running for Luther College and right at his induction in 2011. He was also elected to the Luther College Sports Hall of Fame in 1998.

Grundy Center has a great tradition of distance runners that many people may not realize. It started with Don Purvis in the 1930s, who held the school record for nearly 25 years until it was broken by Al Harberts in 1957. Both are Hall of Famers. Al's record stood over 50 years until Hall of Famer Dana Schmidt broke it in the 21st century. But the fastest known mile time ever posted by a Grundy Center native as of 2016 was clocked by Hall of Famer Tim Williamson.

A tall, lanky kid who moved to Grundy in the fourth grade, Tim tried his hand at the usual sports like football and basketball. But Tim felt he wasn't built for or coordinated enough for either, although he gave both sports a try. What Tim did find out as he got into high school was that he could run. Specifically, he could run distance. Just a freshman in the spring of 1968, teammates remembered this green kid took to high school track quickly from the start and was running with the upper classmen in the half mile and mile runs pushing them in both practice and in meets.

There weren't any distance stars on the Spartan track teams in the late 1960s. That is until the last year of the decade. As a more mature sophomore, Tim Williamson not only out-ran his upperclassmen teammates in practice (this author was one of them), he was winning dual meets, triangular meets, and placing high in various invitationals. His race times steadily improved and Tim was soon anchoring medley and distance relays. That sophomore year, the two-mile relay team qualified for

State with Tim running anchor. One year later, Tim led the two-mile relay team to a State title while setting a school and State record of 8:12, running with teammates Lee Luhrs, Brian Borchardt, and Mark Carter.

Tim Williamson was the anchor leg for the Spartans' 1970 two-mile relay team that won the Class 1A State championship setting a school and State record with a time of 8:12. The team consisted of Lee Luhrs, Williamson, Mark Carter, and Brian Borchardt.

Tim also ran cross country. He was undefeated as a junior and senior in the mile and two-mile runs and set the course record in Grundy Center at 10:56. As a junior, he finished second in the State cross country meet running 10:19. The following year, Williamson finished second again, and therein lies a story.

Leading the whole race and pulling away with a comfortable margin as he neared the finish, Tim somehow missed seeing a course marker and went the wrong direction. He had to double back to avoid disqualification and run around the missed marker. By this time, he was passed by the second-place runner and didn't have enough time to run him down before the race ended.

In one of his State wins, Tim remembers what an odd race the State cross country one-mile championship was. It was run on a track instead of a typical cross country course. Although Tim won this race, he said the starting line was just packed with so many runners, it made for a crazy environment, especially as Tim and the front runners started lapping slower runners near the end of the race.

As a junior in track, Tim continued his winning ways and among his notable wins was the Leonard Thompson Mile in record time at the Spartan Invitational meet. But as a senior, he did not repeat. Tim ran a lot of the relay races including the two-mile relay and the Medley Relay where they placed second in the State meet. He also won the State indoor 1000 yard run.

Certainly Tim had a very successful track career in high school, but it was at Luther College where he really made his mark earning letters all four years in both track and cross country. His accomplishments were so outstanding at Luther, they elected him to their Sports Hall of Fame in 1998.

One of the records for his relay teams still stood after more than 30 years and many others were among their Top Ten times. Williamson was also captain of both squads for several years. One of the things Tim is most proud of was being voted the Most Inspirational Athlete for track and cross country. His best mile time in college was 4:10, which may be the fastest mile time recorded by a Grundy Center runner.

Some of his accomplishments running for the Norsemen include:
- All Conference all four years;
- Conference Mile Champion three years;
- Conference 3 Mile Champion two years;
- First place Conference Cross Country Meet 1972 and 1973; tied for first place 1974;
- Conference Most Valuable Player for cross country in 1973 with a five-mile time of 25.06;
- Captain of NCAA Division III fourth-place team 1972;
- He also set four records at various conference cross country courses.

Tim's biggest regret is missing All-American status. As a sophomore he just missed the cut-off in cross country and as a junior, he had a complete and total crash just yards from the finish line. Then, as a senior, he ran hurt following a sprained ankle injury that happened while merely walking around the Decorah campus.

Despite this disappointment, Tim completed a stellar track and cross country career at Luther College and then went on to University of Iowa where he became a certified physical therapist.

Sports Hall of Fame
Grundy Center, Iowa
Established 2004

Carla Iverson

Carla Iverson was an integral part of the amazing girls golf teams during the late 1990s and a four-time State place-winner. She went on to golf for the University of Northern Iowa lettering each of her four years on the team.

When Carla Iverson talked about her exceptional golf career, she didn't come across as a highly-competitive personality for a highly-accomplished athlete. Rather, she came across as one that played the game for fun and embraced the joy of competition. Of course, it's certainly a lot more fun when you're winning and that's just what the girls golf teams of Coach Rick Schupbach did in the late 1990s. In fact, as an integral part of those Spartan golf teams, Carla helped lead them to three State championships and a complete rewrite of the school's golfing record books.

It all started pretty early in life for Carla. As a youngster, she often played softball, baseball, and basketball with the neighborhood boys. Her parents, Carol and Sam Iverson, were also very supportive of her activities around sports. Sam had her swinging a real golf club by the time she started kindergarten and the young Iverson took to it quite well.

Growing up and making new friends, Carla found a group of girls who also embraced sports and especially golf. Friends like her older sister Sarah, Hall of Famer Trina Dirks, and Abby Oglesby were regulars at the Town & Country Golf Course. By the time they reached high school, they were already very well-schooled in the game and soon gelled into one of the premier teams in all of Spartan sports history.

For Carla, it was all about having fun. Of course, it is a lot more fun when you are as good as Iverson and her teammates. They all loved to play golf and hang around together. It hardly seemed like competition when they were winning most of their

meets by 50 shots or more! They were relaxed, confident, and just plain good. But for Carla, it centered around having fun and sharing in the success of her teammates and the many successes of their teams.

In retrospect, Carla remembers the great crowd following from the Grundy Center fans along with the support she got from her parents, Sam and Carol. And she especially appreciated Leonard and Donna Ralston who would always score for her at the meets.

Another memory was a trip they took her freshman year. They went to play the course in Spencer where the State tournament would be held in a few weeks. Coach Schupbach got an old Chevy Suburban from the school's fleet of vehicles. This was a vehicle Carla and the rest of her teammates seriously doubted was capable of making the trip to Spencer, let alone making it back home!. But somehow, they made it. And a few weeks later, they finished second in the State. Getting up and back to Spencer in that old Suburban wasn't the only thing that worked out well for the girls golfers that freshman season.

.

Many athletes are very superstitious and those great Grundy girls golf teams of the late 1990s were no exception. Whenever they went to State golf meets in the Des Moines area, they always had to stay in the same hotel even though it wasn't the best hotel or in the best location. They just didn't want to change their luck when they had a good thing going.

The accomplishments of Carla and those Grundy Center girls golfers were impressive. Carla was a four-time individual State place winner, twice finishing runner-up to teammate Trina Dirks in 1997 and 1998. She was also a fourth-place finisher as a sophomore.

As a team, the 1995 Spartans of Carla's freshman season finished runner-up in the State tournament. For the next three years, the Spartans won the State championships in 1996, 1997 and 1998.

To illustrate just how good these Grundy golfers were, they also won the overall State championship twice beating the Class 2A and 3A schools. The 1997 team also logged the second lowest score in State history. Carla contributed to seven different team school records in her career and by the time she graduated, she held two of the top-five season scoring averages in school history. In addition, Carla held records for low conference 18-hole scores and low Regional 18-hole scores.

Coach Schupbach stated that Carla had the best short game of any player he ever coached. Because she was not a long ball hitter, it was her short game that brought her success and helped her compete at the college level.

Carla was one of three girls from Coach Schupbach's teams that went on to compete in college. Carla golfed at the University of Northern Iowa and lettered all four years for Panther Coach Kevin Kane.

During her college career, Carla competed in the top five starting squad all four seasons. She fondly remembers those great spring break trips to Florida, Alabama and California as perks for being on the Panthers' golf team. Wrapping up her college career, Carla graduated with a degree in elementary education in 2003.

Sports Hall of Fame
Grundy Center, Iowa
Established 2004

___

Class of 2012

Forrest Meyers* 1916

J.A. Abels 1962

Beth Stock 1970

Lara Geer 2001

Nicole VanderPol 2005

The Hall of Fame Class of 2012 is shown above: Front row: Mary Gayle Meyers Stowe (representing her grandfather Forrest Meyers) and Beth Stock. Back row: J.A. Abels, Lara Geer, and Nicole VanderPol.

Sports Hall of Fame
Grundy Center, Iowa
Established 2004

___

Forrest Meyers

The late Forrest Meyers is shown left from a photo of his high school basketball team around 1916 and center in his later years. He was a multiple sports star for Coe College from 1917-1921. His granddaughter, Mary Gayle Meyers Stowe, represented him at his induction in 2012.

It's a challenging task to find good information on Grundy Center athletes from over 50 years ago, but with Forrest Meyers, it's been more than a century since he entered high school. Unfortunately, we don't know much about Forrest's high school career at Grundy Center, but more information was available to document an outstanding sports career at the college level.

A 1916 graduate from high school in a graduating class of about 15 people, Meyers attended Coe College and made his imprint on the early years of Coe's athletics. By the time he graduated in 1921, Meyers was regarded as one of the greatest all-around athletes ever to play at Coe, a reputation that lasted for many years.

Forrest won seven varsity letters and two numerals at Coe College. Due to service in World War I, he missed a season of football and baseball for military duty or he probably would have won nine letters. He was known around campus as "Chief".

On the gridiron, Forrest was a halfback who won two letters and earned a reputation as a hard-nosed, determined runner. Two years of varsity football showed him to be a *"fast, smashing heady player"* according to accounts of the day. A newspaper sports article noted that Meyers, *"...never knows when he is downed and usually drags anybody who tries to stop him for two or three more yards."*

Chief was the center and captain of the Coe basketball team and earned all-state collegiate honors as a junior and second team all-state as a senior. For three years he was an outstanding basketball player and he was honored with the captaincy of the 1920 team.

In his third sport on the baseball diamond, Meyers made his mark as an outfielder while earning three letters, but little of his baseball record at Coe remains. Clearly, Forrest was an accomplished athlete in his college career.

His Coe College senior annual states, *"No praise can heighten the honor which this record brings to Chief Meyers"*. A fraternity review of the 1919-1920 school year further noted, *"Chief Meyers will forever stand out as one of Sigma Delta's greatest athletes and one of the best who ever played on a Coe College team"*.

It was a fitting tribute to Forrest Meyers when he was honored during the 1932 Coe College homecoming festivities. A classmate donated a framed grouping of four photographs of Meyers to commemorate his athletic career as part of a refurbishing of Coach Moray Eby's office paid for by the classmate. Three of the photos showed Meyers in his sports uniforms for football, basketball, and baseball while the larger fourth portrait showed Meyers in his World War I Army uniform.

It was amusing to read a copy of the letter to Forrest inviting him to the dedication. Apparently, Forrest was a little reluctant to attend the event, but a paragraph in a letter from a Coe College Vice President humorously stated they would sequester him in a closet if he became embarrassed during the proceedings. Forrest did ultimately agree to attend.

Among the attendees participating in the ceremony were the president of Coe College, Moray Eby, whose office was the beneficiary of the refurbishing, along with several faculty representatives and student athletes. Coach Eby in his remarks accepting the gift said the photos would hang in his office as long as he was there and added that he hoped they would remain in the gymnasium forever. It was a great tribute to "Chief".

Forrest passed away in 1975 and is buried in Grundy Center's Rose Hill Cemetery. He was elected to the Hall of Fame in 2012 and represented at his induction by his granddaughter, Mary Gayle Meyers Stowe.

Sports Hall of Fame
Grundy Center, Iowa
Established 2004

J.A. Abels

J.A. Abels made his claim as a senior level runner setting many records in his age group. He's shown left running in seniors' competition and right at his 2012 induction ceremony.

J.A. Abels brought a very unique spin to his Hall of Fame athletic credentials. Although a very strong track competitor at the high school level, J. saved his most distinguished accomplishments until he was in his 60s!

J. is the son of Leola Abels, long-time math teacher at the junior high school. J's high school track career was solid as he set several individual meet records and participated on record-setting relay teams in the early 1960s.

When J. first started running track, he started out as a miler, but found over his high school career that he really liked the half mile and quarter mile races better. In fact in his senior year of 1962, J. was a State champion in the half mile. He won numerous gold, silver, and bronze medals in individual races and relays, such as the medley relay with speedsters like Dick Lynch and Jack Fistler running the sprint portions and J. usually running the 880 yard anchor spot.

When J. was a senior, the Spartans won the district meet. The Grundy Center two-mile relay team consisting of Darwin Heltibridle, Bob Davis, Dave Willoughby and J. at anchor won first place. That same day, J. also won the half mile with his fastest high school time of 2:04.8. The year before, J, Wayne Katzer, Bill Springer and Darrel Long set a new district record in the mile relay.

After high school, J. went to Drake University because he had his sights on a career in the Air Force and Drake had Air Force ROTC. While there, he did not run varsity

track, although he did win the intramural 440 yard dash three years in a row and played center on the Air Force ROTC basketball team.

After graduation, he entered the Air Force becoming a bombardier and flew on 166 combat missions in Viet Nam on B-52s. While in the Air Force, J. played center on a variety of base basketball teams over the years and continued playing after retiring from the Air Force in local Omaha leagues. In one game in 2004 in a YMCA league for "three-on-three over 50 years old", J. scored 75 of his team's 88 points and outscored the entire opposing team that beat them earlier that year. Then in 2005, J. made an important discovery.

Feeling he was turning into a couch potato as his weight exceeded 200 pounds, J. decided to do something about it. With help from a personal trainer, he dropped 30 pounds from a rigorous training regimen and also reduced his body fat from 24% to 10.2%. His trainer suggested he try running in a track meet against other senior runners. That's exactly what he did winning a silver medal in his first race in the 800 meters and then followed it up by taking gold in the 400 meters. That's how Abels got started in USA National Master's Track & Field.

Motivated even more by discovering this venue, J. started running age equivalent times that were better than he ran in high school. *"Age equivalent"* is an internationally accepted way of comparing Senior and Masters event results to those of 20-30 year old athletes. His accomplishments at state and national levels are long and impressive. Space won't permit listing all his accomplishments or record-setting events, but here are just some of them.

J. achieved world rankings of 15th in the 800 meters and 24th in the 400 and felt very proud to represent his country at that level with a United State flag by his name. At age 66, he became a Masters national champion by winning the U.S. National Championship 400 meter race. He won three Senior Olympic silver medals competing in the 800 and 400 meter races. Additionally, between 2005 and 2011, he earned 16 All-American honors in eight different track and field events.

J. also set the Iowa Senior Olympic 800 meter record and the 400 meter record by running the fastest times in the State of Iowa by men ages 65 to 69. He also set six 800 and 400 meter dash records in Iowa, Kansas, Missouri and South Dakota. Altogether, he competed in 108 state level events and won 83 gold, 17 silver and 2 bronze medals.

Beth Stock

Beth Stock was a two-time State runner-up in tennis and continued playing in college. She continued to play adult and seniors mixed doubles for many years. She is shown right at her 2012 induction with fellow Hall of Fame tennis players Norm Riek (left) and Ed Palmer (right).

Hall of Famer Bob Stock was elected to the Charter Class of this Hall of Fame for his tennis career and was the first in a long lineage of great boys tennis players from Grundy Center. Following the family tradition, Bob's sister, Beth Stock, was the first great girls tennis player in Spartan history. When fellow 2012 inductee Lara Geer was informed that Beth was among her Hall of Fame classmates, her comment was, "*She's a legend!*" Bob and Beth are indeed tennis royalty for all they did to establish the foundation for Grundy Center's rich tradition in this sport.

Under the tutelage of brothers Bob and Bill, Beth got an early start in the sport. When the Stock brothers were only 11 and 14, they would take four-year- old Beth out in the street by their house and toss tennis balls at her. And she could HIT them! When Bob was teaching tennis lessons a few years later, he told Beth to go hit a tennis ball against the backboard until she missed. She was only five or six years old and he finally had to tell her to quit because she hadn't missed! She carried that consistency and focus through her entire tennis career.

Beth remembers playing in her first tournament final at the tender age of seven against an eleven-year-old when she was barely taller than the net. She had success because Bob told her to just hit the ball back. She did exactly that and she won! That turned into Beth's strongest trait as a competitive tennis player over more than five decades. She didn't want to miss a shot and she wasn't going to quit.

Beth had a concentration and focus that brought a tenacity to her play. She was very astute at recognizing her opponents' strengths and not playing to them, but rather exploiting their weaknesses while often putting away winning shots with her strong

166

forehand stroke.

As early as 1963, Beth held the number one ranking in Iowa for girls 12 and under. She continued to hold the top ranking continuously through 1969 and was ranked #38 in the entire country in 1968 for 16-year-olds and under. She attributes a lot of her success to being raised right here in Grundy Center. So many of what seemed like insignificant things, turned out to be critical to her tennis development. These things included playing on those cement courts by the old above-the-ground swimming pool and becoming adept at reacting to odd bounces from balls hitting cracks or weeds growing in them. And practicing in the high school gym where the school's maintenance manager, Glen Willig, would let her and Steve Ehlers in the gym before school to hit against the bleachers and thereby learning to hit on the fast surface of the gym floor.

The tennis environment in Grundy Center helped bring along young players in those early days. Beth remembers that she and Ed Palmer would play doubles against Steve Ehlers and Jim Stevens who were four and five years older than Beth. By playing against accomplished and experienced players, Beth and Ed learned how to hit the ball while it was coming up off the court and not waiting until it was arching back down. Stock fondly remembers Jan Reese, the girls tennis coach in the mid-1960s, allowing Beth, at ten years of age, to practice with the high school team. That is the strong community support Beth cherished.

Beth had an illustrious high school career. Playing in an era when high school tennis had no separate classes segregating large and small schools, Beth played #1 all four years for the Spartans. Four times she won the District tournament and qualified for State. As a freshman and sophomore, Beth made the semi-finals and finished runner-up as a junior and senior. She remembers both those years because the prom was the night before her finals matches and she had to be home by 8 p.m.!

After graduating from high school in 1970, Beth headed for the University of Northern Iowa where she played #2 singles for the Panthers. She transferred to Iowa State as a sophomore in 1972 and played #1 singles for the Cyclones before returning to UNI for her last two collegiate seasons where she played # 1.

Throughout her adult life, Beth continued to both play and coach tennis. She taught tennis in Grundy Center for nine summers and also in Waterloo and Cedar Falls. She even helped out brother Bob as an assistant teaching pro in Ocala, Florida in 1973 before becoming the Head Teaching Pro for the City of Gainesville, Florida for another three years.

Beth continued to play competitive tennis and as recently as the years around 2010

was back in the rankings for mixed doubles. She played with husband, B.E. Palmer, who she met in Ocala. She remembers vividly that he had a beautiful backhand and a "knock-out" smile! Beth and B.E. were the #1 USTA ranked 55-and-older mixed doubles team for the Southern nine-state section in 2007-2008 as well as for the State of Tennessee itself. In 2008, Beth and B.E. played #1 on a USTA mixed doubles team which qualified for the National regionals and in 2009 Beth and B.E. were the #2 ranked mixed doubles team in Tennessee.

Beth continued to participate in the Women's National Team Tennis league playing doubles in the Murfreesboro and Nashville area. You can take the girl out of Grundy Center, but you can't take the racquet out of her hand!

Beth Stock is shown in the photo above with her husband and long-term mixed doubles partner, B.E. Palmer in 2007 after winning this tournament.

Sports Hall of Fame
Grundy Center, Iowa
Established 2004

Lara Geer

Lara Geer was Grundy Center's first girls high school tennis State champion and an elite volleyball player who went on to an accomplished career at Wichita State University.

Lara Geer was certainly one who benefited from the rich heritage of Grundy Center athletics. A 2001 high school graduate, Lara notched another individual State tennis championship for the Spartans, joining Bob Stock and Norm Riek. In addition to tennis, Lara was an elite all-state volleyball player who went on to star in the Missouri Valley Conference at Wichita State University.

Lara got an early start in sports. Her mother, Kim, was an all-state tennis player in Illinois and coached the girls tennis team for the Spartans. Kim and Lara's father, Todd, took Lara and her brother, Nate, to many tennis tournaments when they were just in grade school. Before long, Lara became an accomplished player herself.

By the time Lara was a freshman in 1998, she stepped straight into the #1 singles spot and owned it for the next four years. Lara went 85-3 during high school, never losing a match during the regular season, conference or regional play. Her only losses took place in the State tournament to an eventual State champion. She finished third in the State as a freshman and as a sophomore, second in State as a junior, and culminated her high school career with a State championship as a senior. Interestingly, during the State tournament her senior year, Lara beat three accomplished foreign exchange students on her way to her State title.

Geer was described as an aggressive mid-court player. She was quick and rangy on the court. At 5'11", that was an asset. Lara had strong groundstrokes, a powerful serve, and always looked for an opportunity to finish the point. Lara did admit wanting to get her matches over with quickly so she could sit in the sun and work on her tan while cheering on her teammates.

Lara had Division I scholarship opportunities in tennis and in volleyball. When it came to college, she chose volleyball over tennis because of its team aspect. She felt she could play tennis for the rest of her life, so she wanted to play volleyball in college.

Lara was not exposed to volleyball until middle school. She found it fun and enjoyed the team aspect as a contrast to singles tennis. Geer credits Grundy Center's strong volleyball tradition to her high school coach, Darwin Sents, who transformed Spartan volleyball into a perennial powerhouse.

While in high school, Lara was a three-time first team all-conference player, and was conference Most Valuable Player as a senior. The Spartans made it to the State semifinals in 2001. Lara was third-team ell-state as a sophomore and as a junior. Her senior season, Geer was first-team all-state, named to the State All-Tournament Team, and was named to the elite all-state team. Lara was also the runner-up Gatorade Iowa Volleyball player of the year. She was also one of five finalists for the Wendy's Heisman Athlete of the Year.

Lara chose to go to Wichita State University for college to play volleyball. She was impressed with Shockers coach, Chris Lamb. She liked the way he recruited athletes and turned them into volleyball players. Lamb helped bring out Lara's leadership qualities and named her floor captain of the team her last two seasons. Lara was almost always on the court. She was strong and quick defensively, as well as having the ability to play well above the net for kill-shot scoring opportunities. Wichita State was consistently ranked in the top-20 NCAA teams during Lara's tenure.

A three-year letter winner for the Shockers, Geer was named to the Missouri Valley Conference All-Freshman team in 2002. She was also chosen second-team Ain 2002 and 2003. Lara was named first-team all-conference in 2004, and academic first-team all-conference in 2003 and 2004. Lara was named the Most Valuable Player of the Missouri Conference tournament in 2004 when Wichita State won the conference regular season and tournament titles, qualifying for the NCAA national tournament.

A back injury cut Lara's college career one year short, after which she completed her BA degree in philosophy, and then earned a law degree. Lara joined the Grundy Center Sports Hall of Fame in 2012 for volleyball and tennis.

Nicole VanderPol

Nicole VanderPol is shown playing tennis in high school, with the 2005 State championship trophy and playing for the University of Iowa. As a senior in high school, she was named the Class 2A Basketball Player of the Year in 2005, a first in Spartan history!

When inducted in 2012, Nicole VanderPol became the youngest member of the Hall of Fame having graduated in 2005. Nicole came from a family of outstanding athletes. Her dad, Steve, the high school principal, played football at Central College and mom, Barb, played basketball there as well. With genes like that coupled with her own natural ability in a 6' 1" package, there was a lot of athletic potential in this young lady.

Nicole remembered the great access she had to the high school gym while growing up with her dad being principal. Her mother would play with her and helped jump-start her basketball skill-building as well as developing a quick shot from the floor. From grades six through eight, Nicole played AAU basketball coached by one of the Spartans all-time greats and fellow Hall of Famer, Kim Van Deest.

Nicole also attributed a great deal of her high school success from being surrounded by other talented teammates she played alongside. Two of them were Katie Schuller and Amanda Harkin, who played with Nicole from the third grade through high school. Another was Kristen Harris who also teamed up with Nicole in both volleyball and as a doubles partner in tennis.

Nicole was introduced to volleyball during her middle school years. Her older sister, Tara, helped spark that interest and Nicole excelled there, as well. In high school under coach Darwin Sents, Nicole and the Spartans were three-time Conference champions and twice qualified for the State tournament making it to the semi-finals her senior year in 2005.

Playing in the middle front to take advantage of her height, Nicole was first team Aall-conference all four years in high school and academic all-conference as a junior and senior. A two-time conference Most Valuable Player, Nicole was sixth team all-state as a sophomore and first team her junior and senior seasons. She was particularly proud of being named to the State volleyball tournament's all-tournament team her senior season.

Nicole also had a solid tennis career under Coach Kim Geer. She won several doubles and singles conference championships and three times qualified for State in doubles. As a freshman, she and partner Angie Shuey placed fifth and as a junior and senior, she teamed up with Kristen Harris to win two regional championships and take another fifth-place finish at State in 2005.

But Nicole's forte was basketball. Like volleyball, Nicole was a four-time first team all-conference and a two-time all-academic selection. Three times the Spartans were Conference champions and those same three years, Nicole was the conference Most Valuable Player. Both her junior and senior campaigns, Grundy made the finals of the State tournament in Class 2A. They finished runner-up in 2004 and brought home the State championship trophy her senior year of 2005. And therein lies a story and a poignant memory for Nicole.

The Spartan girls carried the #1 ranking into the title game against #2 ranked Tri-Center Neola. While the referees let them play pretty physically in the preliminary games, the officials in the Finals were calling everything a lot closer. As a result, Nicole got into foul trouble early in the game and only played eleven minutes total. The Spartans were trailing by 12 points with just five minutes to go. Back in the game, Nicole remembers with pride how the whole team pulled together dropping in pressure shots offensively, making key steals defensively, and persevering for a dramatic three-point victory! Later, she heard some Grundy fans watching back home turned off their TVs for those last five dramatic minutes thinking a victory was out of reach when trailing by a twelve point deficit. Those fans were stunned to find out the Spartans did exactly that!

Nicole was named to the All-Tournament team for the second year in a row and topped off her high school basketball accomplishments by being named the Class 2A Player of the Year, a first in Spartan history! She held the school career records for rebounds and points with 1,526.

VanderPol took her talent straight to the Big Ten joining Lisa Bluder's Iowa Hawkeyes for the 2005-2006 season and was quickly introduced to a much faster and more physical college game. Playing in her first conference game against Indiana, Nicole

took a hard elbow to the face and a torrent of blood came gushing out of her nose. It was a rude welcome to the Big Ten.

Although she battled injuries throughout her college career, Nicole saw a lot of playing time at Iowa. In her sophomore season of 2006-07, the only year she wasn't hindered by injury, Nicole played in 28 games starting five of them while leading the Hawks in field-goal percentage. Starting three of the last four games that year, she averaged nearly 12 points a game and over five rebounds. She led the team in rebounding in her last two starts that season. In a home win over Wisconsin, Nicole tallied a career high of 17 points with eight rebounds while shooting 7 of 11 from the field.

Unfortunately, they lost the first round of the Big 10 tournament to Indiana, but Nicole led the Hawks in scoring and rebounds. She felt highly honored to win the coaches' award given to the person who demonstrated the hard work and coachability that they want in Hawkeye basketball players.

Nicole was elected to the Grundy Center Sports Hall of Fame in 2012 for basketball and volleyball.

The 2005 State Champion Spartan girls basketball team of 2005. Nicole is circled.

Sports Hall of Fame
Grundy Center, Iowa
Established 2004

Class of 2013

Dick Lynch 1963

Charlie Peters 1965

Ron Coleman 1977

Matt Bockes 1999

Kylie Dirks 2000

The Hall of Fame Class of 2013 is shown above. Front row: Dick Lynch, Kylie Dirks, and Ron Coleman. Back row: Charlie Peters and Matt Bockes.

Sports Hall of Fame
Grundy Center, Iowa
Established 2004

Dick Lynch

Dick Lynch was a multiple sports standout in high school and went on to a successful career on the State College of Iowa (now University of Northern Iowa) track team.

Dick Lynch was a field events specialist and three-year letterman on the University of Northern Iowa track team at both the long jump and triple jump. Of course, back in Dick's days on the track, it was the State College of Iowa and his events were called the "broad jump" and the "hop-skip-and-jump". But Dick's athletic credentials went well beyond leaping into sand pits at UNI's old O.R. Latham Stadium.

An all-around athlete in high school, Dick credits many talented teammates for his competitiveness. In fact, it was Hall of Fame tennis star Bob Stock who first instilled the desire to compete in Dick when they were youngsters. They would race their bikes up to Red Vogt's ice cream parlor on Main Street to see how many free games they could rack up on Red's pinball machines.

It was another Hall of Famer, Bob Smoldt, who helped teach Dick perseverance by playing Bob one-on-one in basketball practices and not to give up against more talented (and taller) players. Hall of Famer Jim Basye taught Dick how to endure the physical punishment of football when he did tackling drills against Jim, an all-state running back who out-weighed Lynch by more than 50 pounds.

Additionally, Dick credits the 1963 North Iowa Cedar League Champion basketball team for teaching him humility. The Spartans won the Districts over Marshalltown at the old Coliseum and took an 18-1 record to the sub-State game a week later and lost a heartbreaker to East Waterloo. While the opportunity of playing in the State

tournament in Des Moines was lost to Dick and the Spartans at that time, he was rewarded 25 years later when son Tom and daughter Sarah (also in the Hall of Fame) both played in Vets Auditorium in the State tournaments. His son, Rob also played on the 1987 State champion football team. Not a bad legacy for the Lynch family.

Taking a look at Dick's size, you probably wouldn't think of him as a football player, but he was a three-year letter winner starting at quarterback as a sophomore and junior. Then he moved to running back his senior season in the backfield with Jim Basye. The Spartans won the 1962 conference title with a 7-0-1 record under Coach Greg Bice. Dick's speed and elusiveness allowed him to lead the team in both rushing with over 1,000 yards and receiving. Dick was first team all-conference, named second team all-Northeast Iowa, and honorable mention all-state in an era when there no class distinctions.

CAPTAINS--Long, Tack, Basye, Lynch.

Dick Lynch (#34) was one of four team captains for the 1962 Spartan football team. He was joined by Gerry Long (#83), Lee Tack (#70), and fellow Hall of Famer Jim Basye (#45). Lynch countered the size and power of Basye with his speed and quickness in the backfield and they were both named first team all-conference.

One of Dick's most cherished sports memories was from the football field. Grundy Center hosted arch-rival Reinbeck for the Conference championship in the last game

ever played on the former football field adjacent to the old junior high school building. He remembered the coin toss with fellow co-captain Dave Shaw (all of 140 pounds) and facing three large linemen from the Rams. Lynch was wondering what they, as smaller players, were doing out there against these really big guys. But the Spartans took the field and Grundy's all-conference linemen, Noel Rewerts and Gary Appel, dominated the line play as Dave Shaw scored the first touchdown of the game and Dick scored the last two Spartan touchdowns on that old field in a 21-13 victory. It's a memory forever treasured.

Despite his success in football, Dick's real forte was track. He was an excellent sprinter and long jumper and one of the highest point scorers for the Spartan track team, also coached by Greg Bice. It was in track that Dick got another lesson in humility when he beat the school record for the 100 yard dash only to to lose the same race to teammate Jack Fistler. Fistler still held a portion of that record as of Dick's 2013 induction. That same race was the District finals and both Jack and Dick qualified for State in that sprinting event.

Dick's track accomplishments in high school are many as he ran individual sprints, long jumped, and ran in a variety of relay races where they enjoyed consistent success. Lynch broke Harold Aiken's high school long jump record by ten inches with a leap of 21' 11½" as a junior. He was also the long jump conference champion in 1962 and 1963. Dick qualified for State multiple times in sprints, relay races, and the long jump, where he finished third in 1962.

While it is not known how many Spartan track stars won high school events at the Art Dickinson Relays at Northern Iowa, it is likely Dick Lynch is the only Spartan athlete to win there at both the high school and college levels. Dick did it in the long jump where he won the event as a high school senior in 1963 and again as a collegiate sophomore in 1965.

While at Northern Iowa, Dick earned a freshman numeral and then lettered three straight years as both a long jumper and triple jumper for the Panthers. He was one of the top two long jumpers on the UNI team and a consistent point winner for them in dual meets, and triangulars. He posted a fourth-place long jump finish in the North Central Conference championships as a senior.

After graduating from UNI, Dick taught and coached for a few years before returning to Grundy Center and taking over the family farming operations together with his brother Jim. Lynch continued his love for sports over their years in Grundy Center as he and his wife Jo were among the Spartans' most consistent fans and loyal supporters over the years.

Charlie Peters

Charlie Peters was known for his toughness in both football and wrestling. In his later adult years, he began running marathons. He joined the Hall of Fame for football, wrestling and distance running.

If the movie *"Marathon Man"* was cast featuring a Grundy Center graduate, the lead character could have been Charlie Peters. Charlie followed up his competitive athletic career of football and wrestling by taking up long-distance running, meaning Marathons, those 26.2 mile races!

Charlie Peters was a very tough and focused athlete in high school. This showed on the football field when he played center and middle linebacker; lettering three years on the gridiron. He was team captain and first team all-conference as a senior, finishing with a fine 6-2 record with the help of big Chuck Kruse and Jerry Bakker in the line blocking for running back Roger Bertram.

One of Charlie's favorite football memories was when he found out an opponent's nose tackle weighed 260 pounds! He went to Coach Marv Ott and asked how to handle a guy who outweighed him by 100 pounds. Coach Ott said to forget his assignments for the first series and, *"Just go after the guy full force every play; he'll be putty in your hands".* Sure enough, Charlie did exactly that and owned the guy the rest of the game with "heart" winning over size.

The toughness Charlie showed in football carried over directly to wrestling. A four-year letterman, Charlie made varsity on the very first Spartan wrestling team when John Doak began the program in 1961. Coach Doak literally hounded Charlie to come out for the new sport of wrestling his freshman year. Nobody had ever seen a wrestling match, let alone understood the sport. It took some convincing, but once Charlie got a taste of the sport, he was in it for the long haul. This decision had a major impact on Charlie's life because it put him on the map for college coaches and gave him the incentive to further his education.

Like everyone else on that first 1961 wrestling team (including guys like Ken Mutch, Goldie Sealman and Bob Smith), Charlie took his lumps, learning the basics of wrestling as the team went 0-8 in duals. He was pinned once his freshman season and vowed it would never happen again. In over seven years of wrestling in high school and college, it never did. As a sophomore, the Spartans improved to 6-6 and Charlie was named the Most Improved Wrestler on the team. He attributed a lot of his improvement and future success to the stairs Coach Doak made the wrestlers run at the old elementary school. Those stairs helped make the Spartans the best-conditioned team around.

As a junior and senior, Charlie established himself as the leader of the wrestling team. He was not only winning a vast majority of his matches, but he was pinning many of his opponents, too, using that conditioning and his own determination. While wrestling at 145# as a senior, Charlie posted a 22-4 record setting the Spartan season record with 14 pins and a team career record of 23 pins while winning two invitational tournaments. The Spartans finished the season 10-3 in dual meets winning both Sectional and District crowns.

One vivid memory for Charlie was from a meet at Beaman-Conrad, a strong wrestling rival that had a very formidable opponent to face Charlie. While taking a sip of water at a drinking fountain prior to the meet, his opponent came over to him and said, *"I'm going to whip your butt!"* Charlie just glared back without saying a word and walked away. With the Spartans trailing as he took the mat, the *Grundy Register* reported the result as a *"brief, but bruising match"* as Charlie pinned his opponent to tie the team score. That meet went down to the heavyweight match where Chuck Kruse won it for the Spartans.

Charlie Peters was one of the three wrestlers who first qualified for the State wrestling tournament. Charlie joined junior teammates Wayne Wrage and Larry McClanathon by qualifying at Districts. Back in 1965, there were only two classes and eight participants at each weight. Charlie lost his first-round match to Algona's Dave Martin, who went on to become a four-time All-American and National champion wrestler at Iowa State. Back in those days, there were no wrestle backs if you lost in the first round, so Charlie's high school wrestling career was over.

Looking back on his high school wrestling career, Charlie fondly remembered the strong support the team had from the Grundy Center fans, not only for home meets, but also for the great support on the road. He recalled hard-core Spartan wrestling fans he'd always see in the stands Wayne Wrage, Sr., Marv Ralston, Porky Stumberg, Bud Pike, Jim Miller, Roger Mooty, Roger Whitcome, Don Coleman, Martin Sharp, and others.

In college, Charlie was a three-year letterman and varsity wrestler on the Wayne State College team winning over 60% of his matches. Unfortunately, Charlie had to miss his senior season due to a major concussion. The Wayne State wrestling teams those years were all Conference championship teams and two of those teams were inducted into Wayne State's Athletics Hall of Fame.

After graduating, Charlie taught and coached for 13 years and refereed wrestling at both high school and college levels. He left teaching for the robotic business world and found out he was becoming such a workaholic that it was affecting his health and his heart. Charlie was told by doctors to find another outlet besides work to channel his energy.

At age 39, Charlie took up distance running and set a goal to run a marathon in 1989. He did, and successfully qualified for the Boston Marathon on his first attempt. He not only did one marathon, Charlie liked it well enough to run 13 more before his knees and hip forced him to quit running in 1999. By then, he had qualified for the Boston Marathon five times, ran in it four times, and ran marathons around the country in cities like Honolulu, St. Louis, the Twin Cities, Milwaukee, and the Disney Marathon in Orlando.

Since his marathon years, Charlie has channeled his energy and enthusiasm into scuba diving, sky diving, and hang gliding. As a pilot since 1967, he also enjoyed the challenge of flying with Air Combat USA where they actually flew prop plane fighters in aerial combat competitions. Charlie Peters remained an adventurer to the core.

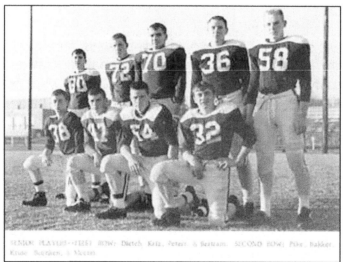

Charlie Peters (#54) is shown next to Rick Kriz (#47) on the 1964 Spartan football team.

Sports Hall of Fame
Grundy Center, Iowa
Established 2004

Ron Coleman

Ron Coleman is shown wrestling his senior year in 1977 for Coach Clint Young. After finishing second in the State in 1976 as a junior, Coleman was gunning for a State championship his senior season when an illness sidelined him. The middle picture shows Ron, wrestling 126#, handling the Walforf 350+ pound heavyweight in college and right accepting his Hall of Fame awards in 2013.

Like many of Grundy Center's Hall of Famers, Ron Coleman took advantage of the town's small school benefits and participated in many sports: football, baseball, track, and his specialty, wrestling.

Despite being relatively short, Ron used speed, quickness, and strength to his advantage earning 12 letters from 1974-1977. He earned three each in football, baseball, track and wrestling. Coleman's speed helped him as a corner back and wing back on the football team, bunting for base hits and stealing bases on the State runner-up baseball team, and doing sprint events in track. Ron had explosive initial speed and could get out of the blocks or down the base path very rapidly. In fact, Ron twice qualified for State in the 100 yard dash and placed at State in relay events. Being able to compete against larger and taller athletes always gave Coleman a sense of accomplishment. And he accomplished plenty!

This explosiveness paid great dividends on the wrestling mat. Ron was a starter as a sophomore for Coach Clint Young, but wrestled two weight classes above his natural weight class due to established seniors in the lineup. After the regular season ended, Ron's dad, Don, would take him to spring and summer freestyle tournaments to gain valuable experience and confidence for his junior and senior seasons. Those times with his dad were cherished memories. Ron competed successfully against Class 2A & 3A opponents and placed well in a wrestling style that aptly suited his wrestling talents: takedowns and throws.

Coming into his own as a junior, Ron quickly showed he fit right in on Hall of Fame Coach Clint Young's high-caliber team. Coleman's teammates included Hall of Famers Dave Ehrig and Kurt Helmick, along with Jim Weber, and Todd Geer. Using his quickness, strength, and leverage, Ron chalked up 95 takedowns in his last two years and set a school record for takedowns in a season with 53 as a junior.

Quite a few of those came from a lethal head-lock takedown Ron perfected where he threw his opponents from a standing position directly to their backs usually resulting in a coveted four or five-point move and often a pin. They didn't keep statistics on this, but one could wager if they tracked who had the most takedowns straight to an opponent's back, Ron could very well be among the career leaders.

Coleman remembers winning a tournament early in his junior year that showed him he was going to be a competitive force at his weight. He won a one-point decision over a good Class 3A State qualifier from Tama-Toledo and then knocked off another outstanding wrestler from Dysart to win his first invitational championship.

Another vivid memory was against Beaman-Conrad, still a fierce rival with the Spartans, even though both schools eventually shared a wrestling team. Coach Young had Ron drop down a weight class to wrestle one of the Comets' best kids. Ron will never forget the astonished "*Oh crap!*" look on the opponent's face when he found out he would be wrestling Ron. Coleman won an easy decision while Todd Geer, who had switched weights with him, also won his match.

Taking a strong 26-3 record into the State tournament his junior year, Ron won Sectionals, finished second in Districts qualifying him for State, and then put together an impressive State tournament performance. Winning the first two rounds, Ron upset a highly-ranked, undefeated opponent in the semi-finals. Coleman handed the wrestler his only defeat of the season by showing him the lights with his signature head-and-arm throw and pinned him! Advancing to the finals, Ron lost to two-time State champion Rod Earlywine, who went on to wrestle for Drake University.

Hungry for another shot at a State title, Ron went into his senior season gunning for anyone in his path. Twice, Ron beat the soon-to-be Class A state champion in his weight. He also wrestled the Class 2A champion in freestyle after the season and beat him, too. He accumulated a 19-1 record while winning the North Tama and Hudson invitationals.

Incidentally, Ron sometimes brought out the worst, not in his opponents, but in their families. Once, an upset mother hit him with her purse after a match against her son. Another time at a tournament, two older brothers of another opponent accosted

Ron in the hallway and were about to get rough with him when Ron was rescued by some nearby Spartan fans who saved him from getting mugged.

Ultimately, fate was not on Ron's side. It wasn't an opponent who derailed Ron's chance at a State championship. It was his health. A high fever and infection put him in the hospital four days and took him out of the District qualifying tournament ending his quest for a State title.

Place-winners for Clint Young's State runner-up team include L-R Jim Weber, Kurt Helmick, Asst. Coach Dwayne Cross, Dave Ehrig (kneeling) Coach Young and Ron Coleman. Four of them are in the Hall of Fame.

After his high school career, Ron went on to star at NAIA Division Waldorf College, then a two-year school. He compiled a record even better than high school in just two seasons with 60 wins against only six losses and a tie. His freshman year, Ron chalked up a 26-4 record, won three tournament championships, and qualified for the NJCAA national tournament. As a sophomore, Ron had an outstanding season with a 34-2-1 mark while winning four more tournaments. He again qualified for the NJCAA national tournament. He was also the captain of the team and their Most Valuable Wrestler. Waldorf was 15-5 in dual meets his senior season and ranked nationally.

Planning to build on his junior college success, Ron enrolled at Winona State University to wrestle only to have them drop the wrestling program. Ron remained at Winona State, where he graduated with a degree in Education.

Sports Hall of Fame
Grundy Center, Iowa
Established 2004

Matt Bockes

Matt Bockes is shown left in a photo from high school, center in two photos at Iowa State University, and right receiving his awards during his 2012 induction ceremony. He was the Cyclone long snapper for four years and also earned a varsity spot on the offensive line.

Many times, Matt Bockes had an unusual view of Iowa State Cyclone football games when he was on the field. His view was upside down and backwards. It was the view of the deep snapper hiking the ball to the punter or field goal kicker. Despite this rather distorted view of the game, Hall of Fame football player Matt Bockes saw a lot of action for Iowa State University as he earned four letters playing in the Cyclones' offensive line.

The son of Roger and Beth Bockes, Matt was a good basketball player and played #1 on the tennis team for three seasons. Despite spending a lot of time and money on basketball camps attempting to be the next Fred Hoiberg, Matt eventually realized that his best sport was going to be football. And he got a quick lesson that ironically gave him a bit of confidence early in his freshman year in high school.

Fellow Hall of Famer, Brad Harms, who later became an All-American lineman at Northern Iowa, hit Matt so hard during a drill during the first day of practice that the back of Matt's helmet was the first thing to hit the ground! Harms reached down and helped Matt back on his feet. Although it was a rough lesson, it actually gave Matt confidence. If he could live through that hit from one of the best players in the state, he could take shots from anyone.

The Spartans didn't always have the best teams when Matt played, but as his senior season rolled around in the fall of 1998, Matt really focused on football determined to play his best. And he did just that as the center on offense and tackle on defense. As captain of the squad, playing offense, defense, and special teams, he was rarely off the field. As a result of his efforts, Matt was named first team all-district, District Most Valuable Player, and first team all-state by the *Des Moines*

Register for Class 1A. He was also selected for the 1999 Shrine All-Star game and chosen a co-captain of the North squad.

A big fan of the Iowa State Cyclones his whole life, Matt aspired to play football there and was a recruited walk-on as a freshman when he red-shirted. Matt had gone to the Shrine Bowl and received his honors in high school for his defensive play, but because of some injuries, Matt volunteered to play center for the Shrine game. The Iowa State coaches saw the game and thought his future was in the offensive line. Matt won the Cyclone's job of snapping the ball for punts, field goals, and extra points. He was always extremely thankful for never having had a bad snap during his career while earning four letters for the Cyclones.

At 6'1" and 235 pounds, Matt was underweight and undersized for Division I football. So he followed the coaches suggested diet plan: *"EAT EVERYTHING!"* He bulked up to 300 pounds and played more and more as his career went along. By his junior season in 2002, Matt was also playing in the offensive line and even started some games by the end of the year.

Those who knew Matt and his family might think the highlight of his college career was beating Iowa four-out-of-five times. He conceded that hoisting the CyHawk trophy above his head on the field of Kinnick Stadium was indeed an amazing feeling. However, of all the experiences Matt had at Iowa State, the two things that he was most proud of happened off the field.

At the 2004 senior banquet Matt's final year, he received the "Player Appreciation Award". This is an award voted on by the trainers, managers, and other support staff and is given annually to the senior who has been the most respectful and treated them the best while being at Iowa State.

The biggest honor of Matt's career came on the eve of the first game his junior year when Coach Dan McCarney asked Matt if he would lead the Cyclones in prayer before and after their game against Florida State. He continued to do this for every game the rest of his career.

Matt credits his parents, Roger and Beth, for being great role models both on and off the field and always appreciated the tremendous support they gave him through his career. Roger and Beth never missed a football game, home or away from fourth grade through college. Matt's sister, Melissa, was his biggest fan and cheerleader who, despite being three years older and extremely busy herself, also never missed a game. Bockes' wife, Tara, although being a volleyball player at Central College before they married, made it to every game she could and was incredibly supportive

even when she couldn't be there. Matt gives 100% credit of his success to God and the incredible support of family, friends, and great coaches.

Matt Bockes probably holds the record among Spartan football players for playing in college bowl games. He played in three bowl games, and one NCAA Division 1 Kick-off Classic. His bowl appearances included the Insight.com Bowl in Phoenix where they beat Pittsburgh; the Independence Bowl in Shreveport, Louisiana; the Eddie Robinson Kick-off Classic against Florida State; and the Humanitarian Bowl in Boise, Idaho. Therein lies a good story about playing Boise State in the Humanitarian Bowl on that gaudy blue field. In fact, Matt remembered the field attracted gaggles of geese that would land there thinking the field was a lake.

But the story didn't happen on the blue turf. Part of the festivities at the Humanitarian Bowl was a "beef-eating" contest at a local steak house between Iowa State and Boise State. They came on separate evenings, but the steak house kept track of which team of three players could eat the most prime rib and Matt was on the Cyclone team. Eating the beef in 24 ounce cuts, the Boise State players polished off 201 ounces, an average of 67 ounces for each of the Broncos. Coach McCarney really wanted to win the contest, so the pressure was on the Cyclones. In front of local TV cameras covering the contest, Matt's two Cyclone teammates only averaged 45 ounces each. But Matt came through to save the day for Iowa State by devouring 113 ounces all by himself! It was also more than any previous contestant and probably a record that still stands today as Iowa State (thanks to Matt) beat Boise State by a mere two ounces!

In a further footnote, TV weatherman, Ed Wilson, Matt's cousin, got wind of the story and played the video footage on WHO-TV in Des Moines as a backdrop to his evening weather report. Roger, of course, thought that was great, but Matt's mother, Beth, was horrified!

Matt remains proud that he was part of the Cyclone football team with the most wins in Iowa State history as they posted a 9-3 record in 2000 during his first year of competition. He also won numerous individual and coaches awards during his football career and graduated in 2004 with a degree in Construction Engineering.

Sports Hall of Fame
Grundy Center, Iowa
Established 2004

Kylie Dirks

Kylie Dirks was a two-time State champion golfer in high school and part of the amazing Spartan girls' golf teams of the era. The Spartans won four straight girls State golf championships during Kylie's high school career.

Grundy Center's golf tradition dates back to Ivan Miller in the 1960s, the first male golfer in our Sports Hall of Fame. Tracey Voss was Grundy's first girls golfer in the Hall of Fame graduating in 1992. From there girls golf took off for new heights and a run of State championships. Kylie Dirks was an integral part of that success.

If anyone had to pick one dynasty team in the history of Grundy Center sports as the best, it would be hard to argue against the girls golf teams of the late 1990s and early 2000s. Those Spartan girls set a standard during their era that is almost impossible to beat. Dirks joined sister, Trina, and teammate, Carla Iverson, in the Hall of Fame when Kylie was inducted in 2013.

Golfing came early for Kylie. Her dad, Dennis, a baseball and basketball Hall of Famer himself, introduced golf to her at five or six years of age. Kylie took to it fast and soon she was playing in junior golf tournaments gaining tremendous experience while honing her skills on the links.

By ages 10-12, Kylie was playing competitively in meets all over the state, sometimes doing two or three a week in the summertime. Her parents, Dennis and Cindy, provided great support to all their kids driving them to the various tournaments. This experience and a strong practice ethic helped Kylie perfect her play. Yet, she credits

the great environment provided in Grundy Center that allowed her and the other great girl golfers on their teams to thrive.

When asked what motivated her in her golfing career, Kylie said it was a combination of things. First of all, it was fun. It was something she and her two older siblings did together. They learned from their Dad, who was a built-in coach to all three spending countless hours working with them. Kylie was also competitive in a positive way competing with herself to do the best she was capable of doing.

Through her hard work practicing and dedication to golf, Kylie became very proficient in all aspects of her game. She was most confident about driving off the tee, but she considered the effectiveness of her short game as the most crucial aspect to make or break a round. Given her success, Kylie's short game was very effective throughout her career.

Dirks' resume while golfing for Coach Rick Schupbach is impressive as she was part of the most decorated sister golfing combination in Iowa state golf history. Together, sister Trina and Kylie won four-straight individual State championships with Trina winning the first two in 1997 and 1998 and Kylie the next two in 1999 and 2000. All four of those years, the Spartans won the State team titles making Kylie the only athlete in the Spartans' storied history to play on four State championship teams. It was also the 1997 and 1998 teams that not only won the Class 1A State championships, but it was also the first time in girls' State golf history that any 1A school beat the teams from all the other classes. And they did it two years in a row!

Kylie shares in a host of team records set during this era including the second lowest score in State tournament history regardless of class. Their team record during Kylie's tenure was 178-3, an astounding 98.3 winning percentage.

Individually, Kylie graduated holding three of the top six scoring averages and tied with her sister Trina for the best career average at 42.4 strokes. Kylie also held records for the best nine-hole score of 33 and the best 18-hole score of 66.

Joining the 1997 State championship team as a freshman, Kylie felt very comfortable. Besides her extensive pre-high school experience, the team was very supportive of all their teammates, including this new freshman.

Kylie remembers they didn't lose confidence or get rattled when they made mistakes. If one player had an off day, another always stepped up with a low score. Coach Schupbach always found ways to bring the team together as well, whether it was team dinners at his house, friendly competition and mentoring in practice, or some

good music on the drive to their meets to calm any nerves. He also struck a deal to let the team shave his head if they advanced to State against some stiff competition.

Kylie placed all four years at the State tournament finishing eighth as a freshman, fifth as a sophomore, and then topping it off with two-straight State individual championships. And when asked which Dirks sister was better, she just pointed to that tie for the best career-scoring average they share and left it at that.

After high school, Kylie chose Central College and played varsity golf as a freshman. She played #1 and liked the smaller school and smaller team atmosphere. She was runner-up in the Iowa Conference tournament and named the Freshman Most Valuable Golfer for the team before retiring to concentrate on her studies.

Kylie was very proud to join her sister Trina when they were inducted together into the Iowa High School Golf Coaches Association Hall of Fame in 2012. She was also proud to see her brother, Jordan, join his sisters and their dad in this Hall of Fame in 2015.

Already winning golf trophies in their youth, Kylie (left), Jordan (lying down) and Trina (teeing it up) took their golf seriously, but also knew how to have fun with it. The results for Kylie and Trina are shown right with each of them winning two golf State championships.

Sports Hall of Fame
Grundy Center, Iowa
Established 2004

Class of 2014

Roger Peters* 1937

Randy Peters 1964

Clint Young 1971-1980

Steve Bergman 1976

Dana Schmidt 2007

The Hall of Fame Class of 2014 front row: Dana Schmidt and Clint Young. Back row: Steve Bergman, Randy Peters and Ryan Peters (grandson of Roger Peters and son of Randy).

Sports Hall of Fame
Grundy Center, Iowa
Established 2004

Roger Peters

Roger Peters was a good all-around athlete in high school, but it was on the baseball field and softball field where "Big Pete" wielded a powerful bat in a long career. He and son Randy were elected in the same Hall of Fame class in 2014.

Sports fans around the Grundy County area in the 1940s and 1950s who followed the exploits of the area's semi-pro baseball and fast-pitch softball teams, understood how the phrase, "*larger than life*" applied to the late Roger Peters.

Standing 6'4" back when that height was really big, Roger Peters graduated from high school in 1937. Respectfully nicknamed "Big Pete" for his size and power, Roger did not play high school baseball because it was not offered. Because he helped on the farm, Roger didn't even play basketball until his junior year after finally talking his dad into letting him go out. However, since his mom came from a clan of 12 children, there was no shortage of cousins for Roger and brothers, Gordon and Marlyn, to learn about playing sports. So when Big Pete finally got to play basketball in high school in 1936, he began by playing with the junior varsity and worked his way into more time in the varsity games as the season progressed. As a senior in 1937, Roger was playing center and was one of the captains on the team. He was offered a basketball scholarship to Drake, but turned it down because he had a chance to rent some land to farm and chose to stay home.

Despite not having baseball as a high school sport, Roger fueled his baseball passion by playing for local semi-pro town teams that were common in that era. He made his mark as both a pitcher and a powerful left-handed hitting first baseman. Throughout the 1940s and 1950s, Big Pete played semi-pro baseball for nearby

Whitten and earned all-state accolades while consistently leading the team in home runs.

In 1941, the spring prior to the attack on Pearl Harbor that pushed America into World War II, Roger and fellow Hall of Fame member Arnie Reynolds were invited to a baseball school in Florida sponsored by Iowa native and Cleveland Indian pitching ace Bob Feller. While there, he was instructed by both Feller and baseball's most famous icon, Babe Ruth. The regret Roger had with that camp experience was he went down there and worked out with the pitchers. Unfortunately, he had hurt his shoulder playing basketball and it hadn't yet fully healed which affected his pitching and the showing he made in Florida. In hindsight, Roger wished he would have worked with the hitters.

Besides semi-pro baseball, Roger played basketball on the Grundy Center Legion team for several seasons, including their State championship team of 1947. He played alongside Hall of Famers Max Appel, Leon Bockes, and Arnie Reynolds as well as others including Bob Grabinski, Russell and Roy Thoren, and Roger's brother, Gordon.

While playing baseball, Roger also spent a lot of time playing fast-pitch softball for Holland and with the Methodist Church team in the local leagues. He would play baseball on the weekends and softball a couple nights a week. As with baseball, Big Pete both pitched and played first base while continuing his power hitting and consistently leading his teams in home runs.

Peters joined the Army in 1943 and was stationed in England. Even *"across the pond"*, he played a fair amount of ball. His Army job was to help prepare and support the bombardiers flying missions out of England to war zones in Europe. After the planes took off on their missions, those on the ground, like Roger, often played baseball or softball to pass the time until the pilots returned.

Grundy Center put together some strong, competitive softball teams in the early 1950s, often beating opponents on the strength of a Roger Peters round-tripper. One local Grundy All-Star team, coached by Hall of Famer Melvin Fritzel, faced bigger city teams in tournament play. Mason City was the heavy favorite to win and advance to State one particular year. But with Grundy Center players like pitcher Alvin Harrenstein, Irvin Cakerice, Dan Yordy, Floyd Senning, Bud Pike, Arnie Reynolds, and Roger Peters, Grundy Center's local team posted the upset winning 1-0 on Big Pete's home run.

Another time, Bud Pike arranged a game between Grundy Center and his home town of Austin, Minnesota and the Grundy boys again won the game on a Peters' home run.

Roger also told the story of playing ball one memorable game with Floyd Senning. Floyd batted ahead of Roger and told Big Pete he was going to hit a home run. So Roger answered, *"If you're going to hit a home run, so am I."* And that's exactly what happened. Floyd hit a home run and sure enough, Roger followed up with one of his own. But it didn't stop there. Floyd hit a home run his next time up and challenged Roger to follow suit and Big Pete came through. And then they both did it again! That made back-to-back home runs for the third time in one game by the same two batters.

Roger did have one dislike about playing games at the Holland field. The right field fence was so short that home runs only counted as ground rule doubles. As a left-handed power hitter, he didn't like that very much.

Roger continued playing softball into the 1960s and although slowed down by age and the wear and tear of nearly three decades of playing ball, Big Pete could still bang the deep ball.

By the 1950s, Roger began bowling to have something to do in the off season. The bowling alley opened in Grundy Center and Roger teamed up with Don Stout and won a State amateur pairs bowling championship. In his bowling career, Peters just missed getting a 300 game by a few pins and put together two different "700" series throwing a powerful ball that carried big pin action. Roger bowled so well at Eldora that he was named to their Bowling Hall of Fame in 2001.

Roger married his wife, Shirley, in 1941 and they had 3 children: Randy, Larry and Susan. They were long time, consistent supporters of Spartan athletics. Roger passed away in 2001 and his grandson Ryan Peters was on hand to accept Roger's awards during his 2014 induction ceremony, along with Roger's son Randy, who was also inducted that day.

Randy Peters

Randy Peters was the first track and cross country coach elected to the Hall of Fame. He was named "Coach of the Year" four times in his career. Left, he is shown as a high school basketball player, then running high hurdles at Wartburg. Right, Randy receives his Hall of Fame award from Terry Haren.

The Hall of Fame had five sets of parents and children inducted into the group by 2016. Harry and Jeff Dole were the first father-son combination and the most recent was Phil Lebo and son, Andy. There is Dennis Dirks and his daughters, Trina and Kylie, who were joined by son, Jordan, in 2015. There is also Dick Lynch and his daughter Sarah. But with the Class of 2014, the Hall of Fame not only added another father-son combination with Roger Peters and his son, Randy, they were inducted together in the same class. And that was a first.

Randy Peters is the oldest child of Roger and Shirley Peters. Like his dad, Randy stood tall. In fact he was an inch taller than "Big Pete" at 6' 5". Following his dad's athletic career, Randy was introduced to sports at an early age. He played football, basketball, and track for the Spartans.

In track, Peters specialized in the high hurdles and also ran the 4 x 400 yard relay. In football, Randy played for the late Greg Bice and in basketball, he played for Marv Ott. Both men were very instrumental in Randy's desire to become a coach himself because of the ways they handled themselves and the way they coached their players.

After graduating high school in 1964, Randy attended Wartburg College and graduated with a degree in Math Education and Coaching. He participated for one season in basketball and gained valuable exposure to another outstanding coach in the Knights' Buzz Levick.

Randy was a member of the track team all four years running the high hurdles. He earned three letters and placed in the conference meets. Randy recalls college track meets where he and Grundy Center teammate and Wartburg sprinter Jack Fistler competed with former Spartan teammate and Hall of Famer Dick Lynch, who specialized in the long jump for the University of Northern Iowa. Altogether, Randy's college experience in basketball and track made the move to coaching those sports a natural transition.

Randy first coached at Nevada High School from 1969-1973 where he was the head coach for boys cross country and the assistant for boys track and boys basketball. While there, he was mentored by Dick Norton and Cecil Rhoads who both had great influences on Randy as he developed his coaching style. It is interesting to note that Cecil Rhoades' young son was usually running around the gym during practices in those days. That kid, Paul Rhoads, ended up running up and down the sidelines at Cyclone Stadium as head coach of Iowa State football some 30 years later.

Randy moved the Quad Cities area in 1973. He took a teaching and coaching position with Class 4A Davenport Central High School, one of the largest schools in the State, where he started as assistant varsity basketball coach. Before long, he was named head coach for basketball. He continued coaching basketball over 33 years, including a stint as assistant men's basketball coach at St. Ambrose College, before going back to the Davenport Central.

While Randy spent over three decades coaching basketball, it was around track and cross country for both boys and girls programs where he excelled. For twelve consecutive years from 1976-1988, Randy coached the girls track program at Davenport Central. He won four conference championships, three district championships and two 4A State titles, those coming in 1982 and 1983. After being chosen regional girls track *"Coach of the Year"* in 1982 and 1984, Randy was also awarded 4A Coach of the Year honors for those seasons.

In his 16 years coaching boys and girls cross country in Davenport, Randy achieved additional recognition. He was named MAC Conference Coach of the Year award and earned his third State *"Coach of the Year"* honor, this time for girls cross country.

Besides the four district championships and three State titles over the years, Randy's boys and girls track teams chalked up seven MAC outdoor conference championships and another four as runner-up, as well as five MAC indoor conference titles.

Although Randy's runners had tremendous success, it wasn't always easy. He recalls one year, his boys 4 x 100 yard relay team made the finals for the Drake Relays with the fourth best time. In the final, which is a flat-out sprint of 100 yards for each team member, the third runner got the baton and came blazing around the backside curve in the lead, only to find his anchorman wasn't anywhere to be seen! Just before the race started, he had gone to the bathroom and didn't realize the race started so soon. He was walking back from the bathroom as the runners in the relay race went flying by. His teammates and Coach Peters were not pleased.

It's interesting to note that Davenport Central had great runners not only with the girls, but the boys. Track coach, Ira Dunsworth, chalked up three State boys track titles in the same 1982-84 time frame that Randy won two girls 4A State titles. When Ira eventually retired in 1990, Randy took over as boys track coach for ten years. During that tenure, his 2005 team won the district and 4A State championships. That boys track team was a very dominant group that also set the Iowa Class 4A record for most points in a State meet. For the success of that team, Randy was awarded his fourth "Coach of the Year" honor for boys track.

Randy attributed the success of his teams to having hard working, tough girls and boys who could perform under pressure. He felt track and cross country allowed him the time to give his athletes additional personal attention, talk them through things, and let them learn from his years of personal experiences in track and cross country. His success over three decades is a great testament to his coaching abilities and why he is a Hall of Fame coach.

Randy retired from teaching and coaching in 2006. He was the first track and cross country coach elected to the Grundy Center Sports Hall of Fame.

Sports Hall of Fame
Grundy Center, Iowa
Established 2004

Clint Young

Clint Young, a State wrestling champion from Algona and NCAA Division II National champion for Northern Iowa, took Spartan wrestling to new levels. He coached five Spartan State champion wrestlers and took the Spartans to a second-place team finish in 1977.

John Doak started the wrestling program at Grundy Center in 1961. After a decade of building the program from scratch, Doak decided the foundation was there and the initial success and reputation of Spartan wrestling was ready for the next generation of wrestlers and coaches. The school was then challenged to find Doak's replacement and new leader in 1971.

What they found was Clint Young, fresh out of the University of Northern Iowa. Young's own wrestling credentials were very impressive. He was a high school State champion from perennial wrestling power Algona and a two-time All-American and NCAA Division II National Champion for the Panthers. Yet, Clint came to his interview with no coaching experience. What he did have was the experience of being coached by the legendary Champ Martin at Algona High School and NCAA Hall of Fame wrestling coach Chuck Patten at UNI. He was also the nephew of the late Keith Young, a legend himself as an undefeated and three-time NCAA national champion who was also the head wrestling coach at Cedar Falls High School. With that background, Grundy Center's administration felt comfortable taking a chance with a rookie coach. It was a great choice.

Picking up where Doak left off, Young brought new energy and a youthful enthusiasm to the job. Clint and wife, Suzanne, settled quickly into life in Grundy Center and the wrestling program produced what are still in 2016 the highest levels of achievement in Spartan wrestling history.

In the Doak era, wrestling practice was in the old elementary school. Clint was able to move wrestling practices from an ancient dungeon that was the old elementary gym to the high school in what was formerly the cafeteria.

In his nine years coaching in Grundy Center, the Spartan wrestlers won 66 dual meets, nine invitational tournament championships, four Class 1A sectional titles, one district title and placed in the top eight at State three times. In 1976, the Spartan wrestlers finished second in the State tournament by a mere half-point, still the highest finish in the program's history. Clint trained his wrestlers to *"never be intimated by an opponent, no matter how decorated they were."* He taught his Spartan wrestlers they could score a fall on anyone *and* no opponent would out-condition them.

The 1976 Class 2A State runner-up wrestling team coached by Clint Young features four future Hall of Famers and the father of another.

The "who's who" of Grundy Center wrestling is dominated by Young's grapplers. It started with the Spartans' first State champion in Mike Draper at 98# in 1973. Heavyweight Dave Ehrig added two State championships and Kevin Ralston another. It's also interesting to note that Young's wrestlers won back-to-back 98# State championships when Hall of Famer Kevin Ralston's championship followed Draper's the very next season. Ralston also chalked up a second-place finish as did Hall of Famer Ron Coleman. And if it were not for an illness right before State his senior season, Clint felt Coleman would have been his sixth State champion. Young's last State champion was Hall of Famer Rick Ruebel.

In his nine year coaching career in Grundy Center, Clint Young sent 29 wrestlers to the State tournament with 16 placing sixth or better. Those place winners included Curt Stumberg, Todd Geer, and two-time place winners Todd Stumberg and Hall of Famer Kurt Helmick.

One of Clint's best memories was when Mike Draper won the program's first State championship at 98#. The Spartans weren't among the top-ten team place winners,

but as the wrestlers drove home from Des Moines, they were met at the seven-mile corner west of town by the Grundy Fire Department and a line of ardent Spartan wrestling fans who escorted their first State champion and the team into town. That was quite unexpected and imprinted a very fond memory.

Another great Grundy Center memory for Coach Young was Rick Ruebel's dominating senior season. Rick went undefeated with 33 wins and hardly had a close match as he breezed to a State championship. Even Wrestling Hall of Fame referee, Mike Allen, was impressed with Ruebel. At the Spartan Tournament that season, the referees were discussing who would get which championship matches. Allen told the group he didn't care which matches he got as long as he got to referee Rick Ruebel. Ruebel always wanted to get a takedown in the first two seconds of a match (and often did) and Mike Allen wanted to see him up close in action.

Young left the Class 1A program at Grundy Center in 1980 when he got the chance to take the Class 2A wrestling program at powerhouse Emmetsburg. Building on his Spartan experience, Clint achieved even grander heights in his 13 seasons at Emmetsburg. They won two team State championships and twice finished runner-up. Clint sent 58 wrestlers to the State tournament, crowned nine State champions (including his own son Mike in 1988) and four runners-up. Six of his Emmetsburg wrestlers became head wrestling coaches and six became college All-Americans. In 1985 he was named Class 2A Wrestling Coach of the Year.

Although it didn't happen in Grundy Center, the most memorable moment of Clint's coaching career was when his son, Mike, won a State championship of his own. Not ranked among the top wrestlers at his weight class and with the top two wrestlers on his side of the bracket, Mike battled his way into the finals and pulled off an upset for Emmetsburg as he joined a very proud Dad as a high school State champion.

More accolades followed Clint after he retired from the coaching ranks. He was inducted into the Iowa High School Wrestling Hall of Fame in 1991 and elected to the Coaches Division of the National Wrestling Hall of Fame in 1997.

Clint was always grateful for the opportunity to teach and coach in Grundy Center. He felt blessed to have worked with dedicated and determined athletes in a community of parents and fans that gave him such tremendous support.

___

Steve Bergman

Steve Bergman, shown left as a high school player, followed his uncle, Bud Bergman, into coaching high school basketball. While winning over 500 games, Steve won five Class 4A State championships including three-in-a row for Iowa City West.

There was another family thread running through the 2014 Hall of Fame induction ceremony. Steve Bergman is the nephew of two Hall of Famers: Max Appel and Bud Bergman. Bud was elected in the Charter Class of 2004 as an athlete, but his coaching credentials are Hall of Fame in their own right. A young Steve Bergman saw the success of his Uncle Bud and drew the inspiration to become a basketball coach from him.

The Bergmans are another great example of why we have a Grundy Center Sports Hall of Fame. What are the chances that two of the most successful coaches in the history of Iowa high school basketball are both from Grundy Center? And that they are related? It speaks volumes to the heritage of sports in this small town.

Steve was a pretty good athlete during his days growing up in Grundy Center. He spent a lot of time playing football, baseball, golf, and basketball. It's what kids in town did in those days and it was very valuable to him later in life. Steve had the experience playing all those sports in a town like Grundy Center, where he often tagged along with his cousin, Jerry Appel (son of Max), to play with the older kids.

Steve's mom liked to tease him about the comments on his elementary report cards. His teachers wrote Steve was *"too loud and too competitive."* Considering Steve

knew from age ten that he wanted to be a coach, it sounds like he was merely honing the skills he would use later in his coaching career.

Steve Bergman was among four future Hall of Famers and the father of another on this little league baseball team of 1970 coached by another Hall of Famer.

While Uncle Bud Bergman ran the basketball program at nearby Waverly, Steve enjoyed going to his games and watching Bud coach. When he couldn't attend in-person, he often listened to the Waverly games on the radio and tried to put himself in Bud's coaching shoes and anticipate game strategies.

In high school, Steve played football, baseball, and was the all-conference power forward on the Spartan's 1976 basketball team under Coach Jim Brousard. He also had some court-time playing for the Spartan team that finished second in the Class 1A State tournament his junior year. Bergman gives a lot of credit to both Harry Dole and Jim Brousard for their influence on him. He took note of how they worked with the Spartan teams of the day and managed their players. Steve wished he could be more like Harry Dole in temperament, but it isn't his personality, although it is something he continually strove for even with more than 25 years of coaching.

Bergman continued playing basketball for two years at Southwest Community College and a year at Winona State University where he started alongside Spartan teammate and Hall of Famer Orrin Brown.

Steve graduated from Cornell College, but was unable to play basketball due to the transfer rules in effect at that time. Next was the challenge of finding a teaching job to go with the coaching. Until he got his teaching certificate for Special Education, those jobs were hard to find. He coached without a formal teaching position for Iowa City Regina, Iowa City High, and his first head coaching job at Monticello.

An opportunity presented itself in 1987 to spend a year in Reykjavik, Iceland coaching both a youth and adult basketball teams. While most of the men spoke English, some did not. Steve would find himself trying to instruct a player in what he wanted him to do only to have another player sidle up to him and whisper, *"He doesn't understand a single word you're saying."* Communication aside, the adults played basketball for nine-month seasons versus three months In America. After a year of that, Steve decided to return to the United States and Iowa in particular. One reason was because his son was going to school where the teachers didn't speak English in the classroom and his family hadn't mastered the local language.

Back home, the opportunity came up to take the head coaching job at Class 4A Iowa City West. At the time, he was advised by peers to not go there. It was considered by some to be a coaching graveyard. The potential was there, but Steve thought the culture and structure of West High basketball needed to be changed. Steve took the challenge and discovered the kids he had to work with were eager to become winners. In his fifth season, his team qualified for the State tournament. By his eighth year, he achieved the biggest thrill of his coaching life when Iowa City West won its first of five 4A State basketball championships.

That first title was memorable, not only for being his first, but West was a big underdog to Des Moines Hoover. Yet Steve's team showed their tenacity with strong defense, big-time determination, and good team discipline. With a minute to go in the game, West had the ball, missed three consecutive shots, rebounded all of them, and as the fourth-consecutive missed shot went up at the buzzer, his player was fouled. All it took was making one of two free throws to win that first championship. And that's exactly what happened as the first free throw went in the bucket.

Another great achievement was holding the Class 4A record for 60 consecutive wins done over three different seasons from 2011-2014. His State championship team of 2012 finished as the 21st ranked team in the nation and the 2013 State champions were ranked sixth. Then in the 2014 basketball season, Steve coached his Iowa City West team to their third straight State championship. At the end of the 2016 season, Steve won his 520th basketball game surpassing Uncle Bud's 519 wins. It also gave this Grundy Center uncle and nephew over 1,000 combined career basketball victories!

Iowa City West also had some strong Grundy Center ties as Hall of Famer Kay (Riek) Dileo coached there and her son played basketball for Steve. Additionally, Kerri (Dole) Barnhouse, daughter of Hall of Famer Harry Dole, was an English teacher at the school. It is indeed a small world in many ways.

Sports Hall of Fame
Grundy Center, Iowa
Established 2004

Dana Schmidt

Dana Schmidt was a record-setting distance runner for the Spartans and went on to a great college track career. He broke Al Harberts' 50 year old record for the mile and was the 2A State champion at that distance. He is shown right accepting his awards from Terry Haren.

Dana Schmidt was the youngest member elected to the Hall of Fame as of 2014, having only graduated a mere six years prior to his induction. He carried on a great Spartan tradition of outstanding distance runners going back to Don Purvis in the 1930s, Al Harberts from the 1950s, and Tim Williamson from the 1970s. All are in the Hall of Fame and Dana Schmidt is a worthy addition to that group with many record setting achievements and All-American performances.

Dana, the son of Kirby and Joyce Schmidt, claimed he didn't really find a passion for track until he got into high school. He was more interested in hockey, baseball and basketball while growing-up. He did some running in junior high for Judd Lyons and liked track, but he had not yet developed a passion for it. Dana's freshman year was anything but stellar. He even threatened to go out for tennis! But fortunately, Spartan track coach, Clint McMartin, talked him out of it.

It really wasn't until cross country his sophomore year that Dana had an epiphany. Running for Coach Sam Iverson, he was probably the second or third best runner on the team, a Spartan team that won the Conference and qualified for State in 2005. At that State meet, Dana finished fourth which really inspired him. After that, girls golf coach Rick Schupbach, challenged Dana to strive for his potential, so he began to truly focus on running.

Dana's sophomore year in track was a precursor for things to come. Coach McMartin's Spartan track team won the Conference and Dana took first-place honors in the 3200 meter (2 mile) run. At the Class 1A District, he not only won at 3200 meters, but Dana placed second in the 1600 meters, which is equivalent to the mile. Going on to the State meet that spring, Dana chalked up a fifth place finish at 3200 meters and eighth place in the 1600 meters. Therein lies a story.

While waiting for his first race at the State meet, Dana was warming up in the indoor track and was also checking on the Spartans' girls track team that was also participating at State. Suddenly, he saw that his race was next on the scoreboard! He raced down the stadium stairs, hopped over a railing, stripping off his warm-ups as he hurried across the field to the starting line. He arrived a mere ten seconds before the race started. That was a close call!

In cross country his junior season of 2006, the Spartans had their highest finish at State in its history placing fourth. Personally, Schmidt finished first in four meets and second in five others during the regular season. The team won the Class 1A Districts leading to their fourth-place finish at State where Dana finished fifth individually.

The track season of 2006 was a special one for Dana. He won five 3200 meter races, seven 1600 meter races, and qualified for the Drake Relays in both events. He also broke the 50-year-old school record for the mile held by Hall of Famer Al Harberts. The Spartans again won the conference and finished fifth at the State meet. Personally, Dana won the State at 1600 meters and finished second in the 3200 meter race.

Poised for a great finish to his high school running career, Dana did not disappoint. In cross county, the Spartans won 10 of 11 regular season meets and Schmidt earned all-state honors by finishing second in the State meet, the highest finish ever by a Spartan cross country runner.

In track, the record setting continued. Again, Coach McMartin's Spartan track team won the Conference for the third year in a row. Dana broke the school record for the 3200 meters previously held by Paul Neher. Dana also won the district championships for both the 1600 meter and 3200 meter runs. At the State meet, he again won both events, as well as finishing fifth in the open 800 meter run. Additionally, he participated on the Spartans 4 x 800 meter relay team that finished fifth. At the Drake Relays that spring, Dana broke both his own school record in the 3200 meters with a 9:19 time and his 1600 meter record with a 4:22.9. Both records still stood as of 2016.

To be successful against the higher level of college track and cross country competition, it was necessary to pay the price in training. In high school, Dana would run about 35 miles a week. Going into the college ranks, he upped that to 60-70 miles a week. By the time he graduated, his weekly distance increased to 80-90 miles.

Dana's first two years were spent at Minnesota State University in Mankato. Red-shirted for cross country as a freshman, he ran track and won conference championships in both the 5K run and the 3K steeple chase. As a sophomore, he ran cross country as part of the Minnesota State team that qualified for Division II nationals. In track, he continued his success at the 5K distance winning both the indoor and outdoor conference titles. Dana also ran on their medley relay team that placed third at the Drake Relays, beating out a Concordia University team from Nebraska who eventually became his teammates.

Following his future wife, Danielle Zimmerman, who graduated from Minnesota State, Dana transferred to Concordia for his last two years of college competition. In his first season of cross country, Dana finished fifth in the NAIA national meet earning his first All-American status as the team finished second. In track, Dana won the indoor 5000 meter title and earned his first track All-American honor with a sixth-place finish at Nationals. He repeated that finish at the same distance in the national outdoor meet and earned another All-American certificate.

Capping off his last year of competition in 2012, Dana was awarded conference "*Runner-of-the-Year*" and earned his fourth All-American honor in cross country. In track on the indoor circuit, Dana was conference champion in the 3000 meters and also won the 5000 meters in conference record breaking time. He then earned his fifth All-American status with a fourth-place finish in the 3000 meters.

Outdoors, Dana had the greatest day in his career at the conference meet at Northwestern College, Coach McMartin's alma mater. He won three events: 10,000 meters, 1500 meters, and Schmidt set a conference record in the 5000 meters while taking home the "*Outstanding Athlete of the Meet*" honors. To cap it off, Dana earned his sixth and final All-American certificate with a third place in the NAIA National Steeple Chase.

Class of 2015

Steve Ehlers 1966

Mike Draper 1975

Rick Ruebel 1980

Jordan Dirks 1995

Bobby Ayers 2005

The 2015 inductees are front row: Rick Ruebel, Mike Draper, and Bobby Ayers. Back row: Steve Ehlers and Jordan Dirks.

Steve Ehlers

Steve Ehlers was the second in a legacy of great boys tennis players for Hall of Fame Coach John Doak shown together left in 1966. They reunited for Steve's induction in 2015. Steve lettered three years playing tennis for the Iowa Hawkeyes.

The legacy of high-caliber tennis in Grundy Center started with Hall of Famer Bob Stock in the late 1950s and early 1960s. The next standout in this lineage of premier tennis players was left-handed Steve Ehlers. A Grundy Center graduate of 1966, Steve was a regular fixture at the local tennis courts and at summer tournaments around the state and Midwest region.

Steve was introduced to tennis as a youngster because he lived close to the old Grundy Center above-ground swimming pool. On the west side of the pool were two concrete tennis courts and one of them had a set of back boards where players could practice strokes by themselves.

Steve's first introduction to tennis was waking up many mornings at 7 a.m. to the rhythmic sound of *"thunk, thunk, thunk"* coming in his bedroom window. One of those mornings, a young ten-year-old Steve rode in the car with his dad, local pharmacist John Ehlers, along the west side of the park and he finally saw the source of that *"thunking"* noise. He asked his dad, "Who is that and what is he doing?" John answered that it was Bob Stock and he was practicing tennis. Steve thought that was pretty cool and looked like something fun to do.

As a result, Steve signed up for lessons with Stock and began learning the game of tennis under his tutelage. In the years ahead, he was joined by future Hall of Famers Ed Palmer, Norm Riek, and Beth Stock, Bob's sister. Bob would take Steve to Cedar Falls to play with kids who would push him more and give him a higher level of competition. Steve eventually took over the program of tennis lessons when Stock went off to college leaving Steve as the Grundy Center tennis tutor.

During his teen years, Steve was consistently ranked in his age classes on a State level. As a 15-year-old, he was ranked fourth in Iowa and by age 18 he was third. Regionally in the Missouri Valley area, Steve was ranked #10 and #44th nationally. Those were great rankings for a youngster from little Grundy Center, Iowa!

Once Steve started high school in the 1962-1963 school year, the left-hander never lost a high school singles match in four years of dual meets, although he did lose a tryout for #1 singles once. Just when Steve thought he was about to play his toughest opponent from Campus High School in Cedar Falls, Coach Doak had Steve tryout with teammate and doubles partner Jim Stevens, another very good Grundy Center player in his own right.

They played a one-set challenge at the blacktop court that used to be on the south side of the old elementary building. Steve played a terrible set and lost to Stevens. Jim then went on to get beat by the Campus High School lead player. Steve never lost another high school tryout after that.

The 1965 tennis team went 11-1 under Coach John Doak with junior Steve Ehlers (circled) going undefeated in his #1 singles play.

Ehlers also paired with Jim Stevens in doubles to make a formidable team, but singles was what Steve loved to do. He qualified for State twice as a sophomore and senior. His junior season, Coach Doak had Ehlers and Stevens focus on doubles for the State tournament qualifying, but they unexpectedly lost in Districts. Steve made it to the semi-finals as a senior back in the day where tennis had only one class and he lost to eventual champion, Steve Houghton of Iowa City, who later became the University of Iowa tennis coach.

After graduation, Ehlers was looking at various colleges to play at the next level. He looked at Texas Christian University and was probably leaning towards the University

of Oklahoma when fate stepped in. Steve played in a tournament where Iowa tennis coach Don Klotz was watching from the stands. Steve remembered he was red-hot that day and could hardly miss a shot. Klotz was so impressed, he offered Ehlers a full-ride scholarship to play for the Hawkeyes.

Most college sports in the 1960s, including tennis, did not allow freshmen to compete on varsity. As a sophomore in 1968, Steve broke into the singles line-up and stayed there finishing runner-up at his respective positions in the Big Ten tennis tournament all three seasons and was selected Hawkeye team captain as a senior.

One of his vivid memories of playing for the Hawkeyes was during a Big Ten tournament. He woke up that particular morning of his first-round match and couldn't lift his left arm. Being a left-handed player, that's a major problem and Steve knew he was in trouble. He tried to get loosened up, but the best he could do was get his arm shoulder high.

His opponent was from Wisconsin and someone who beat him in their dual meet. Steve literally served under-handed during the match and hit both two-hand forehands and two-hand back-hands before that was popular. He lost the first set big, but then his opponent lost his focus and went cold while Steve was starting to loosen up. Ehlers found his stride and began hitting his shots and won the next two sets to advance to the quarter-finals. Again, serving underhanded, he managed to eke out another win. By the semi-finals, his shoulder finally loosened up and Steve was able to play normal tennis again winning the semi-finals and taking second place for the tournament.

While going to Iowa, Steve spent summers teaching tennis in Rochester, Minnesota. After graduating, he soon gave up competitive tennis for himself in favor of teaching tennis on a full-time basis, which he did until 1983. While in Rochester, Steve coached numerous Minnesota state junior champions in various age divisions. He also coached Howard Shoenfield, who tennis aficionados may recognize as a winner of numerous national titles including World Junior Championships at both the U.S. Open at Forest Hills and Wimbledon in 1980. (See Dave Ralston's biography for a related story.)

During his tennis teaching career, Steve Ehlers served as tennis pro, director of tennis, general manager, and owner/operator of various tennis and racquet clubs in Rochester and the Minneapolis / St. Paul area. He retired from the tennis game and started his own financial services business in the Twin Cities area before retiring in 2015.

Sports Hall of Fame
Grundy Center, Iowa
Established 2004

Mike Draper

Mike Draper was Grundy Center's first State wrestling champion winning the crown at 98 pounds in 1973 wrestling for Hall of Fame Coach Clint Young.

"*Records are made to be broken*," goes the cliché. And Mike Draper set plenty of records during his Spartan wrestling career and still held a few of them at his induction date in 2015. While records are made to be broken, "firsts" are forever. And Mike Draper was Grundy Center's *FIRST* individual State wrestling champion. Nobody can ever take that away.

Growing up through his elementary and junior high days, Mike was a small guy, one of the smallest in his class. He was too little to play football and he was pretty short for basketball. Introduced to wrestling in the fifth grade, a sport where physical size didn't really matter, Mike found something that fit him well, even though he claims he wasn't very good at it initially. But he stuck with it.

By the time he started high school in the fall of 1971, Mike still only weighed 90 pounds and he was surrounded by some very talented wrestling classmates including the late Mike Krull, the late Dave Hartke, and future State champion and Hall of Famer Kevin Ralston. It was like wrestling at the State tournament in practice every day with all that talent around him.

Additionally, Mike came into high school when wrestling had a changing of the guard. In 1961, John Doak started the wrestling program at Grundy Center from scratch. After a decade, Doak decided the foundation was there and stepped down for the next generation of wrestlers and coaches. And that next coach was Hall of Famer, Clint Young.

Picking up where Doak left off, Young brought his energy and youthful enthusiasm to the job. During his tenure, the wrestling program produced what are still as of this writing in 2016, the highest levels of achievement in Spartan wrestling history. Mike Draper was among those at the forefront of that evolution.

After wrestling junior varsity his freshman season of 1971-72, Mike came into his sophomore year in the fall of 1972 finally weighing over 100 pounds and wrestling at 98#, the lightest weight bracket. Still battling the state-caliber competition on his own team, Mike didn't break into the starting line-up until January of 1973. His first competition was the Hudson tournament where he won his first match against the third seed, then beat the second seed in the semi-finals, and vanquished the top-ranked wrestler in the finals.

From there, Mike went on a streak winning all his dual meet matches and winning sectionals before losing his first match of the season in districts. His third-place finish qualified him for State. At State, he avenged his district loss with an overtime win in the semi-finals. Mike then capped it off by winning the Class 1A 98# State championship in Des Moines over a tall, lanky youngster from Lisbon. That victory made Mike Draper Grundy Center's first-ever State wrestling champion. It was a proud day for the history of the program. Mike finished the season with an outstanding record of 20-1.

One of Coach Young's best memories of Mike was after he won that first championship. The Spartan team wasn't among the top ten place winners, but as Mike, his coaches, and his teammates returned home from Des Moines, they were met at the "*7 mile corner*" west of town by the Grundy Fire Department and a caravan of ardent Spartan wrestling fans who escorted their first State champ into town. That was quite unexpected and a very fond memory for Coach Young.

The following year for Mike was one of transition. Having grown a little more, 98 pounds was no longer an option. Kevin Ralston was at 105# and won a State championship of his own that season in 1974. So Mike wrestled at 112# and posted a respectable 16-5-1 record that set the stage for his final and record-setting senior campaign during the 1974-75 season.

Now fully grown into the 112# weight class, Mike had one of the best seasons in Spartan history. He posted an undefeated dual record, won three invitational tournaments, and was positioned with a 25-0 record after winning Sectionals and heading to Districts. Among those 25 wins, Mike posted a record 16 pins and broke Dave Pike's career pin record in the process finishing with a total of 33 falls for his

career. That is still third in Spartan history behind only Dave Ehrig and Bobby Ayers, wrestling for the Tri-County Wildcats, both Hall of Famers.

Mike lost his first match of the season in the district finals to Bret Hagen of Britt, who went on to win two State titles. After that match, Britt's coach told Coach Young that Hagen never wanted to wrestle Draper again because Mike pushed him to his limits.

At the State tournament, Mike was battling an illness and lost a match to the eventual runner-up and he finished in fifth-place, capping off a highly successful season with a 30-2 record. In fact, at the State Tournament March of Champions, Bret Hagen, still sporting mat burns on his face from their match the week before, told Mike he was glad he wasn't wrestling him!

Mike Draper held many Spartan career records when he graduated in 1975, including most pins in a four-year career and most points in a season.

Coach Young looks back on Mike Draper's career with a lot of pride. Although Mike was quiet and not a "*rah-rah*" type of leader, Clint saw a hard worker who led by his example, by his work ethic, and by his determination to be a State champion.

Mike received many awards and accolades during his career. Among his many accomplishments besides that first State championship were most career pins, highest career winning percentage of 89%, most falls in a season, most career team points scored, and most team points scored in a season. He also won the Wayne Wrage Sr. Pinners Award, twice won the Ralph Schmidt Memorial Award for most team points scored, and was awarded the Jordan Larsen Athletic Citizenship Award for 1975. Overall, Mike placed in 14 tournaments in his career winning ten times. After graduation,

Mike went to the University of Northern Iowa and wrestled his freshman year for Coach Chuck Patten.

Sports Hall of Fame
Grundy Center, Iowa
Established 2004

Rick Ruebel

Rick Ruebel capped a great Spartan wrestling career by compiling an undefeated senior season in 1980 going 32-0. He won the Class 2A 155# State championship for Coach Clint Young. Ruebel went on to a strong college career at Drake University.

During Clint Young's tenure as the Spartans' wrestling coach, he had five State wrestling champions. Hall of Famer Mike Draper was the first. Hall of Famer Kevin Ralston followed Draper the very next year, and Dave Ehrig, a member of the Charter Class of this Hall of Fame, won two titles as a heavyweight. But Young's last State champion was probably the most dominating: Rick Ruebel.

Clint trained his wrestlers to *"never be intimated"* by an opponent. By the time he was a senior, Rick Ruebel was doing the intimidating! He was perhaps the most intimidating wrestler the Spartans ever put on the mat! In the Doak era, there were intimidators like Charlie Peters, Wayne Wrage, and Doug Van Gelder. Opponents were not eager to take the mat against them. Rick Ruebel fit right into that mold with that same mat mentality.

Ruebel put in the work off the mat that it took to be a State champion. He did extra running, weightlifting, and drilling on moves in both the off season and during the season. Young described Rick in his senior year of 1980 as, *"the most tenacious and determined wrestler he ever coached."*

It all started on the mat for Rick Ruebel in the fifth grade. Friends told him he had to come out for Doug Van Gelder's youth wrestling program. Doug was a very successful Spartan wrestler in the late 1960s and worked with the young kids, taught them the fundamentals, and made it fun. Back in the 1970s it was going strong and Rick remembers wanting to emulate the wrestling stars of the day in the late Dave Hartke and future State champions Kevin Ralston and Mike Draper.

Duane Cross was the coach in junior high and both Rick and classmate Todd Stumberg went through seventh and eighth grades undefeated showcasing the great talent coming up the ranks for Coach Young.

As a freshman, Rick wrestled a few matches at 132# while mostly backing up Hall of Famer Ron Coleman. When Coleman graduated, Rick stepped right in to the 132# spot and posted a very respectable 20-8 record in qualifying for State. He recalls four of those losses were to the same Hudson wrestler, two of them in overtime. Rick was on a roll at the end of the season winning both Sectionals and Districts, but had to default his first match at State due to an ankle injury.

Moving up to 145# as a junior, Rick built on his previous success with an even stronger showing. He posted a 20-3 record with a team-leading 12 pins for the season and earning the Wayne Wrage, Sr. award for most falls. He finished the regular season with just one loss, but a shoulder injury cost him a couple weeks of matches and conditioning.

At sectionals, Ruebel lost to the second-ranked wrestler in the State, then lost a 2-1 match to another tough opponent from Osage. Failing to qualify for State again was not only a huge disappointment for Rick, it turned into a major motivator for his senior campaign. He intended to claim that elusive State championship and nothing was going to stand in his way. Coach Young knew Rick would turn that disappointment into motivation and predicted that Rick would win State in 1980 in a comment he wrote in Rick's 1979 junior yearbook.

Rick Ruebel's dominating senior season stands out as a strong memory for Coach Young. Rick went undefeated with 32 wins, led the Spartans with 17 pins, and only had one close match as he bulldozed his way to a State championship. The close match was in the finals of the Hudson tournament where Rick beat a ranked wrestler from Riceville 12-10. Rick got his bell rung in the match and didn't even remember the third period, but still managed to win.

One of Rick's goals was to get a takedown in the first two seconds of a match. He was pretty good at it, although he occasionally got caught jumping the whistle. Even legendary referee, Mike Allen, later the supervisor of college referees for the NCAA, was impressed with Ruebel. At the Spartan Tournament in 1980, the referees were discussing who would get which championship matches. Allen told the group he didn't care which matches he got as long as he got to ref Rick Ruebel. Mike wanted to see him in action up close and personal to see if Rick could get the opening takedown in two seconds.

Ruebel also had an unorthodox move called the "*Grundy*". He would do the move as a counter to an opponent shooting a single leg on Rick. While his opponent was on his leg, Rick would over-hook the head and under-hook the arm, and then do a "*butt-roll*" to put them on their back which usually resulted in a pin.

When Rick finally reached the State tournament, he remembered being very focused on taking "*one match at a time*" and not anticipating any future match or potential opponent. It worked to perfection as Ruebel won the State 155# Class 2A championship by a score of 4-1 over Miles Erickson from Mediapolis. That tied-in very nicely to the theme song the team adopted, "*We are the Champions*" by Queen. And in reference to another Queen hit song, Rick Ruebel did indeed "*Rock*" them.

After graduating, Rick looked into several colleges to continue his wrestling career. Al Baxter at Buena Vista recruited him hard and he made a visit to Dan Gable and Jay Robinson at Iowa. However, he decided to go to Drake University where his former teammate Todd Geer was wrestling and who helped influence his decision.

Rick wrestled two years at 158# for the Bulldogs and posted two very strong seasons for them. He went 19-8 as a freshman and 20-6 as a sophomore under Coach Lonnie Timmerman. During those two years, Ruebel wrestled a lot of quality opponents including Andre Metzger from Oklahoma, a multiple-time Division I national champion.

Rick transferred to the University of Northern Iowa for his last two seasons and sat out a redshirt year under the transfer rules of the day. He wrestled two years for the Panthers for Coach Don Briggs. After graduating from college, Rick went into teaching and coaching. He coached wrestling a total of 15 years, 13 years as a head coach.

Sports Hall of Fame
Grundy Center, Iowa
Established 2004

Jordan Dirks

Jordan Dirks was one of the Spartans' most accomplished golfers during his high school career. A four-year letterman, Dirks was named Class 1A boys golfer of the year in 1995 and finished runner-up in the Boys State tournament. The middle photo shows Jordan with dad, Dennis Dirks, and at right receiving his Hall of Fame award.

Until the Class of 2015, the Hall of Fame had but one male golfer, the legendary Ivan Miller. With the induction ceremony of 2015, two more were added with Bobby Ayers and Jordan Dirks.

Dirks brought another family thread that often runs through the Hall of Fame. Within the membership are a grandfather and grandson, several sets of siblings, uncles and nephews, and cousins. But none of these family relationships run as deep as Hall of Famer Dennis Dirks and his wife, Cindy. Both of Dennis and Cindy's golfing daughters, Trina and Kylie, were inducted and in 2015 their son, Jordan, joined the family of Grundy Center Hall of Fame golfers.

Jordan got an early start on his golfing and had a club in his hands at age five. Playing golf together quickly became a family tradition for the whole Dirks clan, one they continued over decades. Those early years weren't just about Jordan playing rounds, it was also about putting in the time to work on his technique from tee shots, to the short game, to putting. That investment in practice time certainly paid off.

Like many of the accomplished golfers from Grundy Center, Jordan started playing in the Waterloo junior golf leagues while in elementary and junior high school. He played in tournaments there as well as Cedar Rapids, Des Moines and other places

around the state. He also took lessons from Northern Iowa's golf coach Ken Green to further hone his skills.

Entering high school in the 1991-92 school year, the Spartans had a lot of good golfers coached by Jordan's dad, Dennis. Jordan remembers Tony Briggs as a mentor and leader on that team. Even as a freshman, Jordan's scores counted toward the team total right away and his contribution helped the team win the conference championship.

Jordan considered his sophomore year of 1993 as probably his most consistent season. He was medalist for the Spartan Invitational, tied the school record for nine-holes with a 34, tied the school record for an 18 hole score with 72, and set the school record for lowest nine hole stroke average in a season with 38.8. Jordan also won the conference championship as did the team.

The Spartans boys golf team continued to build and improve for Coach Dirks in 1994 and Jordan recalls they had a very solid team finishing fourth in the State in Class 1A. Again, the team won the conference while Jordan won medalist honors. Jordan broke his own records for nine holes with a score of 32 and 18 holes with a 71 that season. He also recalls having to play a round when he lost a contact and forcing him to hit with only one lens.

If his sophomore year was his most consistent, Jordan's senior season was most memorable. Jordan won the conference championship for the third time and the Spartans won conference for the fourth time in his high school career. Jordan set the records for lowest score in a nine-hole meet with 34, lowest score in an 18 hole meet with 71, and best nine hole stroke average for a season with 38.5.

Jordan had always dreamed of earning medalist honors at the State meet, but after a disappointing State tournament finish his junior year, he was even more determined and poised for the challenge entering the State meet his senior season. Jordan posted an even par round of 72 for day one of the tournament to lead the Spartans into a first-place tie with Aplington-Parkersburg. Additionally, Jordan had a two-stroke lead in the medalist competition. Then the rain began to fall all night long dumping between four-to-five inches on the golf course.

The next morning, State golf officials were set to name Grundy Center and Aplington-Parkersburg co-champions and Jordan as the 1995 medalist until Coach Dirks became involved in the discussion. His Spartan team wanted to play, despite the course conditions. They didn't want to share the title, they wanted to win it out right. So they played.

Unfortunately, as a result, the team finished in third place, four strokes behind Aplington-Parkersburg and Jordan ended up losing a three-hole play-off by a single stroke to finish as the medalist runner-up.

Despite the disappointing finish, Jordan was named Class 1A Golfer of the Year. Locally, he received the Royal Briggs Award for team Most Valuable Player and the Jordan Larson Athletic Citizenship Award.

Jordan played both basketball and baseball for the Spartans. While baseball interfered with his golfing, he still managed to earn first team all-conference as a senior. On the basketball court, he earned second team all-conference as a junior and first team his senior season as the Spartans won the district tournament in 1995.

After graduation, Jordan went on to golf at Simpson College. As a freshman he won his first collegiate tournament highlighted by an eagle on the first hole of play! He was named "Newcomer of the Year", team Most Valuable Player, and earned all-conference honors.

Transferring to the University of Northern Iowa for his sophomore year, Jordan played for the Panthers and competed in nine tournaments, most memorably the Big Four tournament with Iowa, Iowa State and Drake. He had UNI's best score and played with future Masters Champion Zach Johnson, who played for Drake at the time. Jordan redshirted as a junior and then concentrated on his studies before graduating from UNI.

Looking back on his career, Jordan had two particularly fond memories. One was playing in the State two-man best ball with his dad at Ames where he got his only hole-in-one. The other Jordan claims was the best shot he ever hit in his life and it wasn't even in a competition.

Jordan had just hit off the #9 tee at the Town & Country Golf Club in Grundy Center. He was playing with Brad Dellit when Brad took off with the cart leaving Jordan in his dust. With his driver inhand and one ball in his pocket, Jordan hit a ball that went dead-on at the run-away cart. Brad looked back and saw the ball coming right for the cart and made sudden course correction to avoid getting a direct hit.

Dirks later developed a new passion for distance running and ran marathons in Chicago and one in Berlin, Germany.

Sports Hall of Fame
Grundy Center, Iowa
Established 2004

Bobby Ayers

Bobby Ayers was a State champion golfer and holds the record for the most career victories in wrestling. He was inducted for both sports in 2015. An all-around athlete, Bobby earned 15 sports letters for the Spartans.

Bobby Ayers brought multiple talents to the Grundy Center Sports Hall of Fame. He was best known for his golfing and his wrestling from 2001-2005, but Bobby was also an accomplished football player and spent time on the baseball diamond while earning 15 letters during his high school career. Bobby Ayers joined the Hall of Fame as an all-around athlete whose exploits in football and wrestling complemented his success in golf.

On the gridiron, Bobby earned the first two of his four football letters playing defensive back for the Spartans. He often played the *"nickel back"* role in the secondary. For his junior and senior seasons, he turned his talents to the offense and quarterbacked the Spartans. Ayers was a throwing quarterback, but he was also blessed to have an excellent running back in Tom McKendree to challenge opposing defenses. Bobby was able to successfully manage the offense and was very capable of making reads and changing the play at the line of scrimmage. He played under three different football coaches in his four years and earned all-district honors as a senior. He also put his football experience to work in Grundy Center by coaching youth football.

When the winter sports started, Bobby turned attention to his favorite sport, wrestling. Since Grundy Center no longer had its own wrestling program, Bobby wrestled for Coach Randy Omvig and the Tri-County Wildcats, made up of grapplers from Grundy Center, Beaman, Conrad, Union, Whitten and Liscomb. He lettered as a freshman at

125# and won a conference championship before moving up to 135# as a sophomore and averaged 28 wins each of his first two seasons.

Continuing his junior season at 145#, Bobby was Sectional tournament runner-up, won 29 matches and scored 15 pins to lead the team. Wrapping up his senior campaign, Ayers won the sectional tournament and posted an outstanding record of 30-6.

For his career, Bobby totaled a Grundy Center record-setting 115 career victories. He captured the Wayne Wrage, Sr. pinner's award, had 58 career pins topping the previous record of 55 by Hall of Famer Dave Ehrig, while winning four tournaments. In one of those tournaments, Ayers won all five of his matches by falls in the first period! Bobby continued to work with youth wrestling in Grundy in hopes of generating enough interest to restart the Spartan program.

Bobby's biggest success for the Spartans happened on the golf course. Starting golf back in the fifth grade, Coach Rick Schupbach showed him the way and built that early interest for Ayers which helped lead to future successes. By junior high school, Bobby was playing regularly in the Waterloo Junior Golfers Association and entering many weekend tournaments. He won the Waterloo Junior Open in seventh grade when things really started to click for him on the links. He was also the Elks State Junior champion during those years prior to high school.

Bobby stepped into a strong boys golf tradition in high school developed by Hall of Fame coach Dennis Dirks. As a freshman, Bobby found out from both the coach and the upper classmen that they took their golf very seriously. Ayers discovered they weren't there to horse around or just play some rounds of golf. They were there to hone their skills in all areas of the game and become accomplished golfers.

During Bobby's four seasons as a Spartan golfer, he lettered each year and was in the top five on the team even as a freshman. Competition was outstanding just within the Spartan team. Grundy Center won the State Class 2A golf tournament both Bobby's sophomore and senior seasons of 2003 and 2005 and Bobby was a major contributor. Coach Dirks described Ayers as a *"first-class young man with a passion for the game and a desire to be the best."* That determination resulted in Bobby winning the boys Class 2A State championship individually in 2005 and being named Class 2A *"Boys' Golfer of the Year."*

Both Coach Dirks and Bobby have similar memories from that 2005 State tournament. Ayers was leading comfortably after the first day, but during the first nine holes of day two, he shot the worst golf of his career! However, Bobby pulled it

back together and shot one under par on the back nine to come back and win State by a couple of strokes.

Interestingly, while the boys won the State team title in 2005 by 19 strokes, they used the top four scores of their six golfers. And Bobby's second day score wasn't one of them! That just goes to show the depth of the Spartan golf team. Four Grundy golfers were first-team all-state: Grant Stevens, Taylor Schupbach, Zach Swalley, and Bobby Ayers. That was a powerful team!

Another memory from his State championship happened during the medal ceremonies. Just as he was getting called to accept his first-place medal, Bobby got a nasty nose bleed. He barely got through the award ceremony and missed some of the photo opportunities because it took nearly 45 minutes to get the bleeding stopped. They were almost ready to take him to the Emergency Room when he finally got the bleeding under control.

When Bobby graduated, he owned several golfing records. He had the third-lowest career scoring average with 40.2 strokes, he was medalist 14 times, and he set the record for best score on a par 36 course with a four-under 32. As another aside, Bobby also scored two holes-in-one within 16 days!

After graduation, Bobby continued his golfing career at Waldorf, an NAIA program. He was team captain as a freshman and, in fact, was team captain all four years in the program. He chalked up multiple top-10 finishes in college tournaments and was named all-conference his senior season.

Bobby Ayers shown running around North Tama defenders as quarterback of the Spartans.

Sports Hall of Fame
Grundy Center, Iowa
Established 2004

Class of 2016

Dave Ralston 1974

Kurt Helmick 1977

Jeff Crisman 1978

Adrianne Alexia 2010

Phil Lebo 1980-2006

The Hall of Fame Class of 2016: Dave Ralston, Kurt Helmick, Jeff Crisman, Adrianne Alexi, and Phil Lebo.

Sports Hall of Fame
Grundy Center, Iowa
Established 2004

Dave Ralston

Dave Ralston was the last in a long legacy of boys tennis players for Coach John Doak. He was also an outstanding all-around athlete who played football, basketball and baseball while earning 11 letters for the Spartans. In the second photo, he is receiving the first Deke Behrens Award and far right his Hall of Fame award from Coach John Doak.

The legacy of high-caliber boys tennis in Grundy Center under Hall of Fame Coach, John Doak, is well represented in the Hall of Fame. It started with Bob Stock from the early 1960s and continued with Steve Ehlers, Ed Palmer, and Norm Riek. All went on to very successful college careers and Dave Ralston, was no exception.

The son of Leonard and Donna Ralston, Dave was a natural athlete and spent his youth playing the sport of the season with other youngsters in town. Whether it was football, basketball, baseball or tennis, Ralston developed skills in all of them, but especially in tennis. By graduation, Dave earned 11 letters for the Spartans with four in tennis, three in football, two in basketball, and two more in baseball.

Steve Ehlers was the first early tennis influence on Dave when Steve taught for the City's recreation program in the mid-1960s. Ehlers worked with nine-year-old Ralston and encouraged him to compete in youth tennis tournaments. At ages 10-12, Dave was a highly ranked youth player in the state and enjoyed many early successes. At the age of 10, he and Norm Riek teamed up to win the Waterloo Open 12 and under doubles title.

As a 12-year-old, Dave remembered how Steve Ehlers, then teaching tennis in Rochester, Minnesota, asked his parents if Dave could come up to his clinic and play with a 10-year-old student of his. Dave wondered why he would play with a 10-year-old kid, but he journeyed North. When Dave and his young partner played doubles, they won their tournament and then the 10-year-old beat Dave in the singles semi-finals! Steve Ehlers noted the youngster turned out to be a tennis prodigy named Howard Shoenfield who later won National singles championships in both 16 and 18-

year-old divisions and was ranked #1 in the World junior division! Ehlers remembers Dave's loss, *"… was a close one…and may have been his best one!"*

Back at home, Dave played with Ed Palmer, Beth Stock and Norm Riek with additional coaching from John Doak. In high school, Coach Doak remembers Dave as, *"a very sound tennis player who was fundamentally skilled in all shots and a very smart player. He would analyze his opponent's weaknesses and would patiently and consistently force his opponents to make errors."* With Dave teaming up for two years with Norm Riek, Doak's Spartans fared very well, even when playing much larger schools. Dave qualified for State as a freshman, but his biggest disappointment came as a sophomore.

In 1972 when Norm Riek won his State championship, Dave expected to qualify for the State tournament again. Many teams were putting their best players in doubles to avoid Norm and Dave in singles. But Dave unexpectedly missed out on State when he lost in districts in a match he felt he should have easily won.

Coming back in his junior and senior seasons of 1973 and 1974, Dave qualified for State both years and won his way to the semi-finals. As a senior, he lost to the State's #1 ranked player. Dave was the only opponent who took him to three sets all season. Ralston wrapped up his Spartan career, the final link in the chain of outstanding boys tennis players under Coach Doak before John retired.

The 1971 boys tennis team went undefeated and sent both Norm Riek and Dave Ralston to State. Shown above are: Coach Doak, Dave Ralston (circled), Randy Robertson, Tim Wolthoff, Rod Ragsdale, Mark Weber and fellow Hall of Famer, Norm Riek.

On the gridiron, Dave was an excellent running back and linebacker playing for Coach Rod Nelson along with teammates like Buddy Brockway, Jeff Saylor, Jerry Voss, Randy Ragsdale, Danny Szegda, and Dave's brother Tim. Weighing about

155 pounds, Dave frequently found the end zone and was named first team all-conference as a junior and senior. One of his fondest memories was being the first-ever recipient of the Deke Behrens football award as team's most outstanding player.

Playing basketball for Hall of Fame coach Harry Dole and Jim Brousard, Dave was a point guard joined by some great talent like Hall of Famers Greg Goodman and Orrin Brown as well as Randy Robertson, Jerry Voss, and brothers Bob and Chuck Riek. Dave prided himself as a strong defensive player, a trait common to Coach Dole's Spartan teams. Offensively, he was more likely to make an assist than score points, but was recognized for his skills with a second team all-conference designation and winner of the Rev. John Connell Basketball Award his senior year.

Oddly enough, one of Dave's favorite memories of basketball took place when he wasn't even in the game. The Spartans were engaged in a hard-fought road game against Traer. Time was about to expire with Grundy trailing by one point, when Dave fouled out of the game. Coach Brousard substituted with Dave's brother, Tim. With seconds remaining, Traer missed their foul shot and Tim grabbed the rebound, dribbled to mid-court, and launched a desperation shot that went in the basket! Game over! Grundy Center wins! But the story didn't stop there. Dave remembered an overjoyed Tim ran down to the basket, grabbed the ball, and ran into the locker room placing it in his duffel bag intending to keep it as a souvenir. But the referees hunted him down and retrieved the ball, much to Tim's disappointment.

On the baseball diamond, Dave again played for Coach Dole as a catcher while earning two letters. He had the highest regard for Harry Dole as great coach who knew how to bring out the best in his players and even get them to play above their abilities.

Following graduation in 1974, Dave had scholarship offers from Northeast Missouri State, Northwest Missouri State (where Norm Riek was playing) and Northern Iowa. Dave chose Northeast, now Truman State University, and lettered all four years. Starting out as the #3 singles player and the #2 team in doubles, Dave took over the #2 singles position for the next three years and alternated between the #1 and #2 doubles teams. Ralston placed high in the conference tournaments several years and finished runner-up for #2 singles as a junior.

Dave continued tennis as a career for a few years as a teaching pro in Milwaukee and then moved to Iowa City as the Head Pro at the Iowa City Racquet Club. Soon after, he decided to put his accounting degree to work and took a job in banking in the Twin Cities starting a whole new career path. He spent over 35 years as a very successful commercial banker.

Sports Hall of Fame
Grundy Center, Iowa
Established 2004

Kurt Helmick

Kurt Helmick set the season rushing record in football and held multiple records in wrestling when he graduated. He was elected into the Hall of Fame for both sports.

It's interesting to note that Kurt Helmick was a freshman when fellow 2016 inductee, Dave Ralston, was a senior and that they were teammates in football. In fact, it was Kurt Helmick who filled Dave's shoes at the running back position the fall of 1973. And fill them, he did indeed.

Fortunately for Spartan athletics, the Helmick family moved to Grundy Center just before Kurt started his freshman year in high school in 1973. Kurt's first memory of Grundy Center was going around with his parents as local banker, Bud Pike, showed them houses and helped acclimate them to their new town. Kurt jumped right into football playing for Coach Rod Nelson. He was the running back on the junior varsity team which posted a solid winning record. He also played linebacker on defense.

That winter, Kurt gave wrestling a try. Although Kurt only wrestled twice in junior high, wrestling ran strong on his mom's side of the family. The Chelsvig's had several State place-winners in the family and growing up, Kurt attended many dual meets and tournaments. Now wrestling for Hall of Fame Coach Clint Young, he had to learn the sport in a hurry. Kurt won the varsity spot at 126# and compiled a respectable 12-12 record while learning wrestling the hard way: the school of "*hard knocks.*"

Kurt's sophomore year in football was epic. While still playing linebacker and replacing Dave Ralston in the offensive backfield, he used his quickness, speed and balance to hit the hole and break into the secondary behind some big and talented linemen like Hall of Famer Terry Crisman, Earl Slinker Bill Itzen, Don Appel, Gerry Buchanan, and Jerry Voss. Kurt specifically remembered the second game of the

season when they beat SEMCO 39-14. He ran the ball 20 times for 285 yards, and three touchdowns while only playing 2 ½ quarters!

Kurt also vividly remembered a road game at NU High where they trailed late in the contest in a pouring rain. But the Spartans scored two touchdowns in 51 seconds before time ran out to win the game!

Helmick set the Spartan season rushing record that fall eclipsing the 1944 record set by Bud Peterson gaining 1,236 yards in nine games, an average of over 137 yards per game. He finished the season strong and was named first team all-conference, first team all-area, and honorable mention all-state as a running back.

Wrestling his sophomore year, Kurt remained at 126# and Coach Young led the team to a 9-1 dual record. Kurt notched 21 wins against 7 losses and a tie and won his first tournament at North Tama. He finished second in Sectionals and third in Districts.

Expectations were high for Kurt's junior season in football. Coach Nelson did not disappoint and led the team to an 8-1 record. The Spartans were ranked as high as eighth in the State, but unfortunately did not qualify for the playoffs. Kurt rushed for 1,084 yards despite missing one game with an ankle injury, but still averaged over 135 yards per game. He was again first team all-conference, first team all-area, and honorable mention all-state. He was also nominated as a Prep All-American.

Kurt moved up to 138# in wrestling his junior year and put together an excellent season. Coach Young remembers that Kurt's two greatest assets were balance and quickness. Clint remembered Kurt won many matches with those two attributes, but he also praised Helmick for his leadership. In a sport that requires a lot of intensity, Young noted that Kurt had a great sense of humor that helped keep practices, travel, and match stresses from building-up with his ability to lighten the mood when it was needed.

Helmick posted another strong season with a 29-5 record, losing three of those matches to LaPorte rival Hal Reiter Helmick wrapped-up the season with a sixth place finish at the State tournament while the team placed second in Class A, the highest ever in Spartan history wrestling. The Spartans crowned a State champion in Dave Ehrig and a State runner-up with Ron Coleman, both fellow Hall of Famers.

The 1976 Spartan football team in Kurt's senior season was co-Conference Champions with a 7-2 record. Despite missing two more games due to his re-occurring ankle injury, Kurt rushed for 988 yards which brought his career total to a

record-setting 3,955 yards. While his lowest rushing total in his high school career, the 141 yards per game average was his highest. Besides his third straight first team all-conference, all-area and honorable mention all-state accolades, Kurt was voted the Most Outstanding Back in the conference.

Kurt Helmick was a prolific running back for the Spartans in the mid-1970s and an excellent wrestler as well.

Switching one last time to wrestling and moving up to 145#, Kurt posted another outstanding season. He was 27-3, won five tournaments including Districts, and finished fourth in the State tournament. His combined record as a junior and senior was 56-8 and his career record was 89-27-1.

Kurt held many Spartan wrestling records for his career when he graduated. He had the most career wins, most team points in a career with 453, and most place winnings in tournaments with 21. He scored over 100 team points three years in a row, and his 169 ½ points in one season was also a record. Kurt was awarded the Ralph Schmidt Award for outstanding wrestler and was captain of the team.

Besides football and wrestling, Kurt was also a four-year letter winner in track and twice qualified for the State meet on sprint relay teams for the Spartans.

After graduation, Kurt went to the University of Northern Iowa and wrestled two years for Coach Chuck Patten. He was part of the Panthers' Division II National Championship team of 1978 and had worked his way to the second spot in the depth chart before a knee injury ended his career.

Sports Hall of Fame
Grundy Center, Iowa
Established 2004

Jeff Crisman

Jeff Crisman is one of the trilogy of Crisman brothers in the Hall of Fame. Jeff was a four-year letterman in football at Luther College, a two-year team captain, and earned first team all-conference honors at defensive end.

Jeff Crisman fits neatly into the legacy of the Hall of Fame and the Class of 2016. A 1978 graduate, Jeff was a teammate of fellow 2016 inductee, Kurt Helmick. He's also the middle brother between two other Hall of Fame charter members in older brother, Terry Crisman, and younger brother, Joel. With Jeff's induction, he made it a trio of Crisman brothers in the Hall of Fame.

The Crisman family didn't move to Grundy Center until the early 1970s when Jeff was just in junior high. That was certainly a great benefit for Spartan athletics! Moving here was like moving to the "big city" to young Jeff and a little scary! But it didn't take long to assimilate. Growing up, Jeff and brother Terry played with the other kids in pick-up games of football, basketball, and baseball.

Looking back, Jeff fondly remembered the cohesiveness of his classmates that played those ball sports with him. Vince Klosterboer, Mark Hamm, Tom Riek, and Rick Venenga were among that group of boys that did everything together.

The coaches of the day included Rod Nelson, Jim Brousard, and Don Kramer. For Nelson, Jeff lettered three years playing linebacker, defensive end, and tight end along with some occasional plays at running back. He was named first team all-conference and special mention all-state as a senior.

Crisman vividly remembered the fall of 1975 in his sophomore year. Fellow Hall of Fame inductee Kurt Helmick hurt his ankle and had to miss the Homecoming game. Before it started, Jeff had never felt so nervous before a game! But he

accorded himself well by rushing for 98 yards and scoring a touchdown while contributing throughout the season to the team's 8-1 record.

Playing basketball, Jeff was a forward and lettered as a junior and senior. Their junior season, the Spartans were 21-2 winning the Conference, Sectionals and Districts before losing in sub-state to Central Webster of Burnside. The Spartans featured players like brother Terry Crisman, Tim Clark, and Kent Hitchings.

Jeff's senior year, the Spartans had another strong season under new head coach Dave Johnson. They won the Conference again, but lost in the District finals, finishing 19-3. Jeff earned first team all-conference honors and was a team co-captain while averaging over 12 points per game.

Jeff's baseball career at Grundy Center started out his freshman season of 1975 where he was a spot player on the Spartans' State runner-up team. Jeff remembers the few freshmen on the team had to wear older uniforms than the varsity players like his brother Terry, Tim Clark, Jim Weber, Danny Szegda, and others, because there weren't enough new uniforms to go around.

As a sophomore in 1976, Jeff stepped in as Don Kramer's right fielder and the team again qualified for the State tournament, but lost in the first round while posting a season record of 16-9.

Jeff's junior year, the Spartans recorded a strong 14-3 record in winning a Conference championship, but lost early in the State tournament series. Jeff culminated his senior year on the diamond as second team all-conference catcher.

After high school, Jeff still had a desire to play at the college level. He didn't feel at 6' 2" tall that basketball was in his future, although truthfully, Jeff enjoyed basketball more than football! Unrecruited, he chose Luther College to play football for the Norseman. He boldly walked into the head coach's office and asked Coach Naslund if he could try out for the team as a 185 pound defensive end. Even in the late 1970s at a small college, Crisman was still small!

But Jeff had some very sage advice from brother, Terry. He told Jeff it was important to make the coaches notice him. Luther coaches didn't know him, so Terry said he had to, *"Do something to be noticed."* Whether it was practices, extra workouts, running wind-sprints, or something else, Terry emphasized that Jeff had to make his coaches notice him.

Jeff did exactly that. Luther had graduated both their defensive ends from the previous season, so that provided an opportunity. Starting the pre-season workouts, Jeff was fourth team on the depth chart and leading up to the first game, that's where he remained. Following Terry's advice, he tried to be noticed by out hustling everyone in practice and winning almost all their conditioning wind sprints.

As the team finished their last workouts before the opening game, the defensive coach came up and said to Jeff's surprise, *"You're my starting defensive end."* It was a role he maintained over a very successful four-year career at Luther. By the time Jeff graduated, he grew to 205 pounds, still light, but now stronger and faster. His team voted Jeff a team co-captain as both a junior and senior, something only done once before in Luther football history.

As a junior, Jeff was nominated by an opposing coach for first-team all-conference, but he lost out by one vote. By an odd oversight, nobody nominated him for second team, so he didn't make the all-conference team at all that season. It was not only a disappointment to Jeff's coach, but Crisman also got a letter from the Luther College president lamenting the fact Jeff, in the president's estimation, was deserving of an all-conference honor. That was rectified Jeff's senior season when he was voted first team all-conference defensive end. It was a great cap to an outstanding college football career.

Jeff also played baseball at Luther. Most of their games were played as double headers, so Jeff typically played one game at catcher and the other game in left field. He lettered as a sophomore and junior. However, he didn't play his senior season due to working a college internship program off campus.

Jeff fit right into the three Crisman brothers' great legacy in Spartan sports history. He was honored to have Terry and Joel present him with his Hall of Fame awards at his induction ceremony in 2016.

The Crisman brothers are the second trio of siblings to join the GC Sports Hall of Fame.

Sports Hall of Fame
Grundy Center, Iowa
Established 2004

Adrianne Alexia

Adrianne Alexia was one of the best runners in Spartan track history and went on to an outstanding career for the University of Iowa while earning four letters as well as all-academic all-conference honors.

Adrianne Alexia is the daughter of Dr. Barry Alexia and Grundy Center graduate Glenda Grimmius Alexia. Adrianne felt she got a good deal of strong running genes from her Dad. Barry was an intermediate and high hurdler in track in both high school and college. She may have come by the running naturally, but with Adrianne's height at 5' 5", hurdles weren't the best fit. Regardless, her parents were a strong influence and inspiration throughout her entire sports career.

Adrianne's interest in running intensified in middle school when the late Sam Iverson got her interested in joining the track and cross country teams. She looked back on that time and truly appreciated the way Coach Iverson got her started, made it fun, and how Sam also became one of her biggest fans as her career developed.

In high school, Adrianne also played basketball. She was a three-year letterman primarily playing guard for Coach Laurie Willis with teammates such as Jocelyn Onnen, Abby Graves, Amanda Stefl, and Morgan Appel. She prided herself on being a good team player where she was strong on defense and took advantage of being both fast and quick on her feet.

Adrianne also led the Spartan cross country team for Coach Iverson and was the team's Most Valuable Player all four years in high school. Individually, she qualified for State her junior and senior seasons as did the whole team her senior year of 2010. While running mostly sprinting events in track, Adrianne enjoyed the distance

running. She remembers how Coach Iverson created *"Ice Cream Van Runs."* That was an annual event where Sam would ask the team a running-related question at the start of a workout. If you answered correctly, you got to ride in the van. If you missed, you had to run five miles. Each mile, the team would get another question and if they missed, they would have to get out and run the rest of the route. So the team had incentive to get the right answers. At the end of it all, Sam treated them to ice cream, thus the name *"Ice Cream Van Runs."*

Adrianne had a spectacular high school track career for Coach Todd Rohler. He was influential in helping her strive to be better and instilling confidence in her abilities to run with the best in the state.

Strategically for the team, Adrianne ran in a lot of relay races, usually running the anchor legs of the sprint medley, the 400 meter relay, the 1600 meter relay, and the distance medley relay. In 2009, she teamed with Abby Graves, Megan Krausman, and Morgan Appel to set the State record in the sprint medley relay. Then they came back in 2010 to win it again and break their own record!

This 2010 Spartan Sprint Medley Relay team won the State and set a new school and State record in the process. The team consisted of Abby Graves, Morgan Appel, Megan Krausman, and Adrianne Alexia.

Adrianne also anchored school-record setting relays for the 400 meter relay, the 1600 meter relay, and the distance medley relay. She anchored the 1600 meter relay of Abby Graves, Megan Krausman, and Sarah Frisch to a State championship in that event in 2010. While she didn't run too many individual races, Adrianne did set the 400 meter school record with a time of 58.18 seconds.

Alexia tallied many honors in her track career. She was an eight-time conference champion, three-time first-team all-conference, three-time State relay champion, first-team all-state in track, and she was twice selected the conference's Most Outstanding Woman Athlete in 2009 and 2010.

Besides a Hall of Fame running career, Adrianne was outstanding in the classroom. She was the valedictorian for her class, chosen for National Honor Society, and won several prestigious academic awards.

Several colleges were interested in Alexia and recruited her as a runner, including the University of Northern Iowa, Iowa State University, Wartburg College, and others. However, she chose the University of Iowa, her first choice academically. Adrianne was technically a recruited "walk-on" as a freshman, but earned an athletic scholarship her junior year. She also found college track was quite different and a lot more intense than high school in terms of much harder workouts and top-notch competition at the Big Ten level. She remembered fall practices were particularly grueling, but in spring, when they competed in their meets, she had more fun and she enjoyed the traveling to Big Ten venues and elite national meets.

Another change was going from basically a sprinter in high school relay events of 400 meters or less to running the 800 meters individually. Alexia ran a personal-best and Hawkeye season-best indoor 800 meters of 2:08.9 in 2013, which was also the fourth fastest indoor time in school history and one of her proudest accomplishments. Another was qualifying for the NCAA Regionals and placing ninth at the Big Ten championships. Besides running mostly 800 meter races, Adrianne was bumped up to the 1500 meter run and helped the Hawkeyes where they needed it. She was named to the Academic All-Big Ten team all four years for the Hawkeyes.

Adrianne also ran a few relays. She ran the third leg of the 2013 team-leading indoor 1600 meter team and the lead leg on the team-leading indoor distance medley relay at the Big Ten Championships producing the tenth-fastest time for that event in Iowa history. Outdoors in 2013, she placed second at the Drake Relays in the 800 meters with the fifth best time in Hawkeye history running her personal best time of her career of 2:08.6, three one hundredths of a second faster than her record indoor time. She also anchored the Hawkeyes' sprint medley team at the Drake Relays posting the second-fastest time in school history.

Adrianne graduated in 2015 with degrees in Biochemistry and Business. At the time of her induction in 2016, she was the youngest member in the Hall of Fame.

Phil Lebo

Phil Lebo was a highly successful and long-term Spartan coach, primarily in baseball and track. In the center photo, he was inducted into the Iowa High School Coaches Association Hall of Fame. Right, he received his Grundy Center Sports Hall of Fame award.

Phil Lebo was the seventh coach to be elected to the Hall of Fame joining John Doak, Harry Dole, Vernon Morrison, Clint Young, Randy Peters, and Steve Bergman.

Coaching came naturally to Phil. In his high school years, he played baseball, basketball, and track. He even played fast-pitch softball. Attending Morningside College, Phil was a catcher lettering three years and played a little semi-pro ball.

One day in 1980, while driving through Grundy Center, Phil liked the looks of the town and thought it would be a good place to live, teach, and coach. Soon after, he was hired to teach Life and Earth sciences and coach high school baseball, junior high track, and be an assistant football coach. Later on, Phil also coached eighth grade basketball for a number of years.

Taking over the Spartans' high school head coaching job for baseball, Phil embarked on a 21-year stint that totaled a school record 268 wins on the diamond. For many years, he was supported by fellow Hall of Famer, Dennis Dirks, as his assistant along with Steve Drew and Patrick Brown. Phil produced a conference championship, two district titles, a sub-State title and an appearance in the State baseball tournament.

One of the key elements to Coach Lebo's baseball philosophy was being able to bunt. If a player couldn't bunt, they couldn't play for Phil. Bunting puts a lot of pressure on opponents and Phil would use it aggressively. Traditionally, if a batter had two strikes, teams seldom bunt, but not with Coach Lebo. He would bunt players with two strikes, he would bunt with two outs, he would do suicide squeeze bunts,

and he would do suicide squeeze bunts with two strikes and two outs. Phil made opponents' infielders very nervous!

Perhaps Phil's greatest Spartan baseball highlight was in their sub-State championship game in the 1A State baseball tournament in 1993. Grundy faced perennial baseball power Kee High of Lansing for a place in the State tournament. Playing catcher was Phil's son, Hall of Famer Andy Lebo, who desperately wanted to get the Spartans to the State tournament for his dad. While Andy had two hits and two runs batted in during that game, it was a great team effort to come back in the last inning when trailing by two runs.

The Spartans loaded the bases with two outs when Ryan Block hit a deep line drive to left-centerfield. The Kee High outfielder made a valiant attempt to catch the ball and end the game. He appeared to catch it, fumbled it, and almost caught it again before it dribbled to the ground allowing three Spartans to score and win the game for Grundy Center! Before that rally, Phil had noticed the Kee High fans ready to celebrate with balloons and streamers for a win that never came. It was a sweet, sweet victory for the Spartan boys and their coach.

In 1983, Phil created both the annual Memorial Day High School Baseball Tournament in Grundy Center and later the annual seventh and eighth grade and junior varsity baseball tournaments. He also started and managed the local American Legion baseball team which twice qualified for State. Phil additionally served on the City's initial sports complex board for a number of years and helped coach third base for the Grundy Center Gamecocks town baseball team.

Besides coaching the Spartans, Phil was actively involved in the Iowa High School Baseball Coaches Association. He served on the Board of Directors and did a term as president and served many years as the membership chairman. Phil was named Class 1A District Coach of the Year in 1993 and served two years as an assistant coach for the Iowa High School All-Star game and in 1989 he served as the head coach. He was also a regular contributor to various association baseball clinics. In 2004, he was honored to be selected to the Iowa High School Baseball Coaches Hall of Fame.

Track was also a coaching passion of Phil's and he was the high school track coach for 15 years. During his tenure, the Spartans qualified 27 events and 53 athletes for the State track meet and had nine place winners. His teams also qualified for ten events at the Drake Relays with stars like Justin Schaack, who qualified twice in the high hurdles, and Brad Harms, who qualified twice in the discus, as well as some

excellent relay teams. They also placed in two events at the Dickinson Relays at the University of Northern Iowa.

Phil had fond memories of his 4x100 meter relay team which also ran the 4x200 meter race. The 1993 team of Dan McMartin, Andy Lebo, Justin Schaack, and Mike Rottink placed fourth in the State in the 4x100 relay and second in the 4x200 relay. Those relay teams were the best he had during his track coaching career and he loved to watch them run.

The second-place 4x200 team broke the school record at the conference meet, broke it again at districts, then lowered it further at State with a 1:31.7 time, just three one hundredths of a second behind the first place team. Five school records were set by his track team, three conference records, and Justin Schaack was named the Outstanding Conference Performer for 1993.

Football was another sport Phil enjoyed and coached for 12 years. He was head coach for the eighth grade junior high team and an assistant coach at the high school level, including the undefeated State championship team of 1984 under Head Coach Don Knock. He worked with the offensive line and the defensive ends, along with other assistants Bob Schmadeke and Bruce Huber. Phil also enjoyed working with and learning from long-time Spartan coach Keith Hall and had a lot of fun coaching with Keith.

When Coach Knock left, the school hired Craig Johnson from Upper Iowa University, who came and coached one year before leaving for greener pastures. Phil offered to coach football for a couple years and compiled a winning record both seasons.

Phil's daughter, Jamie, who nominated Phil for Hall of Fame, shared this: *"It was clear to see from a very young age just how much my father loved working with kids and helping them grow and develop as students, athletes, and young adults."* She added, *"I would be remiss if I didn't mention how important my mother, Nancy, was in my father's coaching, as she was always next to him in the dugout keeping score, or upstairs in the press box."*

Phil retired from teaching and coaching in 2006.

Sports Hall of Fame
Grundy Center, Iowa
Established 2004

Hall of Fame Fun Facts as of 2016

- 81 members; 68 men and 13 women have been elected since 2004.
- The break out by decade is:
    - 1910s: 1
    - 1920s: 3
    - 1930s: 4
    - 1940s: 4
    - 1950s: 6
    - 1960s: 16
    - 1970s: 19
    - 1980s: 12
    - 1990s: 10
    - 2000s: 7
- Oldest members: Forrest Meyers (Class of 1916) and Vernon Morrison (1921).
- Oldest living member: Mel Heckt. (1937)
- Youngest member: Adrianne Alexi (Class of 2010)
- Furthest Away: Formerly Hal Leffler, Germany (where he passed away); now Dave Pike, Fleming Island, Florida.
- Closest: An estimated 15 members live in or near Grundy Center.
- Deceased: 12 members (Forrest Meyers; Vernon Morrison; Melvin Fritzel, Dale Smith; Harold Leffler, Max Appel; Leon Bockes; Roger Peters, Jim Basye, Arnie Reynolds, Harold Engelkes, and Orville Allen.)
- Related:
    - Siblings: Joel, Jeff & Terry Crisman; Kay & Norm Riek; Bob & Beth Stock; Trina, Kylie & Jordan Dirks; Mark & Paul Eberline (also the only twins): Jack & Jim Basye;
    - Parent / Child: Dennis and Jordan, Trina & Kylie Dirks; Harry & Jeff Dole; Dick & Sarah Lynch; Roger & Randy Peters; Phil & Andy Lebo;
    - Other: Grandfather/Grandson: Max Appel & Brad Harms; Uncle/nephew: Bob & Dave Smoldt and Bud & Steve Bergman; Cousins: Mike & Doug Stumberg and Lance & Kim Van Deest.
- College athletics: 14 played for UNI; 9 for ISU; 8 for Iowa; 3 Drake, 5 for Wartburg, 1 for Simpson, 3 for Central, 3 for Coe, 4 for Luther, and 21 played for other colleges or junior colleges.
- Coaches / Administrators / Contributors: Vernon Morrison (Coach & Administrator), John Doak (Coach & Contributor), Harry Dole (Coach & Administrator), Randy Peters (Coach), Steve Bergman (Coach), Clint Young (Coach), and Harold Engelkes (Contributor), Phil Lebo (Coach)

Sports Hall of Fame
Grundy Center, Iowa
Established 2004

Final Images

The 2014 Induction Ceremony provided another gathering of Grundy greats. Front row: John Doak, Kevin Ralston, Clint Young, Ron Coleman and Kylie Dirks. Second row: Steve Bergman, Dana Schmidt, Randy Peters, Ed Palmer, and Harry Dole. Third row: Orrin Brown, Molly Thoren, and Ryan Peters (far right representing Roger Peters). Back row: Paul Eberline, Matt Bockes, Dennis Dirks, and Jeff Dole.

FIRST ROW: Palmer, Abels, Stensland, Ford Blackburn, Wical, Sheller, Nuis, Smith, Finke, B. Sealman, D. Blackburn, Manager. SECOND ROW: Hagen, Gruver, Almdale, Catherwood, Shaw, Siemsen, Pike, McMartin, Kruse, Peters, D. Sealman, Mr. Doak, Coach; Ralston, Redding, Johnson, Sprague, J. Frederick, Mutch, Schafer, Fisher, Palmitessa, Saddoris, S. Fredrick, Springer.

This is the Grundy Center Spartans first wrestling team in 1961-62. It featured two future Hall of Famers, the son of one, and the father of another one.

This undefeated Spartan team of 1943 went 8-0 and was one of the prolific scoring teams putting outscoring opponents 242-13 with Bud Peterson (#60) scoring 163 points himself. Front row: Beveridge Nickerson, Carrol Haren, Delroy Connerly, Merle Johns, Max Smith, and Bill Kuhlman. Second row: Kay Reynolds, Don Paulus, Lyle Heltibridle, Harry Boren, Harry Slifer, Dale Canfield, Coach Melvin Fritzel. Back row: Leon Bockes, Vernon Friesner, Bud Peterson, Doug Peterson, Hank Mol and Willis Grabinski. Laying down: student manager Jim Ruppelt.

The 1944 Spartans were undefeated and unscored upon with many of the same players, although they tied Toledo in the first game of the season 0-0 and finished 7-0-1. Front row: Max Smith, Earl Stanbaugh, Delroy Connerly, Kay Reynolds, Don Paulus, Harry Slifer, Troy Anderson, and Meint Bakker. Back row: Coach Melvin Fritzel, Vernon Klosterboer, Dale Canfield, Henry Mol, Merle Johns, Leon Bockes, Bill Wilson, Harry Boren, and student manager Jim Ruppelt. Not pictured: Lyle Heltibridle.

Left, Karen Coffman and Teresa Korando are shown with their runner-up trophy from the District tennis tournament in 1965. As of 2016, Korando was still playing competitive tennis. Right, is the potent battery from the 1954 Spartan team with catcher Jim Wells between Hall of Fame pitchers Bud Bergman (left) and Glen Van Fossen (right).

The Spartans 1969 basketball team finished a strong 19-2 coached by Harry Dole featuring seven future Hall of Famers and provided the foundation for the great 1971 team.

Hall of Fame members Arnie Reynolds (circled left) and Roger Peters (upper right) joined other Iowa baseball hopefuls at a Florida spring training camp in 1941 hosted by MLB Hall of Famer and Iowa native Bob Feller (kneeling with the glove). At that same 1941 Florida baseball camp, Roger Peters had is picture taken (right) with and received coaching from the legendary Babe Ruth.

Front row: S. Stoehr, J. Pieters, B. Katzer, R. Gronewold. Middle row: S. Lynch, T. Weekley, A. Harken. Back row: K. Vogt, M. Thoren, C. Sherer, S. Meester, A. Rouse, M. Hawn, Coach Peterson.

The Spartans 1989 volleyball team features two Hall of Famers.

FIRST. John Doak, Paul Vogt, Don Bakker, Dilman Stachour, Ray Kinton, Don Niehaus.
SECOND: Delbert Kell, Orville Allen, Jake Bergman, Arnold Petersen, Paul Schoon, Norman Bergman, Glen VanFossen.
THIRD. Jim Wells - manager, Carl Voss, Ronald Horbach, Jerry Smith, Darrell Heronimus, James Schaa, Earl Page - assistant basketball coach, Keith Tannatt - head basketball coach, Jim Morrison, Junior Middleton, James Dobson, Gene Grummus, Delbert Sonnenberg, Duane Meester - manager.

The 1952 Spartan basketball team went through their regular season undefeated only to lose in the first round of the State basketball tournament. This team features four Hall of Famers, the son of one, and the father of another. It was one of the best in school history.

The 1971 Spartan basketball team was a mirror image of the 1952 team as a highly ranked, undefeated team going into the State tournament where they, too, lost in the first round. Still, this Harry Dole coached team with six Hall of Famers was one of the best in Spartan history. They are first row: Coach Dole, Mark Kruse, Rod Ragsdale, Greg Goodman, Mark Carter and Steve Kiewiet. Second row: Darrel Dirks, Jerry Appel, Dennis Dirks, Mark Eberline, Dennis Modlin, Paul Eberline, Jerry Moeller, and Tim Williamson.

This 1970 Spartan girls golf team was the first in school history to qualify for the State golf tournament. They were coached by Rick Briggs and were led by junior Ann Engelkes. Girls' golf turned into arguably the most successful sport in Spartan history.

CROSS COUNTRY TEAM - top row: Mr. Dole (coach), B. Borchardt, T. Wolthoff, N. Riek, M. Buskohl, G. Goodman, J. Fenken. Bottom row: L. Freed, J. Bettenga, N. Stumberg, D. Dirks, F. Richards, T. Ralston, N. Andrews.

The Spartans 1972 Cross Country team featured three Hall of Famers including Coach Harry Dole, and the brothers of three more.

Chuck Lehr was Grundy Center band director for over 30 years and his marching bands and pep bands added immeasurably to the festive atmosphere of Spartan sporting events.

The Spartans have been supported by decades of great cheerleading squads including those from 1962 (left), 1967 (center) and 1973 (right). They also add to the great atmosphere of football, basketball, wrestling and other sporting events. Many in these photos are related to a member of the Hall of Fame including three wives, two mothers, and two sisters.

Student managers and trainers fill an important role in a well-run athletic program. Those student managers work hard to see that the coaches and players had the things they needed to practice and compete for the Spartans. This student manager montage features one Hall of Famer, the son of another and the brother of another.

Another Gathering of Grundy Greats in 2016

The newly inducted Class of 2016 was joined by fellow Hall of Fame members after the 2016 induction ceremony. While not neatly in rows, the photo includes from bottom to top: John Doak, Phil Lebo, Adrianne Alexia, Kurt Helmick, Jeff Crisman, Dave Ralston, Molly Thoren, Kevin Ralston, Mike Draper, Paul Eberline, Ron Coleman, Ed Palmer, Clint Young, Steve Ehlers, Tim Clark, J.A. Abels, Andy Lebo, Bobbi Sealman, Harry Dole, Wayne Wrage, Dennis Dirks, Jordan Dirks, and Matt Bockes.

Sports Hall of Fame
Grundy Center, Iowa
Established 2004

Front row: Blain Lage, Chuck Hoop, Tony Briggs, Greg Vogt, Chad Ralston, Chris Getting, Dennis Morey, Wes Calton, Marty Poley, Brett Fisher, Brant Mutch. Second row: Mike Roth, John Freeman, Kevin Yoder, Ryan Kosanke, Kevin Hockemeyer, Darrel Davis, Josh Blake, Evan Meester, Matt Kuester, Lance Kruger, Sean Schafer, Chad Deits. Third row: John Gordon, Chad Mackie, Nyle Wilhau, Jeremy Henson, Justin Appel, Matt Dewater, Joe Henson, Scott Schafer, John Poley, Brian Gordon. Jason McMartin. Fourth row: Chris Stewart, Clint McCord, Clint Stephenson, Scott Foster, Mark Appel, Jim Storke, Brad Newton, Turner Bennett, Phil Barnes, Lance Noble, Jeff Mathews, Erik Stensland. Fifth row: David Harberts, Rhett Barrett, Neal Walters, Brandon Sealman, Jeff Beenken, Matt Barnes, Chad Van Hauen, Marc Lamfers, Kent Venenga, Dan Weichers, Brad Flater. Back row: Coach Schadeke, Coach Itzen, Tim Van Wert, Joel Crisman, Arthur Kunzman, Sean Olson, Jeff Hawk, Coach Huber, Coach Bredlow.

This 1988 team won the Spartans' second State football championship.

And we close with a little celebrating of the many victories Spartan sports teams have brought Grundy Center for more than a century of athletic competition. May there be many more in the years ahead as we "Cheer, cheer for ol' Grundy High!"

Made in the USA
Las Vegas, NV
29 November 2021

35567285R10136